The COMPLETE IDIOT'S GUIDE TO

Managing Stress

Jeff Davidson, MBA, CMC

alpha books

A Division of Macmillan General Reference
A Simon and Schuster Macmillan Company
1633 Broadway
New York, NY 10019

To all the wonderful mentors, gurus, advisory board members, and empowering people in my life—past, present, and future—who have helped me to maintain a relatively stress free life despite the fact that I approach my work and career like a jackhammer.

Publisher
Theresa H. Murtha

Development Editor
Lisa A. Bucki

Production Editor
Phil Kitchel

Technical Editor
Carol Krucoff

Illustrator
Judd Winick

Designer
Kim Scott

Cover Designer
Dan Armstrong

Indexer
Cheryl Dietsch

Production Team
Kim Cofer
Tricia Flodder
Daniela Raderstorf
Beth Rago

Contents at a Glance

Part 1: Facing Up to Modern Stressors   **1**

1   To Be Alive Is To Experience Stress!   3
A look at stress from humanity's early days right up to the present.

2   What Do We Mean By Stress?   15
Turn over every stone in exploring the different aspects of stress.

3   Wouldn't You Know It? The Direction of Stress Has Changed   29
How the nano-second nineties have already witnessed major changes regarding where and when people experience stress.

Part 2: Surviving Your Workplace   **41**

4   I Work, Therefore I Compete...   43
The dissipation of traditional career progression is creating stress unlike anything in previous generations.

5   When Too Many Hours Take Their Toll   55
How to make the best of too many work hours and how to extricate yourself from the predicament, whether you're in charge of your schedule or not!

6   Increased Expectations, Diminishing Returns   67
Strategies to keep stress in check even if you have way too much to do.

7   A Workplace Revolution, or How to Get Out of Jail   83
How the electronic gadgets of today present new paths to stress, and what you can do about it.

8   Whipping Workplace Distractions   93
Safely "manage" interruptions and the stress of being interrupted.

9   Workplace Violence: Stress Boiling Over the Top   103
As the level of violence in society rises, so does the level of violence at work; stay safer with the advice found here.

Part 3: External Stressors   **113**

10   The Stress of Population Density   115
The stressful effects of making your way through the teeming multitudes and taking control without moving to Pocatello.

11 The Information Industry   123
    How to avoid getting sucked into the info-tainment vortex.

12 Overexposure to Unreality   135
    Choosing to be who you are and want what you have.

Part 4: Self-Induced Stressors   145

13 Shortchanging Your Sleep   147
    The inseparable link between sleep and stress,
    and some tips on getting more rest.

14 Unconditioned Personal Environments   159
    Controlling your space and not relinquishing it
    to others who are only too ready to "invade" it.

15 Lack of Completions   169
    Completing tasks yields a marvelous sense of tranquility,
    and is one of the best-kept secrets of reducing stress.

Part 5: Getting Your Stress Level Back Down   181

16 Becoming the Master of Your Environment   183
    This has eluded people since the dawn of civilization,
    but there are many opportunities for you to take control.

17 Perfecting the Strategic Pause   193
    Deep relaxation with only a few minutes to spare.

18 Asking the Magic Question   209
    Taking responsibility for the stress in your life.

19 Choosing When It's Confusing   219
    Flourishing despite an over-abundance of choices.

20 Choosing to Have Less Stress   229
    If you feel flustered, you can choose to embody
    grace and ease.

21 Stressed or Not, You're Probably Going to Live a
    Long Time   241
    How to approach your next 40 years.

    Glossary   251
    Key terms you need to understand.

    Bibliography   253
    Other sources and resources.

    Index   255

Contents

Part 1: Facing Up to Modern Stressors   **1**

1 To Be Alive Is to Experience Stress   **3**

"Brain at Work" 4
That's Amazing 5
Name That Stressor! 5
Minor, Niggling Stressors 8
How Did It All Get So Hectic? 8
Living on the Margin 10
Comfort in Mega-Change? 10
Getting a Handle on Stress 12
The Least You Need to Know 14

2 What Do We Mean by Stress?   **15**

How Stress Manifests Itself in Different Ways 16
     Signs of Stress 16
     Good Stress and Bad Stress? 17
What Means What: Some Terminology
     Related to Stress 17
Is Your Job Inherently Stressful? 19
Stress Dressed Up as Something Else 20
Is Your Stress Unique to You? 22
What Is Your Stress Telling You? 24
If You Want to Control Something,
     Control Your Stress 25
Change of Venue 26
The Least You Need to Know 27

3 Wouldn't You Know It?
The Direction of Stress Has Changed   **29**

How Your Home Life Became More Stressful
     Than the Workplace 30
     Personal Finances 31
     Career Stressors 32
     The Best of the Rest of the Stressors 33
     Happily Ever After 33

To Your Health 33
What's the Matter with Kids Today? 34
All By Myself 34
Sex 35
It's All Relative 36
Neighbors 36
Coming to Work to Rest 37
Is Your Commute Killing You? 39
The Least You Need to Know 40

Part 2: Surviving Your Workplace   41

4   I Work, Therefore I Compete...   43

Compete with Yourself, Not with Others 44
Eliminating the Competition 46
Distinguishing Yourself from the Pack 47
Taking the Task No One Wants 47
Go the Extra Mile 48
When the Cat's Away… 48
Give Credit to the Group 49
Make Your Boss Look Good 49
Become a Mentor to Others 49
Be Aware of Your Boss's Needs 49
Figure Out What's Needed 50
Is Self-Employment on the Horizon? 50
Effective Tools for a New Era 51
How to Hang Loose When Nothing
   Around You Is Going Right 53
The Least You Need to Know 54

5   When Too Many Hours Take Their Toll   55

How Much Work is Too Much Work? 55
Little Gain, Much Pain 56
Ten Ways to Know When You've Been
   Working Too Hard 56
Please, Let Me Work Longer 57
A Little Balance, Please 59
Determining Your Overwork Quotient 59
Stay Fit, Work Longer with Less Stress 61

A Different Kind of Play 62
Making It Too Hard on Yourself 62
Strategies for Pacing Yourself 63
On the Spot Strategies 64
The Least You Need to Know 65

6 Increased Expectations, Diminishing Returns   67

When Did the High-Expectation Floodgates Open? 68
   Sons of Guns 68
Hit Me with My Best Shot 71
   Barely Hanging On…... 71
   No Respect? 72
Avoiding Job Burnout 72
What to Do When Your Boss Wants
   You to Be a Workaholic 74
Paying Homage to the Cycles of Productivity 75
   Employees Establish Their Cycles 76
   Working the Cycle 77
   Reprogramming the Cycle 77
When Nothing Else Works 77
   Accentuate the Positive 78
   Strength for the Future 78
   Have You Stood in Your Boss's Shoes? 78
   Knowing You're Going 79
   Revenge: Sweet or Sour? 79
   Hone Your Diplomatic Skills 79
The Best Companies to Work For 79
The Least You Need to Know 81

7 A Workplace Revolution, or How to Get Out of Jail   83

Darn Those Little Chips 84
The Professionally Elusive You... 85
   Dealing with the Telephone in General 85
   Absolutely Never Use Call Waiting 87
   Use Call Forwarding Sparingly 87
   Slave to a Beeper 87
   Car or Cell Phones 88
   E-mail 89
   Fax Machines 89
Establishing Creative Sanctuaries..................................... 90
The Least You Need to Know 92

8   Whipping Workplace Distractions   93

It's the Disruption, Stupid 94
All About Interruptions 95
   Interruption Management 95
   Multitasking Leads to More Stress? 96
   Focus on What's Confronting You 97
   What Merits Your Attention? 97
The Paper Chase 98
Timing Isn't Everything, But It's a Lot 99
Shake It Up, Baby 99
Mental Methods for Reducing Distractions 100
   I Do So Affirm 101
   The Sacred Hoops Approach 101
   How Do You Spell Relief? 102
The Least You Need to Know 102

9   Workplace Violence: Stress Boiling Over the Top   103

Violence at Work Mirrors the Larger Society 103
When Workplace Stress Is at Dangerous Levels 104
Neither Rain Nor Snow Nor Gunpoint… 105
Workplace Subversion 106
Treating Termination Carefully 106
Dealing with an Abusive Manager 108
A Coworker Whom Others Respect 109
The Least You Need to Know 111

Part 3:   External Stressors   113

10   The Stress of Population Density   115

The Planet and Your Life 115
What Scarcity Is All About 117
   Resources Vanishing Before Your Eyes 117
The Ever-Critical Masses 118
   What About Declining Fertility Rates? 119
   Wanted: Hundreds of Millions of Jobs 119
   The Long Waits Scare Me 119
Back in the USA 120
Strategies to Reduce Stress from Overcrowding 120
The Least You Need to Know 122

11 The Information Industry   **123**

The Great Age of Information Hasn't Arrived 124
     Flip the Switch, Man 124
     An Overabundance 125
Publish and Perish 126
     Information by the Boatload 126
     Today's Additions 127
More Than You Bargained For 128
Knowing More, but Falling Behind 128
     I Didn't Know That, and I Feel Fine 129
     Is No Information Sacred? 130
Reducing Your Information Intake 130
     Organize the Information You Do Want to Keep 131
     Tickler Files 131
     Letting Go of Excess 132
     Handle It Like a Pro 132
A Lifetime Guarantee 133
The Least You Need to Know 133

12 Overexposure to Unreality   **135**

Pervasive and Unrecognized 136
     Undermining Your Town 136
     A World Apart 136
So, You Know Better? 137
     Violence, Cigarettes, and Drugs—They're not
     Just for Breakfast Anymore 137
     Winding Down or Cranking Up? 138
Sucked into the Vortex of Entertainment 138
If It Bleeds, It Leads 139
     Is It "News"? 140
     The Wrath of Rather 141
Express Yourself 141
The Tabloid Mentality 142
     About Me, Placed By Me 142
Fueling Anxiety 143
Stop the Media Insanity! 144
The Least You Need to Know 144

Part 4: Self-Induced Stressors 145

13 Shortchanging Your Sleep 147

A Long-Term Trend in the Making 148
Hard to Stay Awake 148
Nothing New but Definitely of Concern 149
The Danger Signals 149
Not Dangerous, but Not Desirable Either 150
Comparest Thou Not with Others 150
Driving and Dozing 151
It's a Female Thing, You Wouldn't Understand 152
A Man's World? 153
Sleep and Recover 154
    Developing Good Sleep Habits 155
    Sleeping Away from Home 156
    About Napping 156
Have You Had Enough Sleep? 157
The Least You Need to Know 157

14 Unconditioned Personal Environments 159

Making Your Home Your Castle 160
Solicitors and Other Uninvited Guests 161
    The Uninvited 161
    From Whence Comest Thou, Stranger? 162
    No Extremes 162
Dealing with Unwanted Phone Solicitations 163
    A Quick 10k (and I Don't Mean a Road Race) 164
Dealing with Junk Mailers 164
God Bless This Space 166
Retaining Versus Tossing 166
The Least You Need to Know 168

15 Lack of Completions 169

From Incompletion to Death 170
In a Sped-up World, Incompletions Proliferate 171
Getting Complete Now and Again 172
    Your Daily Completions 172
    Completions All Around 173
Completions with a Loved One 173
    Completions in the Face of Chaos 175

Getting Complete in the Face of Too Much Data............ 176
Letting Others Get Complete 177
Completion in the Face of Procrastination 178
The Art of Doing One Thing at a Time 179
When 90 Percent Is Complete 179
The Least You Need to Know 180

Part 5: Getting Your Stress Level Back Down   181

16 Becoming the Master of Your Environment   183

All About the Strategic Pause 184
The Strategic Pause Can Be Illusory 185
  Completely Missing the Point 186
  Breaking a Problem Down 186
What About You? 187
  Breathing Is the Key 188
Second, Third, and Even Fourth Winds 188
  A Plane Seat, Train Seat, Bus Seat, or Back of a Cab 189
  Before Dinner 189
  Before Making Love 189
  During Athletic Contests 189
  When Getting Chewed Out 189
Mastering Your Space 190
  A Nice Place to Visit.. 192
The Least You Need to Know 192

17 Perfecting the Strategic Pause   193

First, What You Don't Need 193
  Heatin' Up 194
  Forget Bio Dots and Stress Cards 194
Stuff That Works 194
Prayer and Spirituality 195
Talking to Someone... 195
Using Humor 195
Visualization 196
  Visualizing the Future 196
  Chicken Soup for Success 197
Guided Imagery 197
Self-Talk 198
Aroma Therapy 199

Massage 199
Taking Vitamins 200
Fresh Air 201
Deep Breathing 201
Meditation 202
   Now, Where Was I Going? 203
   Meditation Variations 203
The Stress Inventory 204
Centering 205
Yoga 205
   Get a Mat 206
T'ai Chi Ch'aun 206
The Least You Need to Know 207

18 Asking the Magic Question   209

How Did I Get into This? 210
What Would a Calm Person Do? 211
Does This Need to Be Done at All? 212
What Can I Draw from This? 213
Reframe and Conquer 214
What Experience Do I Want for My Child?
  For Myself? 215
What Will Happen if I Don't Call? 215
What Is This Stress Doing for Me? 216
Is There Another Way to Proceed? 216
How Do I Feel Right Now? 217
With Every Stress-Related Problem Comes a Solution 218
The Least You Need to Know 218

19 Choosing When It's Confusing   219

The Stress of Too Many Choices 220
An Inability to Choose 220
Beware: Deciding By Not Deciding 221
Where to Begin 222
Choosing in the Face of Rapid Change 223
Narrowing Your Priorities 223
Making Better Purchase Decisions 224
A Prepared Checklist 225
Decisions with Less Work 226
Other Shortcuts Abound 226

Pros and Cons 227
Choosing with Others 227
The Stress of Too Few or Too Many Choices 227
Welcome to Your World 228
The Least You Need to Know 228

20 Choosing to Have Less Stress   229

Choosing to Enjoy the Present 230
Choosing to Master Your Finances 230
About That Divorce 231
Handling Routine Upsets 231
Choosing to Be Prepared 232
Choosing to Work Effectively with a Tough Boss 232
Choosing to Master a Tough Profession 233
Choosing to Overcome Technology Anxiety 234
Flourishing in the Face of Constant Change 235
Upping Personal Energy 237
Creative Choices to Recurring Stressors 237
Success in General 238
The Least You Need to Know 239

**21 Stressed or Not, You're Probably Going
     to Live a Long Time   241**

Surprise, You're In It for the Long Haul 241
Substance Abuse Can't Be an Answer 243
The Last "Will" and Testament 243
To Thine Own Self Be True 244
Out of the Mouths of the Rich and Balanced 244
Remaining Alert 246
The View From Here 249
The Least You Need to Know 250

Glossary   251

Sources   253

Index   255

Foreword

Take a look at *Books in Print* and you'll find hundreds and hundreds of books on the topic of stress from the last few years. In fact, since World War II, along with books on diet and sex, stress is one of the most popular topics in publishing. The obvious reason? Stress has become almost the hallmark of our existence. Having a full-time career, raising children, being in a committed relationship—any major professional or personal undertaking invariably has its own set of built-in stressors.

All around us we see more people leading hectic lives, getting ever stronger prescriptions, popping more pills, while hoping to get through the day in one piece.

With all the changes that have occurred in society in the last decade, and an ever increasing array of changes that we know are forthcoming, is it any wonder that each of us must reassess how we run our lives, and renew our sense of balance and purpose? Is it possible to handle everything and still get through the day with relative grace and ease? I believe it is, and fortified by this marvelous book by Jeff Davidson, I think your chances just improved dramatically.

Jeff Davidson is a dynamic speaker, author of 22 books, and an accomplished career achiever. Yet, on his way to understanding how to keep stress in place, he overcame a number of hurdles. His father, age 60, and older sister, age 31, both passed away suddenly, within 18 months of each other, when Jeff was in his mid-twenties—just a few years after one of his best friends passed away at 19 from leukemia. These events, along with many others of a personally cataclysmic nature, forced Jeff to reassess nearly every aspect of his life—what he ate, how long he slept, how he approached the day, and so on.

Over the last two decades, Jeff has honed and refined his observations about life and work so he could present a book on managing stress that gets to the heart, and the truth, of what's plaguing all of us and what's likely to be plaguing you in particular. The observations and witticisms that he provides are unsurpassed. The tips and recommendations he offers are meaty.

Jeff crafted this book with the express purpose of providing you with highly practical, hands-on solutions to the stress-related problems you encounter. The book is presented in an illuminating, entertaining, and honest manner. Once you get on the wavelength of Jeff's humor, you'll find the ride to be very smooth indeed. Whether you're the CEO of a Fortune 500 company, a mid-level manager, or new in the workforce; white-collar or blue-collar; retired, in school, or in-between, you'll find answers you need.

This book mixes age-old truths with new world realities. Throughout the book, Jeff presents compelling reasons, with irrefutable logic, why simply being alive in our society almost guarantees high levels of stress if you're not skilled at keeping it in check. It concludes with the observation that, stressed or not, you're probably going to live longer than you think, and by understanding the origin and nature of stress you experience and keeping it under control, you have the best chance of having the remainder of your life be quality time.

The last section of each chapter is entitled, "The Least You Need to Know." This is a convention used in all of the *Complete Idiot's Guide* books. It is an effective way to remind yourself of the key elements from the chapter that are worth remembering.

Most of the ideas that Jeff presents can be implemented right away. You won't have to undertake a lot of changes in the way you're currently doing things. Indeed, the changes will be subtle, for two reasons. One is that you already have a lot to do and a lot to keep pace with, and you don't need more tasks and more instructions that are difficult to follow. More importantly, for any changes you undertake to be of lasting value, they must come naturally and easily to you. And, if you only partially follow his suggestions, you'll still receive great benefits.

I suggest you keep this book within reach so you can peruse its pages often. You'll find yourself going back again and again as different situations arise. As you experience early wins in controlling stress, you'll want to read or reread certain passages and chapters so you can master other areas.

Your ability to manage your stress is now in your hands. You can attain significant results reading and following the ideas laid out before you. As you exhibit greater mastery of situations that previously caused you stress, the people around you will notice, and wonder how you were able to change effectively. Share this book with them. You'll find that when you're surrounded by people who also have skills in keeping their stress in check, you benefit as well. After all, a lower stress environment benefits everyone in it.

Congratulations! Your journey is about to begin.

Dr. Terry Paulson,
Author and trainer on organizational change
Los Angeles, California.

Introduction

Being Less Stressed About Reading About Stress!

It doesn't take a genius to know that if you hold any position of responsibility, are raising a family, serve as a volunteer, or care for others in any way, chances are you're experiencing stress—perhaps a lot more than you wish you were.

The one thing you and I don't want to do from the outset is to get *stressed* discussing *stress*. For me, the very word invokes ill feelings. To keep my level of *stress* down while writing about *stress*, I envisioned the word within an ice cube. How *stressful* can the word *stress* be when there's cool ice all around it? If it's comforting for you, whenever you see the word *stress*, think of the phrase *stress-busters*, à *la Ghostbusters*. You could picture a little ghost with the word **Stress** written across its chest, with the red slash through it, meaning **No Stress!**

Whatever you envision, you're on a journey to alleviate stress. On the way, you need to get at the hardcore reality of why you experience stress. Steve Martin said, "Comedy is not pretty." I say hardcore reality is seldom pretty. But once you have your feet firmly rooted in cement—I mean, uh, firmly rooted in *reality*, you have the best chance of taking effective action.

Similar to what I discussed in my earlier book, *The Complete Idiot's Guide to Managing Your Time*, the quest to reduce your stress is a noble pursuit, yet you're probably enduring a fast-paced and frenzied existence. With all that competes for your time and attention, how do you modify the pace of your career and life so you can maintain your control of stress? How can you enjoy what your career and life have to offer and still have time to reflect, to ponder, to muse?

We're going to explore how to reduce your stress level, and hence, improve the quality of your life, for now and evermore. But hey, you're up for the task. To be victorious you have to acknowledge that the changes that you'll implement need to come without too much pain. They must be subtle and, need I say, natural, even easy.

This may sound like a crock, because you and I have been told for a lifetime that we have to grit our teeth and plow through formidable obstacles to achieve lasting change. Yet, lasting and effective change can come from small, incremental steps, as long as they're directed to a common purpose.

Let me give you an example. If you place an egg in boiling water, after a certain number of minutes the egg will become hard-boiled. Conversely, if you place the egg in boiling water for 10 seconds at a time, taking it out for a minute, then putting it back in, the egg eventually will also become hard-boiled. (Nobody wants to mess with boiling water and soft-boiled eggs, so it's easier to just put the egg in, leave it there until it's hard-boiled, and eat the darn thing.) Still, small incremental trips into boiling water will eventually lead to a hard-boiled egg.

Likewise, small incremental changes in the way you go about your workday and life can lead you to the desired result of dramatically reducing the amount of stress in your life. You can achieve an altered state, just like the egg in boiling water. (Fortunately, the changes you make won't result in you becoming hard-boiled!)

If I or anyone else asks you to make changes that are too painful, too upsetting, or too radical from what you're already doing, the changes won't last and they certainly won't be effective. This is an axiom of human nature. Therefore, I ask you to categorically ignore anything you read that represents too much of a stretch for you—for the simple reason that it won't work.

On the other hand, when you encounter something that resonates within you, that gives you a little goose bump, or a feeling of "Gee, I could handle that," then as Conrad Hilton says, "Be my guest," and give it a whirl. Little by little, with a solid framework of knowing what stressors impact you, methods for dealing with them, and a modicum of follow-up, you'll emerge as a less stressed, more balanced person. And people will notice.

How To Use This Book

I've arranged the book so that you can proceed through each chapter in chronological order or, if you wish, tackle chapters at random. Each is self-contained, and will provide nuggets and gems for your cerebral grist mill. I'll move from all-encompassing, culturally based issues to in-your-face work and personal issues, all while maintaining the attitude that, generally, most of the stress you face can be licked.

Part 1, "Facing Up to Modern Stressors," begins by acknowledging the reality that to be alive is to experience stress. Think about it: Is the pace of life speeding up or slowing down? Are you being asked to do more each day, or less? Do you handle more paper despite the advent of the Computer Age, or less? Does anyone pass through this world without experiencing stress in one form or another? I'll discuss the curious phenomenon of how the direction of stress has changed. If this intrigues you, jump right now to Chapter 3.

Part 2, "Surviving Your Own Workplace," explores the angst of holding a job in contemporary society. Although your grandfather learned a skill and was able to use it for a lifetime, that just ain't in the cards for you. Although your pop progressed up the ladder and then, with any luck, hit the cruise control, those days are gone forever for most people—if they ever really existed. I'll examine the effects of competition in the workplace, working too long, being expected to do too much, why there are so many workplace distractions, and when stress boils over the top—the increasing incidence of workplace violence. Chances are you're scrambling for economic survival, and that in itself is stressful.

Part 3, "External Stressors," takes a look at the sardine effect—why we naturally feel more stressed as population density increases. I'll also tackle what the news and information industry do to make your day more stressful.

Part 4, "Self-Induced Stressors," gets at the heart of what you're doing and not doing to affect the quality of your day, week, year, and career. I'll examine the impact of sleep on your stress level, what happens when you don't maintain control of the environment around you, and the effects of leaving too many tasks incomplete.

Part 5, "Getting Your Stress Level Back Down," offers key insights and recommendations on becoming the master of your environment, perfecting the strategic pause, and asking key questions of yourself to help keep you in control. It also discusses how to make choices when you're confused, and how to choose to have less stress. The final chapter is "Stressed or Not, You're Probably Going to Live a Long Time." This will leave you with the proper perspective and a sound framework for having less stress in your life.

You've made it this far in life, presumably on your own. Think how great the coming years can be once you put into practice what you learn from this book! I'm excited for you. So, if you're ready to go where you've never gone before, sit back, take your shoes off, and set a spell.

Extras

I've used some special boxed notes throughout the book to help you learn just what you need. These sidebars are shown here, so you won't be alarmed when you encounter them in the text.

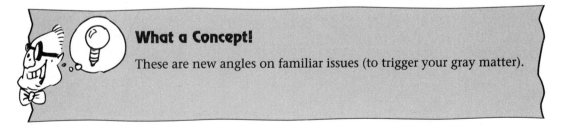

What a Concept!

These are new angles on familiar issues (to trigger your gray matter).

Warning
These are pitfalls to avoid as you reduce your stress.

Etched in stone
These are truths and realities you can depend on.

Word Power
These are new words and terms that can help you know what to look for.

Go!
These are actions to take right away while you're thinking about it.

So, without further ado, flip to Chapter 1 for a look at why to be alive is to experience stress, stressors that everyone faces, and what you can do about them. Otherwise let's roll some credits...

Acknowledgments

Thanks again to all the wonderful folks at Alpha Books and Macmillan General Reference, who keep getting reorganized and put in different offices on different floors, but prevail just the same. They picked me to write this book, and boy was that a good decision! More importantly, they gave me the support I needed to make this book the winner that it is. Thanks to Theresa Murtha, Lisa Bucki, Phil Kitchel, and Brian Robinson for their careful editing, guidance, and all-around excellence.

Thanks to Ellen Greenberg in International Sales for getting this book translated around the world. Thanks to Rachel in Subsidiary Sales for making sure that excerpts are printed all over creation. Thanks to Margaret Durante in Promotion for making sure that newspapers, magazines, TV and radio stations decided to give me a call. Thanks to Gardi Wilks for booking me on shows where the hosts were enthusiastic and supportive. Thanks also to my agent, Trent Price, for his equanimity and balance, in weathering the rigors of getting a book published in this day and age.

Thanks to Brad Diamond for his crackerjack proofreading, Sandy Knudsen for her superfast hands and lightning-quick keyboard, and to Valerie Davidson, now age six, around whom stress is all but impossible.

Special Thanks from the Publisher to the Technical Reviewer...

The Complete Idiot's Guide to Managing Stress was reviewed by an expert who checked the technical accuracy of what you'll learn and provided insights and guidance to help ensure that this book gives you everything you need to understand how to reduce your level of stress. We extend our special thanks to Carol Krucoff, who writes a health column for the *Washington Post* and contributes regularly to numerous national magazines, including *Reader's Digest, Self,* and the *Saturday Evening Post.*

Trademarks

All terms mentioned in this book that are known to be trademarks or service marks are listed here. In addition, terms suspected of being trademarks or service marks have been appropriately capitalized.

Part 1
Facing Up to Modern Stressors

So, you want to reduce the level of stress in your life. Welcome to a club with millions of members in the United States and around the world. Life, even from birth, is inherently stressful. Life's no fun when the amount of daily stress you experience is too high.

You don't need a ton of evidence to know you experience stress. It hits you in the face, the gut, or wherever you personally experience it (maybe it's the base of your neck) often enough. If you learn to manage your stress now, the quality of the rest of your life will be better. Sure, new events and new stressors, like rain, will fall into each life. Armed with effective coping techniques, your future will look brighter and brighter.

To the heart of the matter—these first three chapters examine an array of factors that lead to stress in your life. The stressed-out club has the largest membership on earth! Stress wears many different faces, and more people find their domestic lives are more stressful than their professional lives! Armed with these pleasant notions, let us continue…

Chapter 1

To Be Alive Is to Experience Stress

In This Chapter

➤ Stressors we all face

➤ Stress through the ages

➤ Considering the big picture

➤ Getting off the worst-stressed list

Stress! The very word is stressful for some people, me among them. No one passes through this world without experiencing considerable stress in one form or another. And, from the dawn of humanity right up to the present, each generation and each person, including you, has encountered his/her own set of stressors and stress experiences. Undoubtedly you've heard that there's good stress and bad stress. We'll get to that in detail in Chapter 2. Let me say at the outset that this book is about bad stress, the kind you don't want, don't need, and don't have to have. The kind that limits your effectiveness, chews up your insides, and makes you feel like chopped liver.

The caveperson (or, more politically correct, the Neanderthals) lived on average to age 18 while experiencing a wide variety of stressors, some of which confront humankind today. You're not being chased by saber-toothed tigers, but some of the stressors that you encounter can be just as foreboding. In a way, stress is analogous to electricity. The right amount of electricity powers your radio, lights your lightbulbs, and turns on your PC.

Too much of the same type of electricity blasts out your radio speakers, burns out your light bulb, and causes a power surge that can knock out data on your hard drive.

What a Concept!

When the caveperson encountered a saber-toothed tiger, especially by surprise encounter, he (or she) exhibited stress much like you exhibit it today. The caveperson's body and mind was prepared for either fight or flight. Your ancestors stood their ground and knocked that big cat for a loop, or got out of striking range altogether.

"Brain at Work"

When your brain recognizes or thinks it recognizes danger, it sets a chain reaction in motion, releasing chemicals in your body that put your nervous system into high gear. Your heart starts pumping faster and your breathing accelerates to take in the extra oxygen you'll need, whether you fight or flee. In either case, you're wired. Either you and the saber-tooth duke it out, or you break the record for the hundred-meter dash.

Warning

It may well be adaptive, and even appropriate, for you to exhibit fight or flight stress responses at the onset of a change in your environment. The problem for most people—need I say it, the problem for *you*—is when you stay in this high gear, fight or flight mode long after the initial surprise/shock/bend in the road.

Either way, you have to draw on your physical resources. In fact, so many systems in your body rev up to meet the need at hand, it would take pages and pages to cover them all. Your reflexes get sharper so that you can respond more readily. Your blood clots faster, so if you get clawed, you won't bleed to death…at least not on the first swipe!

Suppose new software was introduced in your department, and you have to learn it in a matter of days. You're comfortable with the old program and you don't want to take on the new, but the whole organization is changing over and you have no choice. So what do you do? You gear up. You put all your energy and intensity into this effort. The problem is, you're "on" the whole time. For the next three days—at work, at lunch, at home, and all points in between—many of your internal systems are revving at inappropriate levels to accomplish the task at hand.

You don't like how you feel, but you don't know how to turn it off. You start swigging cups of coffee, or aspirin, or Prozac, or whatever else is on hand. After work, maybe you belt down a couple of drinks or—if you're wise—do a couple laps around the park. Maybe you get enough sleep that night, maybe you don't. Regardless, the next day, whatever stress control you achieved the day before is quickly lost as you plop down in front of the PC and begin Round Two of Doing Things in a Completely Different Way. You don't like it, but you have to do it, and your body responds by operating in a gear too high to comfortably sustain for long.

That's Amazing

Amazingly (at least it's amazing to me), in nearly every situation you face, nearly all of the time, at least half the battle in alleviating your stress is simply to become more aware of how you react to situations. This sounds too simple to be true, but it is. Moreover, and we might as well get to the biggie right off the bat:

> *For most people, most of the time, most of the stress they encounter is self-induced.*

I know, it's a broad, sweeping, general statement, and you can come up with all types of exceptions. But I'm describing most people, most of the time—and, Bubba, I'm talking about you! Yes, there are traumatic incidents, death of loved ones, cataclysmic losses, and the like. For the most part, this book isn't about those things. For such events, you need case-specific texts, or perhaps professional help—guidance that dwells extensively on the types of stress you're experiencing.

The principle focus of this book is the day-to-day, week-to-week types of stress that John Q. Public and Jane Doe experience simply from having lots of responsibility, living in a frenetic society, and operating at too rapid a pace—the good old-fashioned stress that comes from being alive. The stress that comes from commuting to work, or working for an S.O.B., or having everyone give you grief.

Name That Stressor!

What kind of stressors can the typical professional, somebody like you, experience? The number can be staggering. Actually, almost anything in your environment can be a stressor. For example:

➤ **Your boss** A mean boss, an unfair boss, a disorganized boss, or someone with whom you simply can't get along can be a great source. Such a boss can make your daily work routine miserable. In extreme cases, such a boss can shorten your life, as can many other stressors.

➤ **Co-workers** Everything just said about bosses can apply to co-workers, as well.

➤ **Subordinates** The people who report to you can be an extreme cause of stress, especially if they're incompetent, tardy, unreliable, or untrustworthy.

➤ **Work-related stress** Independent of any particular people involved, the work-place itself can be stressful. Moreover, work-related stress seems to be on the rise.

Whether due to take-overs, down-sizing, mergers and acquisitions, new organizations, or meeting the challenge of hypercompetition, today's professional is likely to be bursting with stress.

This manifests itself in dead-ended careers, emotional disorders, and families torn asunder. More employees, at higher levels, are turning to drinking and drugs than organizations would like to admit. Some employees burst into uncontrollable fits of rage, abuse their families, or turn to suicide. (For more on stress blowing over the top, see Chapter 9.) Even in a non-crisis setting you can have too much noise, not enough privacy, too many distractions, and unrealistic deadlines. Hey, you probably have a mental list of all these and more!

➤ **Occupational stress**   Some people, simply by virtue of where they work, experience oodles of stress. And it's not always in industries you might guess. Airline pilots, for example, tend to live shorter lives. It is postulated that too much flying during the day leads to higher levels of radiation, which over many hours and years shortens one's life. Even sanitation engineers experience occupational stress. (A-ha, you didn't know that, did you?) They have a very high rate of accident and injury. Think about all the sharp, dangerous, or otherwise harmful objects in garbage cans.

You don't have to work in a coal mine to experience occupational stress. People who are around loud noises for too long each day, or who are routinely in high-pressure situations, such as airline traffic controllers, have their work, and sometimes their livers, cut out for them.

➤ **Relationships**   Whether it's your wife, husband, mother, brother, father-in-law, mother-in-law, uncle, sister, second cousin twice removed, great-granduncle on your mother's side, and so on, anyone in your lineage can qualify.

Relationship stress is something to which almost everyone can relate. Who hasn't had stress as a result of a relationship in their life? Even Abraham Lincoln had troubles with his father. David Herbert Donald, in his book *Lincoln*, writes that Lincoln had "not one favorable word to say about his father." He did not even attend his father's funeral.

➤ **Poor nutrition**   You may not have considered this, but if you've been eating junk food all your life and are lacking vital nutrients, you may not have the physical stamina to support your needs. Do you eat some square meals a day? Do you eat any vegetables and fruits? Do you take vitamins? A lot of people don't, and then wonder why it's so tough for them to get through the day.

➤ **Sleep** Study after study shows that Americans, and professionals throughout the world, consistently do not get the amount of sleep they need on a daily basis. Lack of sleep can lower your immunity, increase your susceptibility to disease, and most definitely increase your susceptibility to stressors in the environment. Which leads us to...

➤ **The environment** You don't have to live near electrical power lines to experience stress as a result of your immediate environment. Poor water, poor air, traffic congestion, noise, fear for your safety, and a range of other environmental factors can contribute greatly to the stress you experience.

➤ **Monetary pressures** Meeting the monthly mortgage or rent when you're short on funds, being laid off and not having a bank account, putting your kids through college, getting that operation for your mother, or simply making ends meet has become a continual source of stress for the masses. Then too, spending more than you take in, having what they call "champagne taste on a beer budget," will do you in time and time again.

➤ **Being alone** Has your partner in life passed away? Or has looking for a mate become a long-term struggle? Did someone who matters leave, or get stationed far away? Being alone can be stressful and lead to all types of aberrant, if not unhealthy, behavior.

➤ **Not having time alone** Just the opposite of being lonely, if you never get a spare moment to think, relax, and reflect, a mounting form of stress can ensue. The prototypical "Super Mom" of today, who makes breakfast, gets the kids out the door, holds a full-time job, and barely gets home in time to begin her real work, can fall into this category. "Super Dads" can have equally taxing challenges, which result in the long-term mounting form of stress.

➤ **Your physical self** Do you perceive yourself as too fat, too thin, or too something else? Lots of people do. One poll showed that more than two-thirds of all men and even higher numbers of women are fairly discontent with various aspects of their physical selves, and would like to make major changes. (More on this in Chapter 12, "Over-Exposure to Unreality.") To compensate for perceived deficiencies in their physical self, some people will starve themselves to death. Others will eat themselves to death. Some will go on binges, some will go on feast and famine diets. Someone like that may be holding this book right now.

➤ **Chemical substances** Do you smoke, do you drink, do you take drugs? Do you do any of them to excess? 'Nuff said.

➤ **Other stressors** Add your own here, based on what you do, with whom you do it, when you do it, how long you do it, and so forth. The point is, there are many, many ways to experience major stress in this world.

Minor, Niggling Stressors

Beyond what's listed above, there are an endless number of situational stressors, many of which are highly familiar:

Time pressures You're late for an appointment. Or you're late for a date. Different situations, different sensations, but either way, it's hard to be at your best unless you're armed with tools for keeping your stress to a minimum.

Commuting Maybe you haven't been lucky enough to be on the highway when the guy in the next car pulls out his ten-gauge shotgun, but being stuck in traffic even occasionally is upsetting, let alone having to crawl in a moving parking lot every day just to get to work. Which leads of course to…

Being in lines Despite all the advances and technology, we seem to end up in lines—*long* lines—all too frequently. Whether you're at the bank, the supermarket, the movie theater, or, God forbid, the license branch, the post office, or any other government agency, it's a reasonable bet that you'll be waiting in lines for the foreseeable future.

As if those weren't enough, *Redbook* surveyed its readers and found that the following factors may also contribute to stress. Do any of these apply to you?

➤ Living in a rural area

➤ Having had a major health problem within the last year

➤ Having unsatisfactory child-care arrangements

➤ Having no close friends or relatives in the community

➤ Living in a high-crime area, or an area that you perceive to be unsafe

➤ Having a spouse who doesn't do a fair share of housework

How Did It All Get So Hectic?

Is there something indigenous to our culture that led to the development of a high-stress society? Or did we just luck out? I believe factors were at play that, in retrospect, are easily identifiable now. With each advancement in transportation, communications, and technology in general, human capability increases, and then in the next nanosecond, so do expectations. (Chapter 6 focuses on this in detail.)

Warning
When you're bombarded with more messages and more information than you can possibly respond to, it can get stressful.

For example, in 1803, Robert Fulton, disproving those who thought it folly, was able to propel a boat by steam power, sparking a revolution in transportation and commerce. A scant 60 years later, the railroad hastened the development of migration to the western U.S. In another 40 years, the Wright brothers successfully flew a powered plane at Kitty Hawk.

By 1911, Charles F. Kettering developed the first practical electric self-starter for cars. In 1923, Henry Ford, having already established the Ford Motor Company 10 years earlier, developed the assembly line to produce the affordable Model-T. Today, 170 million registered motorists just in the U.S. own, drive, or have responsibility for 400 million registered vehicles. In some sections of some cities, there are literally more vehicles than parking spaces. In all cities throughout the U.S., traffic has become a drag and a major source of stress.

In communications, Johannes Gutenberg printed a 42-line Bible at Mainz between 1453 and 1455, known surprisingly as the Gutenberg Bible. In 1729 Benjamin and James Franklin began publishing *The Pennsylvania Gazette*, confirming that colonial America could in fact support more than one newspaper (who would have thunk it?). In 1844, empowered by Congress, Samuel Morse completed the first telegraph system linking Baltimore and Washington. By 1861, the system extended to California. In 1866, the Transatlantic Cable was successfully laid between Newfoundland and Ireland. A scant 10 years later, Alexander Graham Bell invented the telephone.

You know what's happened since then. In the 1980s, we witnessed the development and enhancement of cellular phones, fax machines, voice mail, and all the rest. Soon, on-line communications via cable rather than telephone lines will speed images and data to us 28 to 30 times faster than they are commonly received now. Capabilities for gathering and disseminating information will be greatly enhanced. At the same time, our expectations will increase manifold.

Etched in Stone
As soon as a breakthrough is perfected, adopted, and widespread, social expectations rise immediately to meet the new found capability.

Today, it's not uncommon for a corporate executive to receive 100, 200, 300, or more e-mails a day.

Even the simplest breakthrough, which may seemingly have no down-side, in the end, contributes to increased expectations and ultimately to stress. What do I mean? Take the washing machine. Prior to its development and widespread use, people commonly wore the same clothes several days in a row, or at least several days in a week or a month, before washing them. With the advent of the washing machine, higher standards of cleanliness developed. Soon, it became standard, then mandatory, then unthinkable not to wear a freshly washed shirt to work. Wisk, the staunch defender against ring-around-the-collar, still sells today because of the sociocultural expectation that no one ever dare be caught at work without a freshly washed shirt.

I could offer examples in many other industries but the net result is always the same.

Living on the Margin

In his book *Living On the Margin*, Dr. Richard A. Swenson says that there's a specific point where we reach overload: "...where the demands on us exceed our limits. We have, as a culture, crossed that line." Swenson points out that 268 million Americans are all "hitting the wall together." He believes that the demands on our time and energy, and our ability to cope with these demands, can be mapped and plotted with the same accuracy as the path of a comet.

As science and technology vastly outpace our ability to keep up, we predictably find our responses to our surroundings are not what they used to be.

Swenson says we're not just up against time hurdles, it's mental, emotional, and physical energy. For example, he points out that by the time your days are up on this earth, you'll have learned how to operate some 20,000 different devices, from can-openers to camcorders. Name a generation in the history of the earth that's experienced even a 20th of that.

Comfort in Mega-Change?

Professor Charles Hardy writing in *The Age of Paradox* says, "We stand at a crossroads, seeking our way to the future. It is a place of paradox, confusion of simultaneous opposites, of unexpected consequences, of altered meanings and oxymorons. What was once obvious, like the necessity of economic growth, is now hedged with qualifications. We thought we knew how to run organizations, but the organizations of today bare no resemblance to the ones we knew. We're confused because things don't behave the way we instinctively expect them to behave. What worked well the last time around is not guaranteed to work well the next time."

That in itself could be stressful, but I tend to find comfort in it. Why? Because everyone is essentially in the same boat. There's a certain equality among this flock of human beings as we encounter the brave new world. The changes will come swiftly and no one will have an edge.

Professor Lowell Catlett, noted author and professor at New Mexico State University, says that the rate of change in the United States and Canada is such that a new high technology is produced in the market-place every 17 seconds. That's more than three a minute, more than 200 an hour, and well more than 5,000 a day. With each new high-technology product comes at least 100 related services. Yet, in just a few years there will be 17 new high technology products produced every *second*.

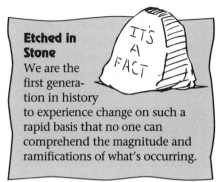

Etched in Stone

We are the first genera-tion in history to experience change on such a rapid basis that no one can comprehend the magnitude and ramifications of what's occurring.

You can't eat more than one dinner at a time (unless you're a real glutton), drive more than one car at a time, sleep in more than one bed at a time, or appreciably speed up bodily functions in some vain, ludicrous attempt to stay on top of "it all." Nor will you have to.

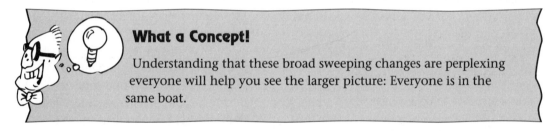

What a Concept!

Understanding that these broad sweeping changes are perplexing everyone will help you see the larger picture: Everyone is in the same boat.

Everyone experiences stress, in some cases major stress, in many cases unprecedented levels of stress. It's not exactly the same stress that you're experiencing, but on balance, person to person, professional to professional, the nature and level of stress often is surprisingly similar.

Consider this. The Gallop Poll surveyed a cross section of Americans and asked, "How often do you experience stress in your daily life?" Forty percent of respondents said Always, 39 percent said Sometimes. This is 79 percent responding affirmatively to daily stress. Also, by some estimates, stress-related symptoms now account for about 60 percent of office visits to doctors.

When asked, "Would you take a 20 percent income cut if you or your partner could work fewer hours?" 33 percent said yes. (It would be interesting to know what the results would be if is was only a 10 percent income cut.)

During stressful times, almost half of respondents said that they prefer to be alone.

Finally, when asked "Is the amount of stress in your life within your control?" 76 percent said yes.

I'm not surprised that three-quarters of respondents said that stress was under their control. After all, with all the psychology we've been exposed to in the last several decades, most people understand that they bear the most responsibility for the quality of their lives. You knew that—that's why you picked up this book. The key to reducing stress to an acceptable level is to apply what you learn to make a difference in how you feel.

Getting a Handle on Stress

The future will unfold at a rapid pace. Yet, there may be nothing quite as stressful as attempting to be someone different from who you really are. It takes a great deal of energy, like a power surge too high for your radio, your light, or your PC, to maintain the posture of someone you're not. It's less stressful to give in to who you are. This is not such a bad thing.

Go!
What's important is to learn measures of control that enable you to stay on a more even keel throughout the day.

Research on identical twins separated at birth but reunited later in life shows that genetics may have more to do with personality than we previously believed. Lawrence Wright, reporting on twins research in *The New Yorker* says that the latest findings suggest that, "The life experiences we think have shaped us are little more than ornaments or curiosities…and that the injunctions of our parents or the traumas of our youth which we believe to be the lodestones of our character may have had little more effect on us than a book we have read or a show we have seen on television."

Wright believes that if identical twins, growing up alone, can "sort through the world of opportunity and adversity and arrive at a similar place, then we may as well see that as a triumph of our genetic determination to become the person we ought to be." So, you get bent out of shape when traffic moves along at four miles an hour? Chances are you always will. The key is to not get so bent out of shape that it does internal damage, or upsets your whole day.

After reading this paragraph, I want you to put down the book and participate in the following exercise. Sitting in your chair, notice areas of your body. Where is there tension? In the back of your neck, in your shoulders? That's common for people who work at a desk. Does your back ache? Is your stomach tied up in knots? Wherever you're feeling discomfort, be it a headache, a backache, or what have you, it's your body's way of signaling that your not getting the rest, relaxation, nutrition, or some other element it needs to operate more effectively.

Does the typical baby walk around with a frown on his face, fretting over what he didn't get done today? The natural state of the human being is alertness, health, well-being, mental clarity, and—dare I say it?—a tinge of happiness.

Okay, so what can you do right now? Here are a variety of ways to reduce some of the stress you experience in your life, starting with some simple maneuvers moving up to the more involved or costly:

Drink water. Half the time, when you're under stress, simply taking a sip of water will immediately make you feel better. A dry mouth seems to accompany many types of anxious situations. Hydrate, hydrate, hydrate.

Sit still. For the next minute, stare at your watch, or if that's too boring, think about something pleasurable you're going to do today. Your perception of the length of a minute will differ vastly from using that minute to listen to the news or read a page from a magazine.

Twist and shout. Physical movement can relieve tension. You can take a walk around the block, stretch right within your office, and use the stairs instead of the elevators. After work, blow off steam by going places where it's okay to yell—sports bars, baseball games, conventions, or pep rallies. By the way, when barreling down the highway alone in your car, some therapeutic singing may also help reduce stress. Yelling may even work.

Improve your posture. Have you noticed that you begin to slouch when you get a phone call, or you slink further and further into the easy chair when you watch television? The body was made to be upright and erect. When you talk, eat, walk and sit with full and proper extension, your systems work better and minor stresses melt away.

Contemplate pleasant thoughts. Whether it's a waterfall, the picnic you had last Sunday, what it will be like when you're with your lover next, or getting a $10,000 check in the mail, visualization can calm the mind and soothe the soul. You don't have to get heavily into meditation or yoga; simply develop the ability to take two to five minutes out of your day to peer out the window, or simply close your eyes. Get into a quiet space, and feel good about aspects of your life.

Use visualization. Tomorrow morning as you get ready for work, rather than switching on the radio or TV, quietly envision how you would like your day to be. Include everything that's important to you—the commute, entering your building or your office, sitting down at your desk, handling tasks, and taking breaks.

Envision interacting with others, going to lunch, conducting or attending meetings, using the phone, finishing up projects, and walking out in the evening. With this exercise alone, you'll begin to feel a greater sense of control in aspects of your job that you may have considered uncontrollable.

Buy a hand gripper. A tennis ball, a racquetball, or a hand-gripper at your desk is a marvelous stress reducer. Squeeze it when you feel tense to achieve a release.

Buy a joke book. If *The Far Side* by Gary Larson or *Cathy* by Cathy Guisewite bring a smile to your face, keep such cartoons within easy reach. One good laugh, and your whole temperament can change, plummeting the stress you feel back down to a manageable level.

Build slack into your schedule. A paradox among accomplished people is that the more they achieve, the more they believe they can achieve, and with less effort. If you think something is going to take two hours, plan on it taking three and schedule accordingly. This is a great stress reducer. If you finish in far less than three, fine.

Volunteer. Serving others helps you to increase your self-respect and sense of accomplishment. When you stay in isolation, your worries intensify. So, serve soup or pick a cause. Choose one cause or one issue, and take some kind of action outside your home. There's little use in intellectually resonating with the world's challenges and problems. Action is customarily invigorating. Your ability to make a real, if minute, difference will immediately lessen your concerns about attaining some breathing space.

Reduce some of your costs. Living beyond your means is one of the most stressful forms of existence in our society. What can you do right now to eliminate some onerous monthly expenses? Can you trade in your car? Can you sell vacation property? Can you eliminate subscriptions? Take a look at what you don't need.

The Least You Need to Know

➤ Everyone in Western or industrialized societies who holds any position of responsibility is experiencing the effects of increasing change. These effects manifest themselves in various forms of stress.

➤ Changes in technology invariably lead to enhanced capability, and in the next nanosecond enhanced expectations.

➤ Because everyone is in relatively the same boat, there's no need to excessively worry about the future. Human physiology changes very slowly, nowhere near the ultra-rapid pace of technology.

➤ Simply understanding this socially pervasive phenomenon that is impacting all humanity in itself can be stress-reducing. Awareness counts.

➤ You have at your disposal many techniques for minimizing stress at any given time. These range from taking a walk to visualizing something pleasant to reducing some of your costs.

Chapter 2

What Do We Mean by Stress?

In This Chapter

➤ How stress manifests itself in different ways.

➤ Some terminology related to stress.

➤ Is your job inherently stressful?

➤ Is your stress unique to you?

➤ What is your stress telling you?

Before you can keep something in its place, you have to understand the nature of the beast! Dr. Hans Selye, one of the prominent psychologists of the twentieth century, undertook original and breakthrough work in the understanding and defining of stress.

Stress, according to Dr. Selye is the "single, non-specific reaction of the body to a demand made upon it."

What did he mean by a non-specific reaction of the body? When there's some situation, irritation, or force confronting you, your body responds in a particular way. This response is far different, however, than your body's response if you step on a thumbtack with a bare foot, walk into a freezing meat locker, or get slapped upside the head.

What's the difference? For the latter three events, your body's reaction is quite specific. You feel the pain of the thumbtack, the chill of the meat locker, or the sting of the slap in a specific location at a specific time. The pain or discomfort is quite specific.

By contrast, an irritating situation is a more nebulous, non-specific stimuli. Both can cause a form of pain as well. This pain however, comes in the form of stress. You don't always recognize it, yet the price it exacts upon your body can be significant.

What a Concept!

Most of the time, you get over a specific reaction to a pain-inducing event. A non-specific reaction to a non-specific irritant, like the droning noise from the equipment in the next office or the fear that the bank may foreclose on your property, can actually do more long-term damage.

How Stress Manifests Itself in Different Ways

Warning

The all-too-familiar tension that accompanies what you know as stress is largely self-induced.

Consider stress as the wear-and-tear on your body. Author Marilyn Manning says that stress is a by-product of pressures, changes, demands, and challenges that you face each day. Nevertheless, the pressures you confront every day don't have to be bad, or to cause stress.

Stress is the way your body tells you that you need to be more attuned to your environment, and as Manning says, "become more attentive and permissive, to let go, and to relax."

Signs of Stress

What are some of the signs that you're experiencing stress? For one, your mouth and throat are dry. For reasons it would take pages to explain, your saliva is less abundant. You might find yourself clenching your teeth or holding your jaw very tightly. If you experience any kind of jaw pain or pressure, you'll know that you've been doing this— perhaps in your sleep.

You're also likely to swallow more air, which can result in bloating or belching. If you find yourself engaging in short, shallow breathing, it's a sign that you're anxious. You're literally depriving yourself of oxygen. Your body has no choice at this point but to request that you yawn, forcing you to take deeper breaths.

You probably already know that stress can make you more prone to colds and flus, headaches of all kinds, and even gas and heartburn. You may not have realized that stress can constrict the blood vessels in your arms and legs while increasing your heart rate, a situation that results in an increase in your blood pressure, perhaps to dangerously high levels.

I was flabbergasted to learn that under stress, you may actually experience fat within your body being deposited in your midsection. Gosh!

Good Stress and Bad Stress?

You've heard that there's good stress and bad stress. Not surprisingly, the term stress is often misunderstood and misused. Even highly paid executives often have misperceptions regarding it—some don't even believe it exists. What is *good* stress all about?

Word Power
Eustress=Good stress.
Distress=Bad stress!

Think of it this way—good stress, or *eustress*, is what gets you up and running, what enables you to get to work, get to the ball game on time, or clean out the garage on Saturday. Eustress helps to make your life enjoyable, even interesting. Such stress provides stimulation and challenges, and is essential to development, growth, and change.

Bad stress, or *distress,* makes you anxious and irritable, dampens your spirits, and shortens your life. Distress is a reaction to some type of pressure, either external or self-imposed, which prompts psychological and physiological changes of an undesirable nature.

No single event categorically leads to stress. Dr. Selye says, "It's not the event but your perception of it that makes all the difference." Two people can be subjected to the same stimuli, and one might not notice it at all while the other is stressed out to the max.

What a Concept!

It's been said that the only person without stress is a dead person.

What Means What: Some Terminology Related to Stress

Among the best definitions of stress that I've come across is the following: *Stress is the psychological and physiological reaction that takes place when you perceive an imbalance in the level of demand placed on you, and your capacity to meet that demand.* In plain English, you're up against something, and you're not sure you have what it takes to meet the challenge. Or, it's so easy that you want to be somewhere else.

In many ways, managing stress means keeping the pressures you face at a challenging, but containable level—the level you might term good stress. When you face a challenge that you perceive to be within your capabilities, you flourish, and, more often than not, meet the challenge.

Unfortunately, maintaining that level is easier to discuss than to achieve. If the pressures you face become excessive, whether real or imagined, you're likely to become "distressed," or for short, stressed.

Note: For the rest of this book, *stress* will refer to *bad* stress.

Doing things that don't stimulate and challenge you can give you a backache, a stiff shoulder, neck pain—you know the feeling. It's too boring to focus on, and therefore difficult to get through. Thus, there's always a fine balance to be achieved.

Stress itself is simply not something out there waiting to get you. You have to perceive and recognize it based on your background or upbringing—have it rub you the wrong way. To become even more detailed in considering stress, you can break down bad stress to its types and causes. C. Leslie Charles, a management trainer and author based in East Lansing, Michigan, categorizes stress into four basic areas:

➤ **Anticipatory stress** is stress caused by concern over the future. Another word for it is worry: You concern yourself with endless stressful possibilities, stewing over something that hasn't happened—and may not. A better strategy? Plan. Planning is different from worrying. If you're concerned about a pending event, figure out how you would handle it and quit worrying. If it happens, you're ready for it; if not, even better!

➤ **Situational stress** is stress of the moment. It's an immediate threat, challenge, or agitation—something that demands your attention right now. How do you deal with it? Breathe! Take a nice deep breath from your diaphragm (not your chest) and let it relax you. Keep your hands open (avoid making fists) and relax your shoulders and jaw muscles. Tell yourself you can handle this (because you can). Stay as calm as possible, do your best, and give yourself credit for coping when it's over.

➤ **Chronic stress** is stress over time. It may stem from a tough experience over which you have no control except to endure or accept, such as the loss of a loved one, an illness, accident, or other trauma. It could be from a strained personal relationship or unfortunate work situation. Chronic stress is best handled one day at a time, with patience, personal strength, support from others, a daily plan, and few projections into the future.

➤ **Residual stress** is stress of the past. It represents our inability or unwillingness to let go of old hurts or bad memories. Come to terms with the fact that you cannot rewrite history, change the past, or magically make things recur the way you want. Let them go.

I've found that by simply recognizing these different faces of stress, I can proceed accordingly. For example, if I experience stress and can recognize that it's situational stress that will pass rather quickly, I can immediately "turn down" my internal stress level because I know that I won't be concerned with it two hours or two days from now.

Go!
You can relieve stress significantly by reducing your anticipatory stress, letting go of your residual stress, and handling the other two as they occur.

Is Your Job Inherently Stressful?

Inquiring minds want to know. A growing number of professionals believe they're in a profession that uniquely contributes to stress. Insurance agents think their industry is inherently stressful. Taxi drivers *know* they're in a stressful job: Recent statistics showed that theirs is the most dangerous profession in America!

A study by the New York State Society of CPAs found that most CPAs agree that public accounting is a high-stress profession. Anyone in the collections department of a major organization can tell you that there are a plethora of built-in stressors that arise when you attempt to collect money from others.

What factors tell you if your industry, your career, your position in particular are too stressful? Try these on for size:

➤ Do you have a difficult boss?

➤ Are you constantly asked to put in overtime, particularly at the last minute?

➤ Do you face role ambiguity, that is, you don't have a clear definition of what's expected of you?

➤ Do you face conflicting demands? If you have one or more bosses, and many people do, sometimes to please one you have to displease the other.

➤ Do you deal with excessive job requirements—tasks and assignments that clearly exceed your ability or training?

➤ Do you lack job security? Are you working someplace, not knowing from day to day how secure you are with the organization?

➤ Do you have an inflexible work environment? Do you have to be in by 8:30 on the button? Are you allowed to leave to pick up your son early one night? If not, stress may be predictable.

➤ Is there a healthy career progression? Do you have enough opportunities for advancement? Does hard work earn rewards?

➤ Do you have responsibility for the performance of others? Have you ever had to fire someone? Even top executives who've fired dozens of people, after many years, still find this to be a highly stressful aspect of their position.

➤ Are your talents under-used? As I mentioned earlier, if your job doesn't offer enough of a challenge, that can be as stressful as one that offers too much of a challenge.

Other indications may include

➤ Intestinal distress.

➤ Rapid pulse.

➤ Frequent illness.

➤ Insomnia.

➤ Persistent fatigue.

➤ Irritability.

➤ Nail biting.

➤ Lack of concentration.

➤ Increased use of alcohol and drugs.

➤ Hunger for sweets.

Stress Dressed Up as Something Else

You don't have to be sucking down a cigarette every three minutes or climbing the walls to be exhibiting signs of stress. Some of the stress you experience is probably exhibited in subtle ways. For example, if you manage a department or lead an organization and you're under stress, chances are you will abandon the judgment and calculated thinking that got you there and fall back on possibly outmoded methods that worked well in the past. Unfortunately, this lack of dynamic flexibility may yield less than optimal results. This is a subtle but predictable display of stress among leaders and managers. Some of the more subtle signs of job stress are:

Warning
One strange aspect of stress is that it isn't always recognized for what it is.

Tending to minutia   Many professionals focus excessively on insignificant minutia when working under stress. This causes them to miss important deadlines. If you think you're the *only* one who falls into this trap, guess again.

Tardiness and absenteeism   And you thought you were just late.

Becoming combative   One of the emotional fallouts of working under stress is that you're likely to become irritable or perhaps aggressive with others. This effects those around you at work and at home, as well as your ability to perform effectively.

Lack of concentration   If you are experiencing excessive stress, don't be surprised if you're less rational, more forgetful, and not quite your old self. The mental effects of working under stress for a prolonged period can lead to indecisiveness and poor decision making. You may even find yourself reading lines in a book over and over. You may even find yourself reading lines in a book over and over.

In one study of workers in the United Kingdom, who now average a longer work week than most of the rest of Europe, many professionals are suffering from what is called *presenteeism*. This is analogous to being among the living dead.

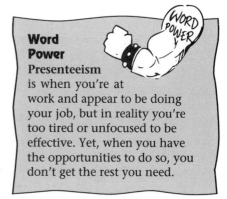

Word Power
Presenteeism is when you're at work and appear to be doing your job, but in reality you're too tired or unfocused to be effective. Yet, when you have the opportunities to do so, you don't get the rest you need.

In what other ways can stress dress itself up as something else?

➤ Having a poor attitude, being lethargic, achieving low productivity, beating yourself up mentally, or frequently letting your mind wander are all potential signs of stress.

➤ Experiencing unexplained depression, nervous giggling, tapping your feet, wishing you could just run and hide, having bad dreams, heightened anxieties, and sociopathic behavior can all be signs of stress.

➤ Feeling like there's no meaning in your life, waiting for Prince or Princess Charming, having no direction or purpose, feeling shallow, feeling uncharitable, or being cold or uncaring can be signs of stress.

➤ Resenting others, not being able to trust others, losing interest in sex or inability to achieve intimacy, feeling ice-layered or depersonalized, or being upset over little things that normally wouldn't upset you at all, are all signs of stress.

➤ Being clumsier than usual, under-eating or over-eating, having migraine headaches, indigestion or irritable bowel syndrome, too much or too little sleep, or becoming easily fatigued are all signs of stress.

➤ Having specific pains in parts of the body, tension headaches, irregular menstrual cycles, frequent trips to the bathroom, nervous twitches, or a racing pulse can all be signs of stress.

Is Your Stress Unique to You?

OK, so far it's clear that the probability of encountering stimuli that result in stress is high. But is your stress unique to you?

The answer is "Yes." After all, what stresses me out may have no impact on you whatsoever. And what I breeze through may stop you cold in your tracks.

Go! You don't have to get angry in a given situation. You could choose to acknowledge the good life you're leading, hum your favorite song, be glad that you live in this country or that your kids are healthy, or think about what's planned for dinner this evening. How you elect to feel is always your choice.

Consider the scenario I discussed in my earlier book, *Breathing Space: Living and Working at a Comfortable Pace in a Sped Up Society*. You're stalled in traffic on the interstate, on a sweltering day in August, when your air car conditioner conks out. On top of that, today you happened to wear a wool tweed suit with no underwear. Do you feel justified being irritated?

The act of choosing is a simple but powerful technique that will further aid you in attaining breathing space (more on this in Chapter 20).

A useful exercise in understanding what's stressful to you and why is to trace back to the origins of your belief system. Suppose being late for an appointment is stressful for you. Could it be that you attach a lot more to the event?

So, you're late for an appointment. What does that mean?

It could mean that you'll incur the wrath of the prospect.

You may not make a sale.

If you don't make a sale, that means your income could suffer.

You may not make quota that month.

Your boss may lean on you even harder.

You may lose your job.

You might not be able to take care of your family.

If this goes on for too long, you might find yourself in poverty.

In extreme situations, you may even starve.

You may even starve to death.

If this scenario seems a little overly developed, consider this: For some people, being late for an appointment is like starving to death. Who knows, maybe it's embedded some-place in their genetic makeup.

Correspondingly, consider the potential stress of being rejected by someone. You ask someone to go out with you. (This *could* be a woman asking a man, you know!) The other person says no. You feel rejected, but it's deeper than that.

They said no. What does that mean?

That could mean that they didn't find you attractive, or desirable.

Maybe you're not worth their time.

What if they're right and you *are* unattractive, undesirable, or worse, unlovable?

Perhaps you'll never find anyone.

Maybe you'll never find a mate.

You'll never have sexual satisfaction.

You won't be part of important social circles.

You won't have children.

No heirs. Nothing to leave behind.

There will be no heritage.

You'll have lived a drab and despicable existence.

Historians will reflect on these shortcomings in your life if you become famous.

Go! Mark Victor Hansen, who was a neat guy even before he found world-wide fame with *Chicken Soup for the Soul*, told me that there's a key word he recites to himself whenever he encounters rejection: "Next!"

If this sounds far-fetched for you, consider that for some people, the stress of being turned down is synonymous with being lonely for the rest of their lives.

Let's try one more. Suppose you're a high school student and you just got rejected by one of your top choices of colleges. It's still early in the year, you've always been a good student. Nevertheless, what kind of scenario might ensue?

Maybe they'll all reject me.

Maybe I won't get into college at all.

Then I won't get the proper education.

I'll get a low-paying job.

I'll live in low cost housing.

I'll fall out of my circle of friends.

I'll be old before my time.

I'll have to live off of Social Security.

But Social Security's going bust.

What's the use? I'll probably starve.

Not so curiously, getting rejected from a college, although probably more significant than getting rejected on a sales call, can invoke the same type of response in people. For some, the underlying fear is that they'll starve to death or be a social reject.

If these are the kinds of equations that are hard wired into your consciousness, it's easy to see why such relatively minor events can provoke highly stressful reactions within you.

What Is Your Stress Telling You?

If you experience undue stress at being late, rejected, early, or accepted, which are also quite possible, look at the situation at hand, experience the stress in all it's magnitude, and then consider it your best friend. Best friend?

What a Concept!

Avoiding or attempting to avoid the stressful information that you receive doesn't give you any power.

The sensations that you experience, problematic stress for seemingly minor events, author Robert Fritz observes, are dynamic, creative forms of information.

Regarding your problematic stress response as a friend, from Fritz's perspective, enables you to benefit from what he calls the law of reversal: Use the negative energy surrounding the problem to propel you to positive forces available to achieve a solution. The more stress you experience in a particular situation, the greater your potential to one day alleviate that stress and live a more balanced life.

The key is to keep asking yourself, "What is this reaction forcing me to learn or to do? Do I need to read up on this, involve others, let go of my tendency to over-control, or simply take things more slowly?"

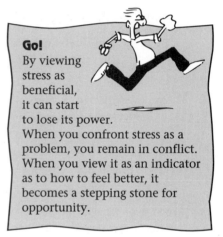

Go!
By viewing stress as beneficial, it can start to lose its power. When you confront stress as a problem, you remain in conflict. When you view it as an indicator as to how to feel better, it becomes a stepping stone for opportunity.

Suppose you're a control freak—just kidding—who needs to be in control of things and becomes discombobulated if you're not. Lack of control is a key issue that causes stress for many people. It's easier to feel successful when you're in control, whereas when you're not feeling in control, any little thing can become stressful.

The less in control you feel, the more you want to *be* in control, which makes you feel even *more* out of control. This spiral adds to your stress.

One paradox of control is that to feel like you have more of it, you have to let go of your need for it. To successfully reduce your need for control, take a different path; attempt counter control measures:

Develop some perspective. Step back from the problem. A month from now, will you even remember what's bothering you today?

Be realistic. Is this a situation in which you can make a difference? Maybe not.

Look at the big picture. Having a sense of purpose or a mission in life routinely offers peace of mind independent of the nitty-gritty problems that you face on a daily basis.

If You Want to Control Something, Control Your Stress

Learning how to keep your stress at an acceptable level is vital to your health and well-being, career success, and personal quality of life. Like the electricity example in the last chapter, when you have the right amount, everything clicks. When you have a short circuit, you're going to suffer in one or more ways.

What a Concept!

The way you respond to the environment around you may actually give you the ability to keep your level of stress in check all day long, day in and day out.

Suppose there were a spectrum with numbers ranging from 1 to 100. 100 would be your highest level of stress. When you're above 80, your entire being is under stress and you're unable to operate effectively, either mentally or physically. When you're at a score of 30 or below, you're calm, relaxed, and have a rare peace of mind. When you're between 40 and 70, you'll be the most productive at work. If you're an athlete, you'll turn in your best performances.

As strange as it may seem, you actually have a choice of where you want to be on the spectrum, almost independent of what is immediately confronting you.

Etched in Stone

Type A behavior is only harmful if you exhibit aggressive and hostile tendencies. If you're a bonafide "Type A," but not aggressive or hostile, and you attempt to be something other than that, your stress level may actually increase.

You may know somebody who exhibits such power, and never consider that he wasn't just born under a lucky sign; he's participating in the process of keeping his stress under control.

You may have heard that if you're a Type A personality, a hard-driving type who works too much, you're likely to be more stressed than others. This isn't necessarily true.

Some people are quite comfortable being Type A's all the time, which isn't necessarily harmful as long as they don't exhibit overly aggressive or hostile behavior. If you're operating the controls and levers of your career and life, then whether you're Type A or Type B, you're likely to avoid this stress which we've been discussing.

Change of Venue

If you feel as if you're part of the proverbial rat race and the rats are winning, here are some suggestions that offer a change of pace, something away from the ordinary, that may help you to achieve lower levels of stress. The later chapters in this book will provide even more suggestions for dealing with stress.

Obviously, not all of these are for you, and I don't suggest for a moment that you attempt to do them all in a relatively short period. If even a few interest you, I suggest you give them a try. Often, simply changing your routine a little is a great help.

➤ Plan a vacation—get brochures, pamphlets, books, or advice from friends on where to go for a relaxing week or weekend.

➤ Go through your bookshelf, pull out the books you know you'll never want or need to read again, and make a donation to your local library.

➤ Challenge yourself to make small improvements in your daily life, such as leaving the house on time or putting on your seat belt before starting your car.

➤ Actually celebrate an upcoming holiday by getting together with friends or family members.

➤ Eat dinner early one night each week to make time for family conversation.

➤ Eliminate all extraneous noise that competes for your attention at dinner. Cut off the TV and radio, and find out what's really going on in your family members' lives—talk to each other.

To win the war on stress requires only small steps, applied consistently. Sure, you can head off to the mountains for a weekend and hang out with the peace and love gurus, but then, hey, you gotta come back to the same world (more on weekend retreats in later chapters). So you might as well make small, incremental changes right where you are!

The Least You Need to Know

➤ Stress wears many faces, not all of them recognizable.

➤ While there is good stress and bad stress, there's no need to focus on the good stress. It works naturally for you. Your goal is to minimize the effects of bad stress.

➤ Stress at work can show up in many different ways, but the common result is you're generally less effective than you could be.

➤ The stress you experience is unique to you, because of the uniqueness of your background, upbringing, and experiences.

➤ Nevertheless, the methods for alleviating stress, such as seeing it as a best friend, letting go of some control, or taking small steps to alleviate it, are common denominators that can work for anyone.

Wouldn't You Know It? The Direction of Stress Has Changed

In This Chapter

➤ Your happy home is stress inducing

➤ The top ten stressors

➤ Stronger families

➤ Getting to work, ready for work

Although 48 percent of Americans say they've taken "steps in the past five years that could simplify their lives," according to a survey conducted by *U.S. News and World Report*, most people's lives are not likely to spontaneously get less stressful in the near future (unless they take appropriate action, such as reading this book cover to cover and following the advice herein). As you proceed in an ever-changing world, life itself, at work and away from work, seems to be getting more stressful.

A *Time* magazine feature on stress and anxiety titled, "The Evolution of Despair," discussed the views of evolutionary psychologists, specialists in a field suggesting that modern life itself causes the stress that we are all experiencing. Human beings, the article observed, seem to be "hard-wired for a different way of life than offered by modernity."

How Your Home Life Became More Stressful Than the Workplace

The nano-second '90s witnessed major changes in where and when people experience stress. Traditionally, you could count on Dad or Mom to bring stress home from the office. Now, the dominating direction has shifted—reports show that most professionals experience more stress *outside* of work! Researchers at the University of Chicago, for example, report that people actually feel more creative, focused, and happy at work than at home.

Warning
Today, Mom and Dad, Ted and Alice, or other significant others are likely to bring more stress to work than they leave with at the end of the day.

The researchers say, "There's a perfect middle zone, often achieved at work, when a task is challenging enough to compel your full attention, yet not so challenging that it completely outstrips your ability."

Let's see what people are saying about sources of stress they experience. In a study conducted by *Prevention Magazine,* the top ten stressors as reported by survey respondents, in order, included:

1. Personal finances

2. Career

3. Too many responsibilities

4. Marriage

5. Health

6. Children

7. Loneliness

8. Sex

9. Relatives

10. Neighbors

I know what you're thinking—items 1, 2, and 3 are all related to work, so how can these Ph.D. types and I assert that the dominant direction in which stress travels is now from home to work? While items 1, 2, and 3 are work-related, people probably spend more time worrying about them *at home*.

Personal Finances

Personal finances are directly related to your work—how much money you make. The number of Americans having money troubles is rising.

Even millionaires are losing sleep over their future finances. A survey published in *USA Today* of the wealthiest 1 percent of Americans having household incomes of at least $200,000 annually, or a net worth of $3 million, found that most people in this category are concerned that they will not have enough money in retirement.

However, the absence of a high income is not the predominant reason people experience financial problems. Not living within their means is. Too many people, for example, are overwhelmed by credit-card debt because they are turning to plastic to pay for things they can't afford.

Some people take the debt that they rack up on one card, pass it onto a new card, and continue to use both cards.

No one, from the largest and most successful nation to the individual household, can run up huge deficits over a prolonged period of time—without making an effort to reduce them—and hope to achieve any measure of economic or psychic prosperity.

The first step to reducing stress away from work is to get your finances in order. Yes, I realize that depends on how much you make at work. Regardless of how much or how little you make, the task ahead of you is to get your checkbook and your finances in order. In short, to live within your means.

> ➤ To reduce a personal financial deficit, place a moratorium on non-essential spending while not shortchanging crucial expenses like food and health care—regardless of what items entice you—until all your credit cards have zero balances.

> ➤ The moment you get your head back above water, begin saving.

Warning
The typical American carries about nine credit cards; in one year, the total credit balance of the typical cardholder increased 23 percent over the previous year.

Etched in Stone
The earlier in life you start saving and investing, and the more diligent you are with the money you have, the more successful you will be in the long run. You want to strike a balance between how much you earn and how much you keep, achieving some relief from financial stress, and a sense of security about your financial future.

Far too many people are caught up in making a living and making ends meet to pay attention to their financial health. Too many people count their earning power as their major asset but fail to apply those earnings to their financial security in any meaningful way. If that sounds familiar, perhaps it's time to come to terms with your tendency to avoid or deny financial matters.

What a Concept!

When Albert Einstein was asked what was the greatest miracle he had ever encountered, his answer was the compounding interest of money.

A plethora of articles in all major periodicals indicate that financial planning is more important to baby boomers and Generation X'ers than previous generations. Why? Because people are living longer (see Chapter 21). You may not have just 35 or 45 years left, you may have 55 or 75 more.

Go!
Whether you are 25, 35, 45, or even 55, you can't go back in time but you can start where you are right now. No need for regrets, just take action. Save some amount every month.

Financial planners say that achieving suitable income and savings requires discipline—something baby boomers and X'ers don't seem to have mastered. The earlier you begin saving, the greater your benefits from the wonders of compound interest.

Example: Say you're 30 years old and you want to retire at 65. You calculate what you think you'll need, and figure you need to save $200 a month to reach it. If you wait until you're 40 to start saving, you'll have to save $600 a month to achieve the same results. If you wait until you're 50, you'll have to save $1,200 a month to accumulate the same sum at age 65.

But this is not a book on personal finances! If personal finances are an issue for you—and there's a good chance they are—check out some wonderful books titled *The Complete Idiot's Guide to Managing Your Money, The Complete Idiot's Guide to Getting Rich,* and *The Complete Idiot's Guide to a Great Retirement.*

Career Stressors

Career is obviously related to work, and as you saw in Chapter 2, concern about job security is epidemic. Since I'll address career concerns in spades in the next chapter and beyond, let's press on! *Too many responsibilities* is also largely related to work, but could represent a blend of work-related responsibilities and domestic responsibilities.

The Best of the Rest of the Stressors

Items 4 through 10, encompassing marriage, health, children, loneliness, sex, relatives, and neighbors, are all "away from work" categories. Consider what has happened to the average man and woman away from work in the last two decades and it's not hard to see why getting to work can be a relief. First, traffic is worse everywhere. If that's not bad enough, you could be wearing a beeper, where you're on call at any moment. If your health isn't an issue for you, chances are the health of your children or your aging parents is.

Let's look at stressors 4 through 10 in detail.

Happily Ever After

It's tough today to maintain a committed, vibrant relationship. Just think about your own! Among the litany of problems and obstacles that marriage partners face today are personal finances, career and dual-career concerns, too many responsibilities, raising their children, health, sex—and many more. All make the top ten list.

Pressed and frazzled by the onslaught of responsibilities, more couples are finding it exhausting to have to "be" with one another—to converse, to empathize, to be responsive. Not surprisingly, the number of families headed by a single adult—usually female—is growing, placing inordinate strains on working individuals with children. Spouses who both earn income may have more *money*, but they invariably experience the stress of two careers.

Millions of couples have no friends, even though many wish they did. Many people are too busy juggling family and career to make and keep friends, so they rely entirely on spouses to meet their needs for companionship.

To Your Health

You could fill volumes with the health-related concerns that people have today—from AIDS, to Alzheimer's disease, to breast or prostate cancer, to irritable bowel syndrome. I think in large measure (so to speak), all you have to do to understand society's health concerns is step on the scale. The number of overweight Americans gained steadily in the past decade. One-third of people over age 20 tip the scales in the wrong direction, according to statistics in the *Journal of the American Medical Association*.

More weight can put stress on your heart and make your vital organs work harder. Most charts that show weight norms in America have been adjusted upward, making people believe their weight is OK because they're part of the norm.

What's the Matter with Kids Today?

What about *children*? Children mean family, and families, it has been widely rumored, are in trouble.

Many people have constant anxiety regarding their children, no matter what the age of their kids. If they're young, there are all types of safety issues. If they're older, there are potential problems related to sex, drugs, alcohol, driving, and so on.

Certainly the continuing breakdown of the nuclear family hasn't helped make home life less stressful. In the United States, U.S. Bureau of the Census statistics show that four out of every ten children no longer live with both biological parents, and the number of single-parent families has doubled since 1970. What's more, the number of children born outside of marriage has increased by 500 percent in one generation.

Around the world, families aren't faring much better. Journalist Tyler Marshall, writing for the *Los Angeles Times* found that in Eastern Europe, "Communism has been replaced by a mixture of economic uncertainty and social confusion, producing what some analysts call a values vacuum that frequently leaves parents incapable of addressing their childrens' questions on what to do with their lives." In one part of India where many fathers spend months working overseas, the divorce rate has jumped 350 percent in just one decade. There are similar occurrences all over the globe.

Marshall says, "Against the backdrop of shifting economic conditions, which have brought millions more women into the labor force" and generated a competition for jobs that frequently sends potential breadwinners away for months at a time, it is getting tougher to raise a family.

All By Myself

Loneliness is making its way up the list of the top ten stressors. More people live alone in the U.S. than at any time in history, and the trend is beginning to take hold in Europe and other parts of the industrialized world. Television, on-line services, and the ability to be connected to the world serve for many people as the most interaction they have throughout the day away from work. Still, in some cases, work is online psychobabble in a chat room.

Is it any surprise that television shows with themes such as *Friends* become instant hits from their first airing? Do you personally receive any vicarious pleasure from visiting with your electronic "friends" every week? (You know, Seinfeld, Kramer, Caroline, Ross, Rachel, and others.)

Here are but a few observations about loneliness and its potential relationship to stress:

➤ Single or divorced men, on average, live much shorter lives than married men.

➤ On any given night, by about 9:30 eastern time, most if not all of the commercial on-line chat rooms are filled to capacity.

➤ The "personals"—advertisements for companionship—in urban and suburban publications are thriving. The ads themselves are placed by a vast range of individuals representing all races, ages, lifestyles, occupations, and sexual orientations.

➤ Among those leaving suicide notes, being jilted by a lover continues to be cited as among the most prevalent reason for taking one's life.

In observing contemporary society, it would not be an exaggeration to say that loneliness is a stress-inducing epidemic affecting people from all walks of life.

Sex

Sex as a stressor? It doesn't look like AIDS is going to go away any time soon. Has there ever been a generation that was constantly reminded of the specter of death for doing what people have been doing since the beginning of time?

Before AIDS came along, herpes was regarded as an epidemic, one that merited continual mainstream press coverage. The bad news is that it still *is* an epidemic, with upwards of one in six of the population having some variety of herpes simplex. The problem is, because it doesn't kill—merely agonizing people for years on end—you hardly ever read about it.

Even if AIDS, herpes, and other sexually transmitted afflictions did not exist, it's likely that sex would still be high up on the list of stressors. The number of harassment cases filed every year is on the increase. What about the quest of homosexuals, bisexuals, and others to gain respectability in mainstream society? Think about the pressure on preteens and teens who would prefer to remain celibate—what incredible peer pressure they incur when surrounded by legions of others who think and behave very differently.

As America ages, as well as the populations of nations throughout the world, new challenges arise for men and women. In the general population, one woman in nine now faces the specter of breast cancer in our society. One man in five faces prostate cancer. Our understanding of one another as a society doesn't seem to be getting any clearer. All this leads to concerns surrounding sex.

It's All Relative

Relatives as a source of stress are nothing new. As Henny Youngman used to say, "Take my wife—please." Whether it's husband or wife jokes, mother-in-law jokes, or what have you, behind the witticisms are age-old grains of truth. When you consider that people are living longer and many people, perhaps even you, now have to care for their parents as well as their children, it's easy to understand the strains that may ensue.

You may be among thousands of readers who have had to become "parents" to their parents. Among many organizations which may be of service to you include:

➤ *Catholic Charities* offers information on community services and supported networks (1-800-886-4295).

➤ *Elder Locator* is a program that helps you find community assistance programs for your elderly parents (1-800-677-1116).

➤ *Jewish Board of Family and Childrens Services* offers a wide variety of programs and services (1-212-582-9100).

➤ Local libraries in nearly every community have a variety of announcements, pamphlets and other information about community groups for the elderly. You may be surprised at the resources in your town.

➤ *National Alliance for Caregiving* has programs to train a family and professional caregivers to care for the elderly (1-301-718-8444).

➤ *National Association for Homecare* offers a list of providers of homecare and a free booklet. Their address: 228 7th Street SE, Washington, DC 20003.

➤ *National Hospice Organization* provides a list of services for the terminally ill. They can be reached at 1-800-338-6819.

➤ Senior Centers and similar organizations are springing up in many communities. They offer social programs, medical screening, field trips, and more. Check the phone book under "seniors."

➤ The U.S. Government's *Medicare Program* offers information on what expenses for your elderly parents may be covered by Medicare (1-800-638-6833).

Neighbors

"Neighbors" comes as no surprise either. As you'll see in Chapter 12, regarding population density, as a general rule at least in industrialized nations, the more crowded an area (and the more people tend to grate on each other's nerves). This is not to say that folks in rural areas don't have their feuds, either. After all, the Hatfields and the McCoys weren't feuding in a thriving metropolis.

Nine out of ten Americans say incivility is a serious social problem, based on a survey conducted by KRC Research and Consulting for *U.S. News & World Report.* When asked how various institutions affect people's ability to get along...

➤ 73 percent said that political campaigns had a negative impact.

➤ 69 percent indicated that prime-time TV had a negative impact.

➤ 67 percent felt that rock music had a negative impact.

➤ 52 percent said talk radio had a negative impact.

A whopping 33 percent felt that schools had a negative impact on people's ability to get along.

In my home town of Chapel Hill, North Carolina, it seems as if every other household in town—about 20,000 of them—has a dog. Not just any dog—a big dog—the kind that makes 90 decibel barks, rapidly, over a prolonged period, throughout the day and night. If the noise weren't enough, these very same large canines, are "walked" each morning by their masters, in search of a safe place in which to poop.

Okay, enough about *my* neighbors. We could fill a chapter or two on your neighbors! Some of them play music way too loud. Some pull in and out of their driveways too quickly. Some have other annoying pets. Some borrow things and never return them. Some leave things with you and never come reclaim them. The list is endless.

Coming to Work to Rest

OK, it's agreed that your non-working life can be, and is, quite stressful. To close out this chapter, let's examine what you can do to at least minimize the stress you *bring* to work. Then in the next six chapters, I'll walk you through making your workplace a little saner, followed by a look at both external and internal stressors that impact you regardless of where you are, leading to getting and keeping your stress level down.

You may be among the masses, given all that occurs away from work, who come in to work to essentially rest. Or you may supervise those who do. If this is so, it is time to realize that you can't do your best work unless you square away your domestic life. The two are part of a system—a system called your life.

Go!
Use all types of domestic services within your budget to free up your time, and make your time away from work less hectic.

Do you really need to be cutting the grass? Do you need to be making pickups when many stores deliver, and at no extra charge? The larger question behind all this is, do you use the same care and precision in managing your domestic life as you do in your work life? I'm not saying to turn your home into an adjunct of your work. By getting the rest you need, however, and marshaling the resources that will help to keep you vibrant, you can come into work more energized, leave work more energized, and have a happier home life. It's a victorious circle.

Here are some ideas to help you get to work, ready for work:

Grocery delivery   Many supermarkets and groceries will deliver for a nominal fee of five to seven dollars. Some produce catalogs from which you can order by phone or by fax. For items you buy frequently, you can establish a standing order whereby every week the market delivers eggs, milk, what have you.

Gift wrap it please   If you're buying presents for anyone, and the store offers wrapping services, pay the extra dollar and have them wrap it.

Pick-up and delivery services   Get in the habit of using vendors and suppliers who come to right your door.

Use any neighborhood or community service that will free up your task list. Here are types of services that exist in your community (but they're called something else):

The Sparkling Touch—House cleaning.

Mr. Fixit—House repair when there's no one handy.

Paul Bunyan & Company—Tree-trimming, hedge trimming.

The Butler Did It—A catering service.

It's On Its Ways—Pick up and delivery.

Pooch Takes a Walk—Takes care of your dog when you're gone.

Gutters 'R Us—Clears your gutters, saves you from roof-duty.

The Jetsons—Airport shuttle service.

Part-time workers—Students (high school, college, and grad school), retirees, foreign exchange students, and interns from colleges can help you with deliveries/pick-ups, cleaning, yardwork, typing, and so on.

Why is it that when someone gets a big raise the first thing they do is elevate their level of expenses? And, at the same time, never give any thought to reinvesting a portion of the new income to maintain the previous quality of life?

If you're making $10,000 a year more than you did a couple of years ago, save most of it for your future, but also take $2,000 or $3,000 of that money, and reinvest in yourself. Spend it on services that enable you to stay rested and relaxed (rather than down payments on fancy cars or other items that will lead to bigger bills), so that you can go into work and do your best work.

Is Your Commute Killing You?

OK, you see the wisdom in getting help with some domestic chores so that you can get to work less stressed. Is your commute, however, maddening? The answer to this question for most people is an emphatic yes. If you let your stress boil over on the way to the top, or on the way to and from work, you're likely to be shortening your life. Your *joie de vivre* is certainly killed a little more each day.

You don't have to have a Ph.D. in psychology to understand the effects of being trapped every day for an hour or more in your car, on buses, subways, and trains.

To make your commute as pleasant as possible, try these techniques:

➤ Spend as little time on the road as possible, by becoming a contrarian. Leave earlier in the morning, and earlier in the afternoon to do your commuting.

➤ Keep your car in top shape. Take it in for servicing if *anything* is askew.

➤ Make your seat as comfortable as possible. Do you need a mat, a cushion, or wooden beads like New York cab drivers use that supposedly massage you while you drive?

➤ Schedule a health club visit *before* you head home. This can help make you more relaxed during rush hour.

➤ Add some leeway into your plans. Tightly scheduled commuting only leads to continual frustration.

➤ Do some stretches in your seat—move some from side to side, rotate your shoulders, lift one buttock, then the other, stretch out one arm past the steering wheel, then the other and so on.

➤ Install a tape or CD player to control the sounds in your environment as you travel to and from work.

➤ Close your windows and turn on the air conditioner. You'll get the same miles per gallon as with the windows open and the A/C off. And your ride will be quieter.

➤ Use drive time to consider what you'd like to do or how you'd like your day to go.

➤ If you're part of a carpool, ride to work with people you like.

Here's looking forward to Monday morning!

The Least You Need to Know

➤ Modern life itself may be causing the stress that everyone is experiencing.

➤ You are likely to bring more stress to work than you leave with at the end of the day.

➤ The ten top stressors include personal finances, career, too many responsibilities, marriage, health, children, loneliness, sex, relatives, and neighbors.

➤ Strive for balance between how much you earn and how much you keep, achieving some relief from financial stress, and a sense of security about your financial future.

➤ By getting the rest you need and marshaling the resources that will help keep you vibrant, you can come into work more energized, leave work more energized, and have a happier home life.

Part 2
Surviving Your Workplace

I've been fortunate over the years to meet many world-renowned authors. In December 1990, I met Alvin Toffler in New Jersey at a Meadowlands exposition. He told me that the contemporary office is a terrible place in which to get any work done. I guess you knew that all along!

Because work is a big part of your life and can indeed be stressful, this section has six—count 'em, six—chapters. Chapter 4, "I Work, Therefore I Compete," looks at what competition is and what alternatives there are. Chapter 5, "When Too Many Hours Take Their Toll," explains why simply working long hours will not propel you further or faster.

Chapter 6, "Increased Expectations, Diminishing Returns," talks about what happens when you try to perform beyond your optimal limit. We'll also discuss how you can engage in what I call the "cycle of productivity." Stay tuned, you'll want to know about this.

Chapter 7, "A Workplace Revolution, or How to Get Out of Jail," focuses on how you can harrass emerging technologies to be more effective, get out of the office, and lead a more balanced life. Chapter 8, "Whipping Workplace Distractions," offers you many ways to stay focused and minimize interruptions. Finally, Chapter 9, "Workplace Violence: Stress Boiling Over the Top," discusses the frightening growth in workplace violence, how to spot potential powder-kegs before they blow, and general strategies for defusing your workplace.

Chapter 4

I Work, Therefore I Compete...

In This Chapter

➤ Compete with yourself, not with others

➤ Distinguish yourself from the pack

➤ Is self-employment on the horizon?

➤ Hanging loose when nothing seems to be going right

Grandpa learned a skill and it carried him for a lifetime. Pop progressed up the ladder and set the cruise control. Today, John and Jane Doe are scrambling for economic survival. With the dissipation of traditional career progression, you may experience an adulthood unlike anyone else in recent history.

Ask people, "Where will you be in five years?" and you'll often be told, "I have no (flaming) idea." A lot of companies have no idea where they'll be in five years. Organizations of all sizes are being hit hard by sweeping changes, forcing them to place increasing pressure on employees—higher expectations for every job and an environment of rapid employee turnover. Employees get the message: Hustle or hit the road. Job security today is less and less of a given.

How stressful, then, is competition in your work place? Some experts believe it's harmful and deleterious to progress. Top performers often thrive, but others who might have made a substantial contribution are placed under tremendous pressure and question their future with the company.

Some companies, particularly the sales division, have a "forced distribution of rewards." Standards are set so high that only 5 or 10 percent of the workforce can earn an outstanding grade. Also, recognition systems in many organizations offer too little recognition too late, and can promote unhealthy competition for the scant recognition that's available.

This chapter looks at new competitive stresses in the workplace, and provides strategies for dealing with them.

Compete with Yourself, Not with Others

You may have little or no control over your organization's ways of doing things. However, you are in charge of competing with yourself.

What does it mean to compete with yourself? You compete with yourself when you challenge yourself to perform better than you have in the past, or to perform better than you ordinarily would based on your history.

This is not to say that you engage in unhealthy, workaholic efforts that deplete your mental, physical, and emotional energy. Instead, you lessen your focus on what others are doing and increase your focus on how you can be the best you can be. John Wooden, the legendary coach of UCLA basketball, guided his teams in the mid '60s and '70s to 10 NCAA championships in 14 years, a feat never likely to be duplicated. He maintained the curious custom of *not* discussing the other team in practice sessions with his own team.

Wooden found it far more effective, and his record bears out his wisdom, to have his players primed and focused, confident in their ability and skills, and ready to execute the right plays as the game evolved.

There are many other examples in sports and business of people who chose to carve their own path, with little or no concern for the competition. Ted Turner in broadcasting, Mary Kay Ash in cosmetics, Charles Schwab in the brokerage business, and Fred Smith in overnight express services, are among career achievers who not only paid little heed to what the competition was doing, but carved out new territory for themselves.

Maybe you've heard these stories before—but what do they have to do with the stress you feel right now? Plenty. On a continuing basis, think about the ways that you can make improvements in what you do. The Japanese call this *kaizen*, which literally means "small, but continual." Remember, small incremental steps can lead to wondrous results. And less stress.

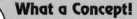

What a Concept!

Small, incremental steps applied to your work will help you to rise to the top.

I find that competing with myself, rather than against others, is a superlative way to proceed in work and life. When I worked for a management consulting firm in Washington, D.C. in the early '80s, everyone was handwriting reports—this was in the prehistoric days, when wild poodles roamed the earth, long before personal computers. I learned how to dictate (usually from an outline or notes) and condensed six- to eight-hour assignments to 30 minutes.

To this day, I dictate everything—I even dictated this sentence, this book, and 21 previous books. After dictating, I hand the tape over to a transcriptionist who types the dictation using a word processor and saves the information in a file on a disk. I then make corrections to the disk file, print out a hard copy, and have another person review the material closely, marking up the hard copy and handing it back to me. It's not rocket science, but it works. I complete articles all day long—sometimes two or three per plane ride. This is one area where *not competing*, but simply seeking to get the best from myself, paid off in wondrous ways.

My best friend Peter, up in Boston, doesn't compete with others. He's in the commercial real estate business, and hardly ever answers advertisements in the paper. He says that by the time something hits the market it's already too late: There will be lots of bidders, and the competition means he's not likely to get a good deal. How did he become a multi-millionaire? He competed with himself. He compiled data on the key buildings in a radius from his location in the Boston area. Over the years, he has added to his database.

Today, he maintains data on the size and number of units, square footage, and so forth of these key properties. He will sometimes submit an offer to an owner who had no idea anyone was interested in purchasing the property. Often enough, he makes a purchase at a very good price, since there were no other buyers.

Peter contends that no matter what your industry or profession, if you keep your eyes open, opportunities will emerge whereby you can forge ahead by virtually eliminating competition.

Eliminating the Competition

On the job, you can eliminate your competition and not even go to jail for it.

Take the case of Jim, the lowest level employee in a supermarket. He was just hired yesterday; if anyone is likely to be fired first, it's him. He's a "bag boy." It's not a glamorous job, and Jim's career prospects don't seem that promising. But let's explore what Jim can do to make himself more valuable to his employer.

Jim goes to the head of shipping and says, "I'd like to put in some overtime in shipping to understand how your department works." Sure enough, he puts in a couple hours there. Another time he goes to the manager of the meat department and says, " I'd like to work with you a little to understand how you wrap the meats and preserve them." At other times he goes to the bakery, security people, clean up, even the credit department.

After three months, Jim has worked in a dozen different areas, so when somebody from another department calls in and is delayed or sick, guess what? Jim can substitute.

Several more months pass. Suppose there's a downturn in business and the store has to lay off some people. Who are they going to lay off? It's not going to be Jim, you can count on that. Suppose there's an upswing in business and they need to make someone a manager. Who are they going to consider?

The same principle applies each time you take an unwanted job or pinch hit for others. Work a little overtime, learn a little more about the organization you work in, and gain a greater understanding of total operations. In a matter of months, you can become one of the most valuable employees in the organization—with no exaggeration whatsoever.

What Jim essentially has done is eliminate the competition, without killing anyone—least of all himself. If the operation expands, who will top management want to have participate in the expansion phase?

What a Concept!

You can moan and groan about the stress that you feel at work, the dead ends that surround you, and the relentless grind of the competition. Yet, is it necessary to compete at all? Is competing even an efficient process?

Distinguishing Yourself from the Pack

Surveys show that job security is the number one concern of most workers. With everything going on in the world contributing to a potentially stressful environment, who wants to work under the constant fear of losing one's job?

If you're not self-employed and you want to have a more secure job, I suggest you distinguish yourself from others. It's highly worthwhile.

A strategy I found most effective, which I highlighted in my book, *Blow Your Own Horn: How to Get Noticed and Get Ahead*, is to practice making yourself indispensable. Listed next are some basic tactics on how you can do this. You want to integrate a few of these strategies without creating more work for yourself—and more stress. Balance your need for security with your need for relief from work pressures. Choose those strategies that you can most comfortably initiate, those you can "piggyback" on top of what you're already doing.

➤ Take the task no one else wants.

➤ Go the extra mile.

➤ Work harder when the cat's away.

➤ Give credit to the group.

➤ Make your boss look good.

➤ Become a mentor to junior or new members of your company.

➤ Be aware of a boss who is feeling professionally threatened, and be supportive.

➤ Figure out what's needed, not what's expected, and do what's needed.

Taking the Task No One Wants

Morrie was new to the consulting firm. He was brought in as one of a well-established group of trainers and instructional designers. Rather than melting into the pot of professionals versed in education, Morrie became an expert in a spreadsheet program that greatly facilitated project planning. Then the company announced that all of the company's financial records would be changed over to this program.

Morrie saw a niche for himself—one no one else wanted or had the skills for. The president of the company needed someone who could explain the software and its features to others in the firm. Morrie stayed after work twice a week to become an expert with the software. Soon, everyone with a question was referred to Morrie. He, in short, became indispensable.

Go!
You can go the extra mile in other ways. Do the little things that make a difference. I prepared client reports monthly in a company three-ring binder. Since this was unusual, I took it upon myself to get this extra work done. It made a difference in the way the reports looked to clients—and my boss.

Like Jim the bagboy or Morrie, you can develop your niche by picking up a skill or technical knowledge that is vital to your company, yet hard to learn. Be the best at something no one else wants to do and you will dramatically raise your level of importance to your organization.

Go the Extra Mile

If you want to get ahead in your own company, take on more work than you are assigned. Volunteer to help on a project that is running over deadline and make yourself available for extra projects. You'll be noticed.

Frequently, companies need assistance with rush jobs. At consulting firms I worked at, I always volunteered to work on proposals. With quick turnaround necessary, volunteers are greatly appreciated. Additionally, working on proposals exposed me to information outside my department and to people I didn't usually work with.

When the Cat's Away...

The scene occurs in thousands of offices every day. The boss is away, on business or vacation. A great sigh of relief goes up the minute he or she is out of the door. People drift into each other's offices, the telephones light up with personal calls, and lunch hours are stretched to the maximum.

Managers generally report productivity to be only two-thirds of normal when they are not in the office. That's why working even at your normal place when they are away will impress your supervisors.

Go!
Not only does staying productive reflect well on you, it also keeps you from having to play "catch up" later, which ultimately reduces stress.

My strategy during this time, always, was to stay productive. I knew the boss was most likely to monitor employee performance following periods of his absence, rather than when he was in the office for a stretch.

To add to your indispensability, when supervisors are away, try to complete jobs they assigned before their departure. There's nothing a supervisor appreciates more after a trip than hearing, "Here's the job you wanted. It's done." The subtle yet deep-seated message you convey is long lasting.

Give Credit to the Group

Giving credit to the group of people you work with can work wonders. This seeming irony—standing out by praising the group—makes sense in the overall business context. Those who make it to the top levels of management are able to motivate others to do their best and to work well in group situations.

What are you really saying when you say "My team did a great job"? Those above you know instinctively that when a group does well, it's because someone exhibited leadership. Highlighting the team is especially useful when you manage the group. It indicates your ability to facilitate good work.

Make Your Boss Look Good

Similar to the concept of giving credit to the group of people you work with or manage, making your boss look good can only reflect favorably on you. Both your boss and his or her supervisors will appreciate this.

The best way to make your boss look good is to handle your work efficiently and thoroughly. If your boss is fair, you'll get credit for the work, increasing your chances of promotion. If your boss doesn't do his share of the work, leaning on you unfairly without giving you the credit, you're still likely to be promoted when he is. Your boss knows you've been doing part of his work and that he can't take a new position without your help.

Become a Mentor to Others

Maybe you're only 28 years old, or maybe you've only been in your job for a year and a half. Nevertheless, with your previous experience and achievements, you may already be in a position to serve as a mentor or informal advisor to others.

This can be done informally, and you can choose how much energy you're willing to commit. Helping junior members of your organization always looks good to those above you, especially at performance-review time.

Be Aware of Your Boss's Needs

We all need to be praised. Yet how often do we praise our bosses? Bosses are people too. If your boss has been extra supportive of you, tell him or her you appreciate it. Remember to honestly praise your boss to your co-workers and other supervisors.

Figure Out What's Needed

One way to become indispensable is to be on top of your job, your department's goals, and your company's objectives. Knowing your job description and following it, or amending it if necessary, protects you from misunderstandings. It also gives you an idea of the part you play in the whole organization—an important factor in your job satisfaction and chance for promotion.

If your job description does not adequately detail the information you must know and the responsibilities you have, change it! Learning your department, division, or project team's goals is important to guide your actions as well as to mark milestones.

Go!
Your company's brochure, annual report, promotional literature, or employee handbook often has the company objective spelled out.

Finally, any organization, from the smallest business to the multi-billion-dollar corporation, has objectives. It could be to expand sales, increase mergers, solidify a market already captured, or make a specific contribution to research.

If you are unsure of the direction to take on a particular project and are not receiving sufficient guidance, look at the problem in light of your company's objectives. Is what you're doing in line with those objectives? Will it be good for the company over the long-range?

Is Self-Employment on the Horizon?

Another strategy for distinguishing yourself from the pack is to prepare for the day when you're not employed by others. (If you're already self-employed, skip this section.) In his book, *Job Shift*, William Bridges discusses one of the curious realities of our time. He says, "What is disappearing today is not just a certain number of jobs or jobs in certain industries or in one country—or even jobs in the developed world as a whole. What is disappearing is the very thing itself: the job."

There's growing evidence to support his contention. For example, in 1994 alone, General Motors eliminated over 69,000 jobs. IBM eliminated more than 38,000, and GTE almost 28,000. Hundreds of thousands more jobs were cut in the same year from other major U.S. employers.

If sometime in the future you do not have a "job," what will your options be? Obviously, you can start your own business. You can become a consultant—in some cases a consultant to the organization that previously employed you, or to similar organizations.

What steps might facilitate such a transition?

➤ If you don't already own one, buy your own PC and develop more computer skills.

➤ Set up a rudimentary office in a corner of your home.

➤ Take a course or two in marketing, finance, record keeping, or entrepreneurialism.

➤ Talk to others who have gone the self-employment route.

Go!
Acquire an awareness of how you'll prosper in an era in which you may no longer have a job.

More people are working within organizations, but under arrangements that you wouldn't call a job. They work as contract employees. If you find yourself in a new employment situation, take heart. More and more companies are willing to work with former employees on an as-needed, contract basis. If you're released due to corporate downsizing, your previous organization or others can begin to rely on your capabilities, and you can charge a premium per hour for your services. You might end up making more and working less than you did. Then again, you might not.

As a consultant, the ability to structure your life in more supportive, balanced ways, however, means you'll be able to earn an income *and* have a life. That's more than those tens of millions of people experience crawling along superhighways on their way to and from the big city.

What a Concept!

Armed with your PC, modem, fax-modem, copier, printer, scanner, and online services, you may be able to carve out the niche you've always wanted. You can cut your commuting time to nothing, maintain a decent income, and have a life. Such a deal!

Effective Tools for a New Era

What are the tools at your disposal during the workday, when your head starts pounding, your insides start shaking, or you feel like you're simply going to explode? Fortunately, there are many:

Maintain a sense of humor. Humor will take you a long way. The ability to laugh at yourself or any situation can defuse almost any stress you're experiencing. Laughter can help to lower your blood pressure. It can mean the difference between blowing up over a situation or sailing past it.

The difference between dead-ending in your career and rising to the top is often a sense of humor in the face of tough challenges.

Stretch. I don't mean join a yoga class (although I will talk about that in Chapter 17). Engage in any type of stretching activity that enables you to "shake out the kinks."

Right now, right where you are, stand up, close the door to your office, if you have an office and door, and reach towards the ceiling. Then, look right, look left. Extend your right leg to the right, extend your left leg to the left. Do deep knee bends.

If you can bring your knee to waist level, and then alternate legs, it'll only take about 10 or 20 seconds before your derriere and posterior side feel somewhat toned.

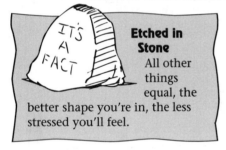

Etched in Stone

All other things equal, the better shape you're in, the less stressed you'll feel.

Don't sweat the small stuff. Ray Perez, an ordinary guy from Gainesville, Florida, believes there are two major events in a person's life. The first is when you're born. The second is when you die. "Everything in between," according to Ray, "is small stuff." Too many people have a tendency to *catastrophize* daily obstacles. Accept the day-in and day-out stuff that *is* going to happen—just don't let it get the best of you.

Take a walk. I mentioned this in a previous chapter. Walking is one of God's many gifts to homo erectus. The key is to not be in a hurry. Walk purposefully, stretching out your legs and swinging your arms as you go. Maintain your best posture. Take good deep breaths while you walk. Notice your surroundings.

Take a drink of water. Notice I said water—not coffee, not tea, not alcohol, just good, old, plain H_2O. Undoubtedly, you've learned along the way that your body is 90 percent water. I suggest keeping a bottle of spring water in your office or nearby.

Change your posture. The mere motion of standing up more erectly enables every system of your body to function more effectively. You can't be as stressed when you're standing up straight as when you're slouched over. It's a physiological impossibility.

Keep a hand gripper nearby. This could be a tennis ball, or a mechanical hand gripper sold in any sporting goods store. Squeeze it a few times throughout the day to release tension. Squeezing the gripper can actually provide a release that satisfies your body's fight or flight response mechanism.

Listen to a relaxation or subliminal tape. Most health food stores have these today. There are tapes for releasing stress, relaxing, visualizing a pleasant scene, and so forth. The tapes run anywhere from 20 to 45 minutes. You sit back in a chair, pop the tape into your cassette recorder, and follow the instructions.

Take a hot or cold shower, whichever feels better. Simply being underwater changes your outlook. Something about going from air to water makes all of the difference.

Leave nice notes for yourself. For example, if you have a rough working environment, when you get home, sometimes it's refreshing to see a note that says you did a great job today, despite all you had to put up with. Such notes could be left on your car dashboard, in your calendar, and in your gym locker.

Warning
"Too many people deplete their health in the pursuit of wealth, and then deplete their wealth attempting to regain their health," says nutritionist Wayne Pickering from Daytona Beach, Florida. It's better to not let stress deplete your health in the pursuit of anything. Then you have a chance of actually achieving what you're after, and saving your money when you get there.

How to Hang Loose When Nothing Around You Is Going Right

Some days, perhaps many, no matter what you do, nothing at work seems to go right. You want to throw up your hands, jump out of the window, or do something equally unhealthy. When nothing is going right, *look for something you can do*—anything—that represents forward progress.

Say you've got a big project due in several days and you're road-blocked. The essential people are not in the office, you can't get the approvals or the resources you need, nothing's working as planned, and you're ready to scream. Look for some small victory. It's might be as simple as reorganizing the project materials, putting them into the proper file folders, or making a couple phone calls you'll eventually need to make anyway.

What a Concept!

When you string together two or three small tasks for which you can get a "win," your outlook improves, and any stress that you're experiencing begins to subside.

I've never had a day that has gone so smoothly, so wondrously, that I didn't experience *some* stress. I'm sure it's the same way with you. By finding the small win in small but worthwhile activities, other roadblocks seem to dissipate, and you can continue motoring down the highway. Then, always conclude your day with these positive steps:

➤ **Leave work at the office.** As the day winds down, even if it was a near disaster, give yourself the mental, emotional, and physical break of separating from your work. Make a clean break, at least for the evening. Have a life for the rest of the night. It'll all be there the next day, and, mercifully, you'll probably have a better perspective with which to tackle it.

➤ **If the spirit moves you, take a different way home, perhaps along a more scenic route.** Stop and get an ice cream cone, if it'll make you feel better. When you get home, change from your work clothes into whatever you wear around the house.

➤ **Talk to people at home.** Especially before dinner, give everyone at least five minutes of your complete attention.

The Least You Need to Know

➤ Nobody knows where they're going to be professionally in five years.

➤ The most effective form of competition is to compete with yourself, not with others.

➤ Making small, continual improvements in what you do can lead to fabulous results.

➤ To distinguish yourself from the pack, take the job no one else wants, go the extra mile, give credit to your group, and become a mentor to others.

➤ Learn some simple procedures for staying limber while in your office. Using humor, stretching at your desk, and taking a brief walk are just a few steps to beat stress at work.

WHEN WAS THE LAST TIME YOU WERE HOME?

WHERE?

When Too Many Hours Take Their Toll

In This Chapter

➤ When work becomes too much

➤ Working longer without feeling stressed

➤ The fundamentals of pacing yourself

Have you been working more and enjoying it less? Have you been feeling overwhelmed and perhaps undeserved? Have you been making gallant efforts on the job, but feeling underappreciated? If so, take a number and get in line! The results are in: Too many hours on the job can yield disastrous effects mentally, physically, and emotionally.

In America, the situation is particularly acute. Americans are indeed working longer. Based on some surveys, men average 50 hours of work each week, while women average 42. Worse still, many people feel constantly rushed on the job. What's more, surprising numbers of people take no vacation in the course of a year.

How Much Work is Too Much Work?

In her book, *The Overworked Americans*, Dr. Juliet Schor says, "In the last 20 years the amount of time Americans have spent at their jobs has risen steadily."

U.S. manufacturing employees today work over 320 hours per year more than their counterparts in France or Germany!

320 hours = 8 more work weeks!

Little Gain, Much Pain

Sure, there have been some productivity gains. However, most people don't use any of the productivity "dividend" to reduce hours: For example, the average American owns and consumes more than twice as much as his counterpart in the late '40s, but also has less free time.

Word Power
Vacation deficit disorder is the inability to take time off even when you've earned it and it's offered to you.

Joe Robinson, editor and publisher of *Escape* magazine, says that "one-fifth of Americans don't even take the vacation time allotted to them." They're too busy working and guzzling laxatives and potions for indigestion. "They can't stop, because if they did, they have nothing else to do."

Robinson says it's not easy in a culture where identities are based solely on jobs.

Vacation deficit disorder won't be a feature on *Nightline* anytime soon. Few doctors are treating it. Yet, it's a threat to your nervous system, quality of life, and potential holiday plans. Some 19 European countries and Australia rank ahead of America in how much time their citizens vacation per year. America is 22nd overall in the world.

Ten Ways to Know When You've Been Working Too Hard

Here are some definite indications that you need to take some time off (in Letterman-style reverse order)!

Warning
You're working longer, buying more, owing more, and hence, working more to pay for what you owe.

10. You've become good pals with the nightly cleaning crew.

9. You think "Ross Perot" is some new type of wine.

8. You and your PC have become "one."

7. You've filed for an extension to complete your taxes for the third year in a row.

6. You think *Dead Man Walking* refers to poltergeists.

5. You have equipment in your office that you've never used, and you can't recall what it does.

4. You've installed a cot in your office and keep forgetting to bring in a pillow, so you roll up your jacket.

3. The word "vacation" has no meaning to you.

2. You missed a gala awards dinner at a splashy hotel, in your honor, paid for by your company.

1. You got lost on the way home last night.

Please, Let Me Work Longer

Given the change in the dominant direction of stress (see Chapter 3 on how stress flows from home to work), there are perhaps some built-in incentives for you to stay longer at work. Actually, the issue is probably not so simple. Many organizations both here and abroad have developed a culture where people are expected to stay late. What are some of the vital indicators, if in fact you are among the many who are working too many hours? Here they are:

➤ During the winter months, you arrive at work while it's still dark, and leave work at the end of the day when it's dark again. In other words, you're not commuting during daylight.

➤ You have no expectation of leaving at normal closing time: 4:30, 5:00, 5:30 come and go, and you're still there.

What a Concept!

Since human beings are creatures of habit, if you're in the habit of leaving the office at 6:30, guess what? You're reinforcing the incidence of leaving on future evenings around 6:30. To reinforce leaving at 5:00, leave at 5:00.

➤ When you get home, you don't have the energy to be a full participant in your household. You want to plop down in a chair and take it easy.

➤ You don't converse with members of your family, you don't help make dinner, and you sure as heck don't want to listen to anybody's problems.

➤ You've started to abandon hobbies, but worse, don't even miss them. You spend less and less time with friends, and more time with electronic media such as television, videos, or the Internet.

➤ A dead giveaway when you're spending too many hours on the job is when you're not only eating lunch at your desk, you're also eating some dinners there as well.

Dan Sullivan, a Canadian author and trainer who runs seminars for entrepreneurs, believes that you'd actually be better off if you had *half as much time* to spend on your job. Why? Then you'd be forced to

➤ Focus on what's important.

➤ Streamline your operations.

➤ Assemble the appropriate resources.

➤ Stay on target more of the time.

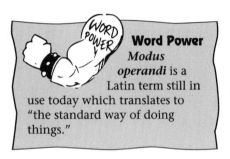

Word Power
Modus operandi is a Latin term still in use today which translates to "the standard way of doing things."

Based on Sullivan's view of work, when you allow yourself to pour 50 to 55 hours or more per week into your job or business, you're practically setting up a situation *in which you will not work efficiently.*

I know, you're thinking, "Buzz off, buddy, I have no choice." But you *do* have choices.

If you've experienced any of the following, you've not only been working too long, you may be reaching the danger level and need to take immediate action so that more damage is not done:

Go!
If you're employed in a highly competitive profession or industry, and it seems like there's no way to get ahead without putting in monster hours, you have to work with greater focus and efficiency for the hours you do put in, and let go of lower priorities.

➤ You experience chest pains on the job, for no apparent reason.

➤ You've experienced any kind of dizziness, fainting, or blacking-out.

➤ You have difficulty digesting food or swallowing.

➤ Chemical dependence has become a way of life to get you through the day.

➤ You've started to experience near misses while driving.

➤ You begin to bump into things, cut yourself accidentally, or in general, are more accident prone.

Only you know what is a comfortable level of work for you. Some people thrive on 60 hours; some people are wasted after 35. If you're an entrepreneur, running your own show, you may actually gain energy from the time you put into your business. I know some people who find it stressful to be *away* from their work, at least if they're away too long.

A Little Balance, Please

Listed below are the activities and resources professionals rely on, when their work and non-work life begins to get out of balance:

➤ Support of family or friends.

➤ Having others with whom you can share your problems or feelings.

➤ Using time as wisely as possible.

➤ Actively engage in hobbies for relaxation or recreation.

➤ Eat at least two wholesome, balanced meals a day.

➤ Have some place in your home as a sanctuary where you can rest, or simply be by yourself.

➤ Maintain a faith or belief system.

➤ Exercise at least three times a week for 20 minutes or longer each time.

Rather than relying on one or two of these resources, I suggest you make three or four, or more, a part of your routine. The more weapons you have in your arsenal, the more effective you'll be at handling the tough challenges you face.

Determining Your Overwork Quotient

With a little calculation, you can determine your overwork quotient—how many extra hours per day and week you can work before it becomes counterproductive.

Suppose as a starting base, working an eight hour day is well within your capabilities. Notice then how you felt on days when you work 8.5 hours, 9 hours, 9.5 hours, and perhaps 10 hours. For many people, someplace between 8.5 and 9 hours begins to feel uncomfortable, and certainly beyond 9 to 9.5 results in noticeable differences in energy level, enthusiasm, and *joie de vivre*.

I begin my work day usually at 7 a.m. and end sometime a little after 5 p.m. During that time I eat a good lunch for 30 to 40 minutes, and usually sleep about 20 minutes. Thus, my average work day is nine hours. On Fridays, it's probably closer to eight hours. Occasionally, I also will work from one to three hours early on a Saturday morning. So, my typical work week is 46 hours. If I average an extra half-hour a day Monday through Thursday, I immediately begin to feel it in terms of energy loss. In other words, while I'm fine at 46 hours, at 48 there's a slight but noticeable difference. At 50 hours, there's a distinct difference.

Jeff Davidson's Average Work Week

Day	Sunday	Monday	Tuesday	Wednesday	Thursday	Friday	Saturday
Start time		7:00 a.m.	6:50 a.m.	7:20 a.m.	7:00 a.m.	7:30 a.m.	9:00 a.m.
Lunch		30 min.	30 min.	30 min.	40 min.	30 min.	—
Breaks		20 min.	30 min.	20 min.	30 min.	20 min.	20 min.
End time		5:30 p.m.	5:50 p.m.	6:00 p.m.	5:10 p.m.	4:00 p.m.	11:50 a.m.
Daily Total		9:40	10:00	9:30	9:00	8:40	2:30

Weekly Total = 46:20

At 50 to 52 or more working hours, life takes on a different perspective for me. Working too much upsets the delicate balance that I need to remain happy in both my working and non-working life.

For you, a 10-hour day, five days a week, may be the norm. Hence, you're putting in 50 hours. Maybe you do some work-related reading on Saturday and Sunday for an average of 52 hours a week. Perhaps you can still go another four hours with no real downside. I doubt it, but maybe you're special.

Conversely, maybe a 40-hour work week is your cup of tea, and even a half-hour beyond that throws you out of whack. This isn't to say you're a wimp or don't have the intestinal fortitude of others. Perhaps you're simply comfortable with a 40-hour work week—do a whale of a job during that time—and don't want to work any more than that. People in government positions or any job where they punch the clock could easily fall into this category. After years of working a fixed number of hours per week, your body and temperament become accustomed to it; a variation in the pattern could cause problems.

If I only get six or seven hours of work in during a day, when I intended to do nine, sometimes that's a little stressful. If I only intended to do six or seven in a day and I do the six or seven, that's fine.

Use the chart to add up the typical number of hours you work per week, then in the coming weeks, take note of your overwork quotient.

Your Average Work Week

Day	Sunday	Monday	Tuesday	Wednesday	Thursday	Friday	Saturday
Start time							
Lunch							
Breaks							
End time							
Daily Total							

Weekly Total = ?

It might be as little as 15 minutes a day, although for most people that won't register much on the Richter Scale. I'll bet it's someplace between two to four hours per week. But why would you even want to know?

Once you have the number that's pretty much right for you, you can align your week and days, so that you stay within your comfortable range. Your goal then is to work productively within those hours, so you don't increase stress trying to get more done in less time and offset any gains you achieve by not working longer. I hope I've made myself perfectly clear!

Stay Fit, Work Longer with Less Stress

If you have to work long hours, how do you make the best of it?

Vigorous workouts help me stay calmer during the day, better able to put in my nine hours—as long as I get a nap—and finish in the evening with enough energy to still have a life.

For several years, the National Sporting Goods Association has conducted an annual sports participation survey. The most popular sport in America, by far, is exercise walking with some 19,770,000 participants, nearly two-thirds of which are women. Exercise walkers engage in this activity an average of 110 times in a 365-day year, or almost once every three days.

Go!
If you've been working too many hours and not getting enough exercise, walking is probably the easiest way to reintroduce yourself to physical activity.

Close on the heels of walking comes exercising with equipment, with some 11,350,000 people participating—in this case, slightly more men than women.

People who exercise with equipment do so nearly one day out of every three. Also, some people in this category undoubtedly are in category one as well. At any rate, exercise is widely known to both improve health and reduce stress, and you can pick any one of a number of exercise types, as long as you make the commitment to exercise regularly.

If you're already exercising regularly, good. If you aren't, there's no better time than now to get started. Since walking is the easiest to initiate and yields great benefits, why not start this evening?

A Different Kind of Play

In organizations throughout the U.S., dress-down days are becoming popular. At many organizations, this is usually on a Friday, and everyone agrees it's a great tension reliever. You save on dry cleaning bills, and see your fellow workers in a different light. Many people are more relaxed wearing the clothes they prefer. (If you're the head of your department, or can initiate such procedures, you might be doing everyone, yourself included, a favor.)

Making It Too Hard on Yourself

It's one thing to work long hours, it's another to heap the pressure on yourself by engaging in activities that tend to speed up your sense of time. Here are several factors that tend to speed up your sense of time during the workday. If you can minimize some of these, then the long hours that you put in may not be so onerous:

Working in front of the clock   When you do this, your perception of time is that it goes by quickly. Hide the clock, and work at your own pace. You'll accomplish more in less time than if you monitor yourself. Of course, you'll still have to keep loose track of the time: if you have kids to pick up from soccer practice, you can bet they won't be sympathetic when you're 45 minutes late!

Having an unrealistic time frame   I've observed that often, many otherwise accomplished people have unrealistic time frames. Normally, if you think a project will take one hour to complete, it might actually take up to two hours. Examine the contingencies, and allow enough time. After estimating the time it will take to do something, multiply that by 1.5 and you'll usually have a more realistic time frame.

Working under pressure   Any time you face a deadline, time will seem to run faster. In some cases, you can't do anything about deadlines. Try to arrange your time so that you don't face them as often and you'll gain a greater sense of control over your time.

Working without the right equipment   If you don't use the right equipment (especially when compared to your competitors), you'll be at a loss. Years ago, I knew a coworker who refused to get an item because the company wouldn't pay the

$200 it cost. I asked him how much time he'd save if he bought it himself, and he figured about an hour a day. That's about 250 hours a year—a return that would pay for the typewriter's cost many times over! Acquire equipment as the need is apparent and when you can comfortably absorb the cost.

Following the unchallenged ritual in your workplace   (Such as reading the morning paper even though you don't want to and it really is no use to you.) Look at the things you do in your workday that represent rituals that may no longer be supportive, productive, or efficient. Some things could be delegated, not done at all, or done a different way.

Increasing your information intake   You can only absorb a finite amount of information. So many activities are going on in the world; attempting to take them all in overwhelms you. Be a wise information consumer—there's no keeping up.

You'll also be amazed at how your sense of time will stop racing and be reduced to a more normal pace.

Strategies for Pacing Yourself

Sometimes the best way to handle seemingly time-consuming duties is through innovative strategies. I once had the opportunity to appear in a full page feature in *USA Today* in which I counseled three busy people on how they could have less hectic lives. One of the people was a pastor who not only put in a full workday, but frequently had to visit members of his congregation who were ill, perhaps hospitalized.

He told me how difficult it was for him to do this and give his wife the attention that she deserved. I asked him how long his visits were to the people hospitalized. He said usually no more than 15 to 20 minutes. I gave him a solution that he enjoyed, and put to practice immediately. Hereafter, I told him that on days when he knew he'd be visiting someone in the evening, to make a date night out of that for himself and his wife. In other words, his wife would accompany him to the hospital, and either stay in the car and listen to music or read, or perhaps come into the hospital lobby.

Since he was only going to be visiting with the patient for no more than 15 to 20 minutes, he and his wife knew in advance what time they would be departing. Hence, rather than have an evening disrupted and his wife more frustrated than ever, *she knew if she could simply weather the 20 minutes that her husband would need, then he'd be totally available!*

His wife was no longer resentful, and even looked forward to the 15 to 20 minute periods in which she knew she could read uninterrupted.

Go!
In every profession, regardless of how long and how hard you work, opportunities to pace yourself exist. You only have to look for them.

You probably work in an office reporting to others. Regardless, there are many, many innovative ways to handle the tasks that confront you, while maintaining a sense of balance.

On the Spot Strategies

Okay, so you're working late again, and for now, you need some immediate help. Here's a potpourri of stressors you may experience, along with some antidotes.

➤ You've been at your desk too long, and you're unable to concentrate, perhaps indecisive. The antidote: Take some long, deep breaths. It may take a few minutes before you're able to breathe slowly and deeply. Let your abdomen expand with each inhalation. Soon, you'll feel calmer, and better able to concentrate.

➤ You've got the sniffles and suspect that a cold or flu is coming on. Antidote: Keep some vitamin C tablets in your desk. When you've been working long and hard, your body can be low on vitamin C. You can safely take up to 1,000 milligrams, perhaps even 2,000, although for some people, stomach irritation may result.

➤ Your neck and your shoulders are aching. Antidote: Tilt your head down so that your chin touches your chest. Roll your head gently left and right to loosen up neck muscles. If you can, let your neck go limp. Reach to the back of your neck and slowly and gently knead yourself. In a few minutes, you'll feel looser. Knead each of your shoulders with the opposite hand: left hand to the right shoulder, right hand to the left shoulder.

➤ You've been clenching your jaw, and this has made your muscles tight. Antidote: Make a fist and place it under your chin. Then, while resisting the jaw movement with your fist, try to open your mouth. If you can hold this for several seconds, pretty soon, the tension around your jaw should subside.

➤ You're experiencing heartburn, gas, or cramps. Antidote: This could be a result of taking in carbonated drinks, caffeine, or alcohol. Eat more slowly, and switch to water on occasion for your beverage during meals.

➤ The muscles in your lower back are tight or sore. Antidote: Clasp your hands in front of you and rest your arms on your knees as you squat down. Hold this for several seconds. If you've been sitting for an especially long period of time, repeat this a couple of times. Your muscles will start to loosen up.

➤ You feel fidgety, ill at ease. Antidote: Whenever you're seated at your desk, and feel the urge to get up and walk around, it's the perfect time to do so. It's best not to ignore such urges. Your body has a way, miraculously, of telling your when it's time for a stretch.

➤ Your mouth and throat are dry. Antidote: Have water nearby. Also, non-sugared cough drops—there are a wide variety today at health food stores—or a piece of fruit or a vegetable will help. Baby carrots are available in almost every supermarket today. They don't need refrigeration, and are edible right out of the bag.

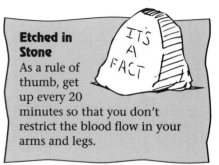

Etched in Stone
As a rule of thumb, get up every 20 minutes so that you don't restrict the blood flow in your arms and legs.

➤ You've been in front of your computer screen too long, and your head is pounding. Antidote: Get some fresh air away from anything that emits electromagnetic waves. When you return to your desk, make sure you sit at least two feet from your computer terminal. (Also, see Chapter 4 on staying in shape in front of your PC.) If you have an older monitor, say earlier than 1994, you may need to get a screen to place over it to limit the amount of electromagnetic rays that you're exposed to. Newer models of monitors have reduced these problems.

The Least You Need to Know

➤ You're working too much when other aspects of your life that were formerly important are getting extremely short shrift.

➤ Determine your overwork quotient, how many extra hours a week you can work, before you start to feel crummy. Then, don't exceed that limit.

➤ Consider working fewer hours per week, which will force you to focus on what's most important, have the mental and emotional strength to let go of lower priority items.

➤ Rely on self-administered remedies right at your desk, when you know that you've been working and sitting for too long.

Chapter 6

Increased Expectations, Diminishing Returns

In This Chapter

➤ When everyone around you is expecting more

➤ When you're expecting too much for yourself

➤ All about job burnout

➤ Paying homage to the cycles of productivity

➤ The best companies to work for

➤ Strategies for doing more while keeping stress in check

Wherever you go today, you hear the same lament from business executives—the pace of business has become immediate. It moves at the speed of voice and e-mail. People are using all kinds of tools and technology, and still the paper mushrooms. Instead of one phone number now, people have six—office, fax machine, car, home, administrative assistant, voice mail, perhaps one for a beeper, and who knows what else?

The more tools of technology that are created to assist you, the more you are asked to do.

When you only had a typewriter that could generate three or four items of correspondence at a time, that's how much you were expected to do. With the introduction of the PC, which allows you to generate hundreds of pieces of correspondence with a few keystrokes, expectations regarding your output are notably higher.

When you can do more, people expect you to do more. These demands don't come from only employers; they come from fellow employees, family members, neighbors; in sum, everywhere you turn.

What a Concept!

People frequently resist change, not because of change itself but because of their attachment to doing things the way they always have.

Perhaps most onerous, as society gets more complex, more stringent documentation is often required by your company, your customers, the government, and others who have the ability to demand it of you. It seems harder and harder to do anything without documentation.

As society becomes more complex, there's a time lag between the introduction of new ways of doing things and the actual implementation of these new methods. In addition, there's unresolved mental clutter, attachment, resistance, and personal agendas.

All of the above means that you're facing more challenges and more situations where you're balancing many tasks, while unconditionally expected to do more.

When Did the High-Expectation Floodgates Open?

In pinpointing the start of the "ever-increasing expectations" phenomenon, I would guess that it was around the second year following the birth of Federal Express. Don't get me wrong, I'm not blaming Fred Smith—he certainly fulfilled an important need, and I've used his and other overnight courier services at least a dozen times a year since the mid 1980s.

The FedEx notion of delivering a package "absolutely positively, overnight," along with widespread use of PCs and growing competition from foreign manufacturers, raised the bar, if you will, prompting more progressive businesses throughout the world, to increase levels of service.

It's hard to argue against the value of having companies dispensing better service. Alternatively, what's required of employees who are responsible for delivering that service has increased. And, as you look at particular industries, it's apparent that expectation levels everywhere are rising, probably *with no possibility of declining.*

Sons of Guns

Meanwhile, your *own* level of expectations regarding goods and services that you acquire has also increased markedly, hasn't it?

Increased Expectations Result from These Goods and Services Provided At Record Speeds

Near Instantaneous

✔ Telephone directory information	✔ ATM Machines
✔ Tele-banking fund transfers	✔ Photocopiers, printers
✔ Fax machines	✔ E-mail
✔ Web sites: news, weather, updates	✔ CNN Headline News
✔ Air phones on planes	✔ Fast-food restaurants, drive through
✔ Microwave	✔ Pay-per-view television

On Demand

✔ Pizza delivery	✔ Gourmet dinner delivery
✔ Groceries delivery	✔ Courier service
✔ Jiffy Lube	✔ State car safety inspection
✔ AAA or motor club response	✔ 911 response
✔ One-hour glasses, contact lenses	✔ 24-hour print shops
✔ All night restaurants, supermarkets	

Next Day, Same Day

✔ Express delivery of packages	✔ Laundry, dry cleaning services
✔ Office supply delivery	✔ Morning-after pill

Nearly Perfected

✔ Education on demand	✔ Just-in-time manufacturing
✔ Universal cellular telephone	✔ 100s of techno-breakthroughs

The Great Expectations Chart of Future Attitudes indicates some of your expectations for the present, and some that are forthcoming. It illustrates how the pressure for speed may increase even further in our lives.

Great Expectations: A Chart of Future Attitudes	
Old Expectations	**New Expectation, Someday**
Using an electric can opener.	Using a laser-driven can opener.
Cook food in 30-60 minutes using a stove.	Cook food instantly with a microwave.
Using a plug-in or portable iron that heats up in 30 seconds.	Using a plug-in or portable iron that heats up in a second and wondering why it takes so long.
Changing TV channels by getting up, walking across the living room, and manually turning the TV dial.	Having a remote control channel-changer and being irritated that channel surfing takes too long.
Going to a video store to rent a movie to watch that evening.	Getting on-demand movies via your TV; soon, using on-demand holographic or virtual TV anywhere.
Booting up your 486, 60-megahertz PC in 30 seconds; retrieving files in another 30 seconds.	Booting your post-Pentium, 440-megahertz PC and saying any phrase from a file to retrieve it in seconds.
Using a high-speed modem to transmit data quickly; sending longer files or documents via mail or overnight carriers and waiting for replies.	Having an advanced ISDN connection, 100 to 250 times as fast as a modem; faxing or downloading files online and wondering why downloading takes so long.
Placing an order by mail or phone and waiting four to six weeks to receive your purchase.	Ordering by phone, fax, or e-mail and expecting the delivery later today—or even within the hour.
Traveling across the country or around the world on a Boeing 767 or an SS Concorde.	Taking a 45-minute half-orbital shuttle to Sydney, Australia from Houston.

Etched in Stone

Technology enables everyone to get more done, while raising expectations about everyone else as well.

Your expectations extend beyond receiving products and services. Suppose you send a letter or e-mail message to your congressional representative and you didn't get a reply. "Why not, that's what they're elected for." Actually, the number of e-mail messages coming into the House of Representatives system just in 1995, surged from about

185,000 messages per month at the beginning of the year to over 600,000 per month by the end of the year. By 1996, messages were up to over one million per month.

Most people can't respond to all of the e-mail they get, let alone your congressional representative.

Hit Me with My Best Shot

The expectations you have for yourself may be the highest of all, and certainly stress inducing. Guilt and perfectionism are rampant among today's professionals. Dads feel guilty that they're not spending enough time with their kids. Working moms feel guilty that they're not doing the best they can at work or the best job raising their kids.

Many people report feeling as if they are not living up to company standards, even though they've been asked to do more with less resources. "I am worried that I'm not living up to my boss' expectations," says a 34-year-old director of marketing at a financial brokerage in Cincinnati. Never mind that this person lost two people from his staff, and endured a 10 percent budget cut.

Barely Hanging On...

If you're a survivor in an organization where many people have been downsized (riffed, or simply let go, depending on the terminology at the moment) it's important to maintain your sense of equilibrium. Many of those around you may be resentful of the situation they face—having to do almost twice as much as before—although they're thankful to be among those retained. To flourish in an environment where you're asked to do more with less:

Pace yourself. In the short term, you can work extra hours, you can work faster, and you can throw yourself at your job. In the long run, regardless of the situation, pacing is the order of the day. For example, you're better off working a regular schedule, even if it's long days, rather than pulling all-nighters and around-the-clock efforts—crashing, getting up, and expecting to be at your best.

Treat yourself well. Too many professionals under heavy stress abuse their gastrointestinal tracts, their hearts, and their heads. They fill up on fatty foods, alcohol, cigarettes, and worse.

Maintain perspective. The higher-ups know they've reduced your staff, reduced your budget, and reduced your resources. If you turn in a superior performance, they're probably all slapping each other on the back, knowing they have such a rare talent in their stable.

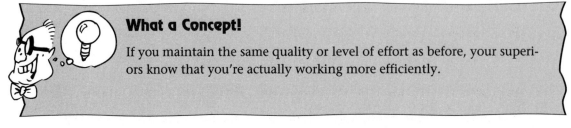

What a Concept!

If you maintain the same quality or level of effort as before, your superiors know that you're actually working more efficiently.

If you're doing the best you can do, truly doing the best you can do, why get stressed out about it? If you're rewarded for your efforts, that invariably offers some release. If your efforts are ignored, there is a reliable way you can bring credit to yourself for the good job that you're doing:

1. Your own organization's in-house newspaper or newsletter is always looking for news and tidbits to fill their pages. If you can develop even a two or three paragraph summary on your accomplishments, you probably can get it published.

2. Here's a mere subset of all of the topics that are suitable for a small blurb on what you've accomplished:

   Services New service introduction, new projects, new uses for existing products, unusual service offerings, and new contracts.

   Your professional activities Speaking engagements, travel abroad, noteworthy accomplishments, civic activities, courses completed, certificates, degrees, seminars attended, mention in trade, professional journals, awards, citations, honors, and affiliation.

   Research Survey results, trends, projections, and forecasts.

No Respect?

What about when you're asked to do more with less and then you are chided somehow? I say your path is relatively clear. You'll have to move on. Any group that asks you to do more with less and then is widely dissatisfied will never be happy with your efforts. And, if you remain in that situation for very long, you'll be a candidate for burnout.

Avoiding Job Burnout

Burnout is a term that has made the rounds in business and general literature over the last decade and a half. It's actually a unique type of stress that involves:

➤ Diminished personal accomplishment.

➤ De-personalization.

➤ Emotional exhaustion.

We will visit each of these items in a moment.

Although researchers are still exploring the nature of burnout for now, it is widely regarded as a distinct type of stress related to demands on the job. Burnout is costly to organizations, but those organizations in which employees feel the effects of burnout often do little to help, unfortunately. How do you know if you're heading for burnout, or are already there?

Have you been evaluating yourself negatively lately? Does it seem like you're not making any progress or even losing ground? If you feel you're not as competent and successful doing your job as you have been in the past, you're experiencing the sensation of *diminished personal accomplishment.*

Another clue to burnout, is *de-personalization.* This occurs when you methodically do what you're supposed to, but withdraw emotionally from what you're doing. In the health care industry, this could be characterized by a nurse who follows correct medical procedures and is cordial with patients, but no longer cares about them personally. In business, de-personalization can be seen as detachment, a blasé attitude toward peers, clients or customers, and perhaps one's organization in general. If you begin to see others as objects rather than human beings, beware, you may be on the burnout path.

The third component of burnout is *emotional exhaustion*—feeling like you don't have the capacity to respond emotionally to others. Your energy level is low. You are irritated or tense. You know that you can't give of yourself like you have in the past. Following a long weekend, or time away from work, you still loathe the thought of going back to work.

Who is most susceptible to burnout? Those in helping professions, or in positions that have significant amounts of interpersonal contact. This includes people in customer service departments, municipal services, health care, and the travel industry.

Also, people who initially may have been optimistic about what they could achieve on the job, with high expectations for themselves, are particularly susceptible to burnout as they experience setbacks and frustration in what they're asked to do, what they want to accomplish, and what they're actually accomplishing.

> **Warning**
> Emotional exhaustion often is the first of the three characteristics to appear when you're in danger of experiencing burnout. Long hours and heavy demands can drain your emotional resources.

Among the antidotes that are emerging are 1) The ability to know, observe, and be involved in the outcome of your efforts, and 2) The opportunity to engage in a self-evaluation.

The first remedy allows you to maintain a mental link between what you do and what results occur. Said another way, it's highly stressful to work at a job all day long, perhaps interacting with many, many people, and not know if what you do is of value, or appreciated.

The second remedy, self-evaluation, involves looking at what you do with some measure of objectivity, perhaps using a chart, checklist, or scale (developed during less trying times), that includes the key components of your job description and responsibilities. The following chart gives you an idea of how.

What I Accomplish					
What I'm Asked to Do	MON	TUE	WED	THU	FRI
Task A					
Task B					
Task C					
Task D					

Etched in Stone
One of the best safeguards for not falling prey to burnout is to accept the input and advice from trusted others.

Your spouse, coworkers, and friends often notice changes in your behavior that may be detrimental to your well-being long before you are aware of them. Please, listen up when somebody says, "Take it easy."

If you've ever watched *Star Trek: The Next Generation*, you know that when Counselor Troi tells Captain Picard to take it easy, he always resists at first. Then he relents and follows her advice. Captain Picard, I postulate, never missed a day on the bridge due to burnout.

What to Do When Your Boss Wants You to Be a Workaholic

Despite the well-known, high prevalence of stress and burnout in the contemporary working world, and the resulting dangers, some organizations still maintain a culture in which employees have it tougher than it needs to be. Too many managers have the misguided notion that only wimps are stressed. These are the same managers who tend to give out stress in abundance. If only they knew that stress is real, and exacts a cost on both individuals and the organization.

Someday, organizations will be held responsible, both socially and legally, for the mental health and well-being of their employees.

Suppose your boss unduly heaps piles of stuff on your desk with little or short notice. What are some strategies you can employ to keep your job, maintain your relationship with your boss, and yet not be overwhelmed?

With great tact and professionalism, offer these words: "I'm really over-committed right now, and if I take that on, I can't do it justice." *Other appropriate responses:*

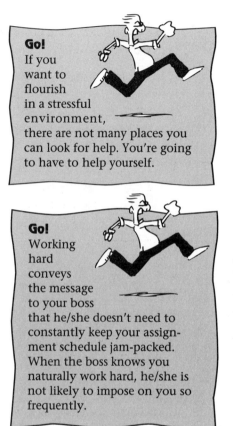

Go!
If you want to flourish in a stressful environment, there are not many places you can look for help. You're going to have to help yourself.

Go!
Working hard conveys the message to your boss that he/she doesn't need to constantly keep your assignment schedule jam-packed. When the boss knows you naturally work hard, he/she is not likely to impose on you so frequently.

➤ "I appreciate your confidence in me, but I wouldn't want to take this on right now, knowing my other responsibilities would prevent me from doing an excellent job."

➤ "I'd be happy to handle this assignment for you, but realistically I can't do it without foregoing some other things I'm working on. Of tasks *a* and *b*, which would you like me to do? Which can I put aside?"

➤ "I can do that for you. Will it be okay if I get back to you in the middle of next week? I currently have blank, blank, and blank in the queue."

➤ "The number and complexity of the assignments I'm handling is mounting. Perhaps we could look at a two- or four-week scenario of what's most important to you, when the assignments need to be completed, and what I can realistically handle over that time period."

All the while, stay as flexible as possible. Frequently, your responsibilities and assignments will change. As you learned in Chapter 4, your ability to adapt to your boss's needs will go a long way in helping you flourish at your position, and help diminish the feeling of being overwhelmed you may be experiencing.

Paying Homage to the Cycles of Productivity

Let's look at a scenario wherein two professionals are able to work with great efficiency.

Linda won't transcribe tapes late in the day or anytime on Friday. As a matter of fact, she has established a personal work pattern in which specific tasks are undertaken throughout the course of the week. Susan, the production supervisor, rarely interferes with Linda's cycle unless an urgent report or letter has to be completed.

Is Linda an obstinate employee, undermining the production needs of her office?

❑ Yes   ❑ No

Is Susan deficient as a production supervisor?

❑ Yes   ❑ No

Should either or both be given the heave ho?

❑ Yes   ❑ No

Okay, put down your pencil.

Is either woman derelict in her duties? No; they are not mutineers. Linda is an extremely effective member of the production staff, and Susan directs the production department skillfully. *Linda has determined her production peaks and valleys over the course of the normal work week, and recognizes her personal cycle of productivity.* For all but urgent assignments, Susan acknowledges Linda's ability to maintain high productivity by handling assignments on those days and at those hours, which achieves a relatively constant "effort to task" ratio.

Robert, Linda's production staff partner, also maintains high productivity by personally prioritizing assignments. Linda and Robert have similar production responsibilities, but each has different strengths and weaknesses, varying energy levels (throughout the work week), and has long since gauged these factors so that each knows what can best be undertaken when. In short, they "go with the flow" of their energy levels.

Employees Establish Their Cycles

If you report to others, read on to see how you might implement this arrangement; if you supervise others and want more assignments completed faster and more effectively, give your good employees every opportunity to establish their own productivity cycle. Within reason, it makes sense to allow your best workers to undertake assignments in a manner that best suits *them*. You know too well that many employees devise countless ways to diminish personal productivity by stretching out assignments or coasting until quitting time.

What a Concept!

Enabling employees to respond based upon personal cycles of productivity results in high job satisfaction and yields a greater long-range output.

However, highly productive employees such as Linda, Robert, and Susan take pride in consistently maintaining high productivity.

Letting productive people follow their own schedules means that they will be less fatigued and less stressed. It's draining to continually meet arbitrary deadlines. Productive employees allowed to pace themselves can accomplish more and remain vibrant.

Working the Cycle

Productive employees have an internal "time grid," which charts their cycle of productivity, even if no formal sketch or chart is ever made. When your best staff members tell you they'd "rather not handle the DEF report right now" because they "can do a better job on it tomorrow morning," and the "GHI assignment could be better undertaken now," believe them!

Here are some basic ways to get the most from productive employees in recognition of their cycles of productivity:

➤ Provide enough and varied assignments so the cycle can be used. If an employee only has one assignment, there's obviously little leeway in undertaking the assignment at the most personally opportune time. With numerous assignments, a productive employee can strategically arrange his/her schedule.

➤ Be flexible with "due" dates when possible. Unlike others we all know, productive employees will finish the important jobs on time. Assignments of lesser importance will be finished as soon as possible. The more flexibility you give a productive employee to complete assignments, the better they can execute assignments in accordance with their cycle. More often than not, given flexible due dates, productive employees will complete many assignments sooner than you anticipated.

Reprogramming the Cycle

If you need a report finished within four days, good employees will prepare themselves and generate the requisite energy to successfully accomplish the task. In the short run, good employees can "reprogram" their cycles to handle a crisis.

Warning
Forcing a good worker to reprogram his or her cycle for an extended period is not recommended. Since he or she is already highly efficient, an extended variation soon becomes an imposition (a drag!).

When Nothing Else Works

Suppose you work in an organization where there are no good role models for you, and to top it off, your immediate boss is just plain nasty! Perhaps you're in a situation where things are so stressful that you'd like to quit—and maybe tell your boss a thing or two.

What a Concept!

If you can work with a nasty boss for a four- or six-month period or longer, you may actually be strengthening your capabilities to work with a wide variety of people in the future.

To shore up your withered work ethic, however, try to remember that you may gain some long-term benefits from the experience of working for a tough boss. After all, if you can weather the rigors of working for an onerous boss, think how much easier it will be for you to work with others in the future. Then too, you might be a better boss yourself, someday, for having the experiences you're having now.

The rest of this section provides a sampling of other "successes" that you may experience in one form or another for having worked with a difficult boss.

Accentuate the Positive

Regardless of the specifics of your work situation and the various reasons for your lack of satisfaction, one point remains clear: It could be worse. You could be working for someone who practices exploitation, is dishonest, makes exaggerated promises, or misrepresents the company. All things considered, your personal dissatisfaction with your work situation, particularly your relationship with your immediate boss, is probably tempered with positive as well as negative factors.

Working in a disagreeable situation is undesirable, but it's better than being unemployed, right? Statistics indicate that it is far easier to obtain new employment while employed than to land a job while unemployed.

Strength for the Future

If you make the best of a bad situation and learn to peacefully coexist with people you don't care for, your ability to deal with people you don't like will improve. You'll be able to apply your ability to successfully undertake tasks and responsibilities in a difficult situation in other business and professional relationships.

Have You Stood in Your Boss's Shoes?

Since you can't unequivocally say that you know exactly what it would be like to undertake each and every responsibility that confronts your boss, perhaps you could try developing a sense of empathy. *Or, maybe the SOB doesn't deserve any, under any circumstances!*

Knowing You're Going

By now you may be ready to scream, because your dissatisfaction in your job may be well founded. Let's assume you are *totally* in the right.

Take comfort in knowing that you are leaving. If you have ever debated about leaving a position for months or even years, you know the relief you feel when the decision is made. You can let all of your mental anguish subside. There is now a light at the end of the tunnel. The daily trials and personal conflicts that you have sought to minimize are now, at least, tolerable.

Revenge: Sweet or Sour?

While you are in your present position, commit to doing a good job and upholding the good name of your organization. To do anything else would be a strong reason not to respect yourself.

Be professional, and take your experiences in stride. Learn and benefit from your experience, but don't waste your energies resurrecting the past, "evening up" the score, or trying to fulfill your personal sense of justice. This will be a waste of time, regardless of any minor satisfaction. The long-term personal satisfaction of getting "revenge" is nil. Moreover, the possibility of something going wrong or being misinterpreted is high.

Hone Your Diplomatic Skills

While coping daily, you are refining your diplomatic skills even if you are not aware of it. Do you think the Secretary of State actually respects all of the people with whom he negotiates? In a work environment, a little diplomacy can go a long way.

Go!
By developing diplomatic skills, you are increasing your professional marketability.

Half a century ago, Andrew Carnegie, the multimillionaire steel magnate, observed that he could hire the functional or technical skills necessary for any business venture. However, the one ability for which he would (and did) pay most dearly was the ability to deal with people.

The Best Companies to Work For

In the last decade several books have been published on the best companies with whom to be employed, among them *The 100 Best Companies to Work For* and *The 100 Best Companies to Sell For*. *The Best Jobs in America for Parents*, by Susan Dynerman and Lynn Hayes, shows you how to go about searching for a good, flexible job whether you're an attorney who wants to work a reduced schedule of "only" forty hours a week, or a pair of secretaries who'd like to share a job. It also outlines negotiating methods that ensure you get the kind of job you want, and explains how to make sure everyone (especially you) is satisfied once you get it.

The companies listed in these books recognize that the needs of their workforce is changing and that retaining good employees today means offering them the kinds of programs and benefits that make for vibrant, balanced workers.

At E.I. Dupont de Nemours and Company, for example, top executives began developing "work-life programs" designed to help their employees handle issues such as elder care, child care, and other demands of holding a job and raising a family in contemporary society. Such enlightened companies acknowledge that pressure away from work definitely impacts employee productivity.

At Dupont, top management points proudly to the 52 percent of staff who have participated in three or more work-life programs and now say that they would "go the extra mile for Dupont." Observers both inside and outside the company agree that such employees are better able to approach their jobs with creativity, energy, and a sense of urgency.

Keep in mind that Dupont's initiatives are business-driven. They're based on improving productivity and competitiveness. They're not based on some squishy notion of "social responsibility," although the end result is that the company becomes more socially responsible.

Companies deciding to employ work-life types of programs need to assess the particular circumstances impacting their employees. At Dupont, nearly one-third of employees were either single parents, or came from two income families that had responsibility toward children age 13 or younger, or for any older adult relative.

If your organization is aggressively progressive, thank your lucky stars that they value you as an employee and want to make sure that you achieve results, but maintain balance and peace of mind in the process. If you're not working in such an organization, you have two basic options:

1. Try to bring about change in your current environment, perhaps getting top management to notice the long-term benefits of installing work-life programs, or

2. Seek employment with those companies that have already instituted such programs (albeit a long shot). You'll then be able to meet high expectations without experiencing diminishing returns.

The Least You Need to Know

➤ The pace of business has become immediate. The more tools of technology there are to assist you, the more you are asked to do.

➤ Your own expectations in terms of acquiring goods and services have also increased markedly.

➤ To flourish in an environment where you're asked to do more with less, treat yourself well and maintain a healthy perspective.

➤ Emotional exhaustion is often the first of three characteristics to appear when you're in danger of experiencing burnout. One of the best safeguards for not falling prey to burnout is to accept the input and advice from trusted others.

➤ You need effective role models to accelerate your learning curve and to let you see that, with a balanced career, success is attainable.

Chapter 7

A Workplace Revolution, or How to Get Out of Jail

In This Chapter

➤ Darn those little chips

➤ Taming the telephone

➤ The professionally elusive you

➤ A little quiet, please

Visualize this scenario. Grok, your typical Cro-Magnon, is exploring the far side of a hill. He finds some caves and, upon entering, discovers that there are some untouched walls. He gathers up some sticks, stones, mud, red clay, and anything else he can find and starts to create a colorful mural. Hmm, what can we paint today? How about a hunting scene, or maybe the dance? Or maybe some of the sacred animals? This is going to be one of the better murals! There's nobody around, oodles of time, and lots of space on the cave wall.

Just then, a pterodactyl flies by and drops off a message. It's from Mamuk, his common-law wife. Hmm, wonder what she wants? Let's see, could he get some of those elderberries on the far side of the hill, some more kindling, and oh, try to get home early today?

In this age, interruptions like the message from Mamuk are coming two or three at a time. The

Etched in Stone
Everybody, in every age, had interruptions and disturbances.

automatic, electronic gadgets of today present new paths to stress. Faxes, e-mail, voice-mail, and (jeepers, creepers) beepers ensure that anyone can be reached anytime. Fortunately, you can use the same technology that exposes you to all types of disruptions to create some sanctuary for yourself, as you'll learn in this chapter.

Darn Those Little Chips

More potential disrupters exist today than ever before—it's not just your perception. We are the most distracted generation in history. By 2001, technical knowledge will double every 11 months. An estimated 17 high-tech products will be developed every second, with an associated 200 new high-tech services.

Word Power Contemporary people who disdain the intrusion of technology are known as **Luddites**. In contrast, **neo-Luddites** believe that the best chance of social survival is through the abandonment of 20th century technology and a return to a more harmonious relationship with nature. Neo-Luddites loathe television and regard it as a drug that lulls one into a passive, lethargic state while creating unfocused anxiety in the body.

Word Power Although technology was developed to supposedly enhance the process of making fare changes and new reservations in the airline industry, the process actually **recomplicated**, or became more confusing. Within a 24-hour period, the airline industry reportedly recorded as many as 600,000 fare changes!

As technology infiltrates every aspect of life, it's easy to understand why some people view the onslaught with disdain. Will anything be left of the world we knew? Will there be any semblance of the privacy we once enjoyed? The Luddites among us, and they're growing in number, want to smash PCs, stamp beepers into the ground, and rip out the lines of the Internet.

Technology has simplified *and* complicated life. What's it called when you make a telephone call to someplace, encounter an automated reception system, have to keep pushing buttons, and still can't reach the right party? And the option you want isn't reachable, and you can't even get to an operator? Answer: Phone mail jail.

The voice mail systems you encounter daily are one of many examples of technology run amuck.

The more you send messages and information around the globe with the push of a button, or are concurrently prevented from reaching others because of technology's inherent capability for fouling up what it was designed to improve, the less anything redeeming gets done.

Professor Theodore Roszak, a professor of history at California State University and the author of *The Cult of Information*, observes that "data merchants have shamefully promoted the importance of bits of information...." Paradoxically, "master ideas," he observes—the moral, philosophical, and religious teachings that are the underpinnings of our humanity—are not based on information at all. The phrase, "All men are created equal," is widely accepted by millions, if not billions of people around the globe. Yet, no amount of information could add up to such a proposition.

What a Concept!

In the affairs of humanity, that which is universally held to be true is often *not* the byproduct of systems configuration or any form of data processing.

The Professionally Elusive You

You can count on it—no one works as effectively when continually interrupted via fax, beepers, phone, or office visitors. A few simple principles, explored here, will enable you to stay connected, stay productive, and keep your stress at a manageable level.

Dealing with the Telephone in General

The telephone continues to be the foremost tool of communication between people who are apart. Depending on the flexibility you have in your current position, I suggest implementing all the following to control telephone interruptions:

➤ Carve out at least one or two hours a day to let it be known that you are not accepting calls. If you have an answering machine, you could simply leave a message that says "I'll be available today from one to three," or "I'll be away from the phone from nine to eleven" or any similar message.

➤ If you have voice mail or a receptionist, protect some portion of your day in a similar manner.

If I discover that Mr. Jones likes to be telephone-free from 8 a.m. to 10 a.m., what do I do? Naturally, I call after 10 a.m. I don't think any less of him because he carves out this time for himself, and I don't see it as an impediment to getting in touch with him. Indeed, *I'd rather know that he was more available after ten.*

➤ Turn down the phone volume to its lowest practical setting. If you're in a noisy machine shop and it's your responsibility to get to the

Go!
People come to understand and appreciate others who have protected a portion of their day by not taking phone interruptions.

phone, maybe you need the volume turned up all the way. My guess is that you work in an office with some control over your environment, and need only the most subtle of rings, beeps, alarms, or chimes summoning you to the phone. Also, inexpensive devices are available that provide a flashing light in place of sound when a phone call comes your way.

➤ If you have two lines, use the one on your business card, stationery, or literature as the inbound line—the one on which everyone can call you—and use the other line for outbound calls. Why? This frees you from missing calls while you're on the line; it also enables you to monitor calls and keep working, if you want.

Most important, it enables you to offer a measured response to the calls you receive. Often it's best *not* to receive calls when they come in, especially if you're in the midst of a call to market your business or product, for example. Sure, it's more costly to dial someone back long distance, but such inconvenience is offset by your ability to gather information for the first party's request, plan what you're going to say, eliminate distracting background noise, and then call the other party when you're ready to deal with them.

Note: This may not be the best for folks working from a home office, who must designate one line as a business line, which becomes the only line for which outgoing calls can be deducted as a business expense.

Go!
You owe yourself a sound sleep every night, and having a phone by your head all but ensures that you won't. If you insist on a phone in the bedroom, at least turn the ringing down to the lowest possible volume.

➤ Avoid sleeping with the telephone by your head. I know people who think there has to be a telephone in their bedroom. I don't know why; perhaps they've seen it in the movies or their parents kept a phone in their bedroom.

The basic argument people offer for keeping a phone close by is that there might be an emergency. They have an aging mother, teenage son, and so on. It's an individual decision, but you have to weigh 10 or 15 years of good sleep versus being able to field the one important call that might come in where you *might* be able to take immediate action. Most of the time, it'll be a wrong number.

➤ When on the road, unplug the phone in your hotel room (see Chapter 16).

Absolutely Never Use Call Waiting

This is about the least productive, most offensive, stress-inducing telephone service I can think of, although you're entitled to your own irritants as well.

When you use call waiting, in essence you're telling both callers that they're not that important, and that you're not that resourceful. You either don't have a receptionist or the proper telephone configuration in your home or office to treat parties with any semblance of respect.

Warning
When you invite constant bombardment by callers, by employing features such as call waiting, all other things being equal, you're going to have a more stressful day.

Some people might say, "I have a teenage daughter who will be calling in around this time, and I don't want her to get a constant busy signal if I'm on the phone with someone." Fine, if you receive a call around the time that you're expecting another, then keep your conversation short.

Use Call Forwarding Sparingly

The ability to receive a call when you're out of your office can be a blessing. However, you only want to use call forwarding when it's appropriate for both you and other parties with whom you'll be interacting. Otherwise, the intrusion and disrespect that you convey is similar to that which you convey when you employ call waiting.

Slave to a Beeper

If you're chained to your beeper, on constant call, I feel for you. Doctors, emergency service workers, high-powered executives, low-powered executives, and all manner of professionals in-between seem to be sporting a beeper. I laugh sometimes when I see them because I've come to understand how *unimportant* most of the calls are.

In some ways, the onslaught of beepers is analogous to the introduction of the PC 10 or 15 years ago. The typists where I worked told me that with the advent of the PC, their job got much easier in some respects and much more difficult in others. Why? Suddenly, people were asking for countless revisions, knowing that with only a few keystrokes, a report could be saved under a different file name. One clerical worker told me that in her office, it got to the point where no report, letter, or document was ever considered finished.

All the unnecessary calls fielded by your beeper represent a similar phenomenon. A technology is introduced, and immediately on the heels of its introduction comes overuse, finally settling into a long-term era of abuse. My strongest recommendation on the use of beepers is this: If you have a receptionist who can field your calls, that receptionist should be among the very few people with your beeper number, so he or she can get in touch with you only when it's necessary.

If you have to wear a beeper and be on call all the time as part of your job, recognize the importance of being beeper-free on a periodic basis. Being on call around the clock is highly stressful to many people. Outside of being the President or a high-ranking diplomat, there are few professions where you have to be reachable *all* the time.

What a Concept!

Brain surgeons, chiefs of police, heads of universities, or other high-profile professionals, you can carve out one day a week, or three or four days a month, where you are not electronically chained to the world.

Car or Cell Phones

If you have children, a car phone or mobile phone (also called *cellular* or *cell phones*) can enable you to stay in touch at critical times during the day. Some cell phones allow for emergency dialing; nearly all have some type of anti-theft alarm; and some will dial your home or office when an intruder attempts to make a call. Many offer wider display screens, brightly lit for easy use at night, speed dialing, speed redialing, and one-touch dialing.

By adding a cell phone to your automobile or carrying one around with you, what happens that perhaps you *don't* want?

➤ Anyone can reach you at any time?

➤ Disturbance of one of the last sanctuaries that you had?

➤ The potential for driving *less* safely?

➤ Added expense as you engage in unnecessary conversations?

➤ Another invoice to examine at the end of the month and another check to write?

The most prudent use of the cell phone, to keep your stress level in check, would be for outbound calls only. At least then you are in control. As with a beeper, how often do you actually need to be contacted while you're motoring down the highway or eating in a restaurant?

E-mail

With the growth of commercial online services and Internet navigation software, use of e-mail has proliferated to the point where many people log on to find dozens, if not hundreds, of e-mail messages per day.

In fact, in some instances, companies may even send you unsolicited e-mail promoting products and services. (On the Internet, this is known as *spamming*—using the Internet for promotional purposes, which is widely frowned upon.) Any message that has one or more of the following characteristics may qualify as "junk" e-mail; be wary of spending your time on messages that:

Warning
Use of e-mail has gone from use to overuse to abuse in record time.

➤ Contain an unfamiliar e-mail address.

➤ Appear in all capital letters.

➤ Are prefaced with "FYI" for "immediate release," or "first, some background."

➤ Take longer than a minute to read.

➤ Have a lengthy closing "signature" of longer than six lines.

Odds are, what's left may actually be worth reading.

Consider getting a private e-mail address, one that you dispense with great reserve so as to maintain a bastion in which you can receive high quality messages—and not too many of them.

Fax Machines

For me, the biggest source of stress from the fax machine is having that awful three-second beep, which happens whenever the darn thing comes on for any reason, even an incomplete reception! I've called manufacturers, and there doesn't seem to be an easy way to silence them.

My second pet peeve is the extensive waste of paper because the senders are not clever enough to submit a concise fax. Do you need one full page announcing that a fax is coming, a second one saying that this represents page two of three, and a third one that simply contains a one-inch paragraph at the top of the page? I think not.

I recognize that you can't control the length of incoming faxes. However, you do have the ability to pare down their length so that you're not besieged by more paper, which in itself leads to more stress.

If you receive a three-page fax, but the vital information you need is in one paragraph on the page three, along with a 3-by-3-inch square on page two that has the sender's information, retain that, and chuck the rest. Thereafter, a single file folder with the pared down, relevant faxes you receive keeps your desk neat and you in control.

Some businesses turn off their fax machines at the close of the business day. This intrigues me! They might be missing orders from customers in the hinterlands. There's no buildup of fax messages the next morning, however, and if someone wants to get in touch with the organization, he will probably try the next day, anyway.

At one division of American Express, employees had to field fax messages almost every couple minutes. That was bad enough, but each fax represented another five or ten minutes worth of work—fulfilling the request, assembling the information, getting back to the party who sent the fax. One supervisor remarked that her staff wanted to "rip the fax machines out of the wall."

The most appropriate solution would seem to be fax-on-demand, where callers are given a menu of information that they can receive any time of day, simply by pressing a few digits on their phone.

Dan Poynter in Santa Barbara, California maintains an elaborate fax-on-demand system. Dan is an author, publisher, and seminar presenter on book publishing and promotion. In fact, he has a fax-on-demand number that automatically sends to your fax machine information on the topic of faxes-on-demand. For the mildly curious, Dan's fax-on-demand information can be sent to your fax by calling him at 805-968-8947 and following the voice prompt to request documents #109, #311, and #313.

The beauty of fax-on-demand is that you can incorporate hundreds of documents on file and assign each of them its own telephone extension, thereby cutting your fax-related workload at least in half and your fax-related stress immeasurably.

Establishing Creative Sanctuaries

No one is as concerned with your career as you. And as you saw in Chapters 4 and 5, you must continually take charge of your career to ensure that you advance at a pace that is both comfortable and rewarding for you.

One key measure of achieving this is to establish mental and physical sanctuaries for yourself on a daily, weekly, and monthly basis.

Do you do your best thinking surrounded by noise and interruptions? Probably not. Are you able to achieve dramatic insights when people are knocking on your door every couple minutes? Could you plan a merger or acquisition, a new product or service line, a new branch or store location, or any other major undertaking in the midst of high rabble? Few people can.

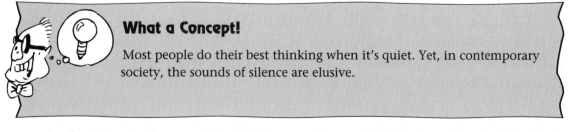

What a Concept!

Most people do their best thinking when it's quiet. Yet, in contemporary society, the sounds of silence are elusive.

Gordon Hempton has recorded wildlife around the world. He's also a staunch advocate of quiet. He believes that the environment is being degraded by noise and that each of us needs a quiet place for a little time each day to truly relax, lower stress levels, and hear the world.

Hempton identified 20 locations in the state of Washington that had more than 15 minutes of silence at a time. He returned five years later to find that 17 had been infected by noise pollution, such that the noise-free interval had decreased to less than three minutes. Only three locations still had noise-free intervals of 15 minutes or more.

With bulldozers, jackhammers, chain saws, small planes and helicopters flying over hourly, car and other engine noise, and loud campers, even the national parks don't represent a haven for quiet anymore.

Etched in Stone
Baseball legend Cal Ripken, Jr., who holds the record for the most consecutive games played, used to listen to the radio or books on tape on the drive to the ballpark. He gave up that listening in favor of a silent ride to better concentrate on the upcoming game.

Given all that you're surrounded with and the impediments that your organization or your work setting impose on you, how do you create sanctuaries for yourself so that you can do your best work and achieve breakthrough or conceptual thinking? How can you be your most productive self, with the least amount of wear and tear on your being? Here are some hints to make it happen:

➤ Barricade yourself in a room and post warning signs.

➤ In advance, identify those places where you will be able to work steadily, when you choose to, such as the company conference room. You'll know when you've found the right spot. You will feel good, productive, and unhurried.

➤ Take the far cubbyhole on the third floor of the library.

I'll examine the notion of becoming the master of your environment in greater detail in Chapter 16. For now, suffice it to say that the observations of Alvin Toffler ring true in office suites worldwide: The contemporary workplace is a terrible place in which to get work done. Nevertheless, stress is a response to your surroundings, not the surroundings themselves.

If you feel that your office and the surrounding technology is deleterious to productivity and personal balance, let any disturbances hereafter serve as a reminder that although you can't control everything, there are ways to turn situations to your advantage.

The Least You Need to Know

➤ Each new office technology offers both benefits and detriments. It's up to you to make the new technology work for you rather than be disruptive and add more stress to your life.

➤ Try to set aside an hour or two each day when you will not receive phone calls.

➤ When appropriate, be professionally elusive to the degree that you can. For example, establish time periods when you won't carry a beeper.

➤ Most people need quiet to do their best work or conceptual thinking.

Whipping Workplace Distractions

In This Chapter

➤ All about disruptions and interruptions

➤ Systematizing interruptions to stay in control

➤ Timing isn't everything, but it's a lot

➤ Mental methods for reducing distractions

You're all ready to start work when your PC monitor starts fading. It flickers back on, then goes off for good.

Instantly, your frustration level zooms up. Why? Certainly you'll be delayed for whatever you're going to do that day. However, you call your company's tech support staff. They can send someone up in 20 minutes to fix or replace your monitor. That time is valuable, but it's not a lifetime. You won't even be thinking about this in a day or two.

Why is this incident still frustrating? Because you had a notion of what you were going to accomplish that morning, and waiting for tech support wasn't among the activities. In the last chapter, you learned how to minimize distractions caused by communications devices. This chapter helps you deal with annoyances in your worklife.

It's the Disruption, Stupid

Let's focus on a second scenario. You just finished a business trip to the West Coast. It went rather well. While you're waiting for your plane in the Los Angeles International Airport, you realize that you've lost your wallet, or perhaps it was stolen. You try to retrace your steps, but to no avail. You go back to the ticket counter, but they haven't seen it.

At the lost-and-found office, you are told that the wallet may show up anywhere from a half hour to a day later. You leave your name, address, phone, and fax number, and leave the office hesitantly.

Fortunately, you still have your ticket and other valuables. For the moment, you don't need your credit cards, and you don't need money. You'll get home just fine. You only had about $11 in cash, one credit card, your license, and a bank card. No one can use the bank card because they don't have your personal identification number. You're not sure what somebody might do with your license, but it won't affect you. You've already taken steps to cancel your credit card, so you're protected there.

Mentally, you skip ahead to the next several days:

➤ You'll have to make an appointment with the motor vehicle department to get a new license.

➤ You'll have to wait a couple days until the credit card company sends you a new card with a new number.

➤ You'll have to make contact with all those places that already have your credit card number so that they can bill you automatically on a monthly basis while you change over to the new account number.

➤ You'll have to get a new bank card, so it won't be easy to withdraw cash for a couple of days.

➤ Oh yes, you'll also have to replace the photo of your spouse and child. Do you even know where the negative is?

As you can see, losing your wallet represents a disruption of activities. But the mere incident itself is not so upsetting. Rather, it is the break in your expectations that bothers you. Being distracted by something you hadn't counted on will consume some time and break your stride. When you understand this concept, you'll be better prepared to take the interruption in stride and work through the consequences.

All About Interruptions

Of more than 15 workplace stressors identified by managers, including demands on their time made by others, work load, organizational politics, responsibility for subordinates, firing someone, reprimanding or disciplining someone, balancing work and personal life, dealing with upper management, conducting performance reviews, working within budgets, and interruptions; which would you guess was cited as the most significant stressor?

If you said interruptions, you're right on the money.

A study conducted by *Industrial Engineer* showed that the average interruption sustained by a manager was six to nine minutes. That, in itself, doesn't seem so bad, but consider that the average time that it took for the managers *to recover* from interruptions was from *three to 23 minutes*.

You don't have to be Einstein to figure out that it only takes a couple interruptions an hour to consume the whole hour, and a couple interruptions a day to throw off your entire day. Is it any wonder that professionals find interruptions the most stressful aspect of their jobs?

> **Warning**
> The typical interruption results in 20 minutes away from the original task at hand.

Interruption Management

Does the phrase *interruption management* seem like an oxymoron?

I once consulted for a supervisor in Minnesota who had six employees. He wanted to use his time more efficiently. He said his employees came to him with questions every couple of hours. That seemed harmless enough, but look at how it built up: If an employee asked a question every two hours, he asked an average of four each day.

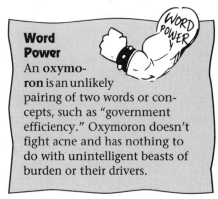

> **Word Power**
> An **oxymoron** is an unlikely pairing of two words or concepts, such as "government efficiency." Oxymoron doesn't fight acne and has nothing to do with unintelligent beasts of burden or their drivers.

With six employees, that meant 24 questions a day, or 120 interruptions each week, resulting in disruptions of the manager's work three times each hour in a 40-hour week! If you throw in how long it took to "recover" from each interruption, potentially, his whole day was consumed by them! Would that be stressful to you? I suggested a system to help him cope with the interruptions and to gain control of his time. I called it the J-4 System. (The "J" was for Jeff. You can use your own initial.)

I had the supervisor put the questions into four categories of manageability. The first distraction, J-1, was already answered in print and did not need a personal reply from the supervisor (it was in the company policy manual or someplace similar). The supervisor could tell his employees, "Please don't concern me with these kinds (J-1) of distractions; review materials you already have to find the answer."

The second distraction, J-2, was a question that a peer or bookkeeper could answer; the supervisor did not need to be bothered and could quickly refer the employee to another person, or ask that certain questions be taken directly to someone else.

Distraction J-3 needed only a straightforward yes or no answer. These questions required interaction with the supervisor, but not much—a quick phone call or buzz on the intercom.

The final category was the J-4 distraction. It was a question that required the supervisor's input—one that the supervisor had to, and desired to, answer.

How many questions were of the J-4 level of importance? Assume that each person asked two J-4 questions per day for a total of 60 interruptions each week. This cuts the number of interruptions in half! Actually, the supervisor achieved an even greater reduction. More important, he was able to better use his time and reduce his level of stress.

When you classify the types of interruptions you receive, you can cut them down by taking steps like referring questions to others and better cope with them. As you do, you'll gain greater control over your work and will feel more relaxed.

Multitasking Leads to More Stress?

What if you're in a position where constant interruption is the norm? For example, you are in charge of a switchboard, a customer-service counter, a take-out lunch counter, or a taxi service? In such cases, you have to learn to practice the art of doing one thing at a time, which I discuss at length in *The Complete Idiot's Guide to Managing Your Time*.

How many automobile accidents and mishaps could be attributed to people attempting to do two things at once—put on makeup, shave, eat, smoke, talk on the phone, or listen to 200 decibel music?

Unquestionably, you can safely engage in more than one activity at a time. Psychologists tell us, however, that only one activity will command "sharp attention." Engaging in multiple activities makes a stressful life even more stressful. It ruins vacations and diminishes the positive effects of leisure time. If you're a high achiever, of greater interest to you, it can cripple your productivity.

The key to keeping your stress level in check, despite the number of tasks that compete for your attention, is to continually focus on the task at hand. No lamenting for what just transpired, no anxiety about what's coming up. Simply focus on the present. There are some variations to focusing on one thing at a time, rather than multitasking:

Focus on What's Confronting You

Recognize that however quickly you speed from task to task, you'll do your best work if you give your complete and undivided attention to the task at hand, for however brief a time that might be. In other words, you develop your concentration so that even if you only have 10 to 15 seconds to focus on what confronts you, that 10 or 15 seconds is highly directed to the task at hand. Let me give you an example:

You're waiting to board an airplane when the flight is suddenly canceled. A swarm of angry customers surrounds the gate agent, looking to quickly reroute their passages. How does the gate agent handle the throng? One passenger at a time, intently focusing on that passenger's previous itinerary, looking at the computer monitor to see what options are available, and working on each customer's needs to completion. Whether it takes one minute or five, a skilled gate agent stays relatively unflapped.

What Merits Your Attention?

Suppose you have five tasks confronting you and you're stymied as to how to proceed. What's the fastest and easiest way to tackle the five tasks and keep your stress in check? The answer: Put them in order of importance and handle them one at a time. Child's play you say—Anyone could have figured that out. *Anyone could, but hardly anyone does.*

Tackling one project or handling one customer at a time rubs up against the very nature of society, which might seem to tell you to do as many things at once as you can. Just get it all done and never mind how stressful it is—jump on your horse and ride off in all directions.

Frequently, I see people at my health club who get on the stair climber wearing a Walkman. I guess they're listening to their favorite tunes, a lecture, or perhaps simply the radio. The other day, I saw a woman get on (but it could just as easily have been a man) who not only was wearing a Walkman, but she also opened a book. This, mind you, while on the stair climber. I almost went over to her and asked her if she wanted some chewing gum!

> **Warning**
> Paradoxically, when you jump back and forth between projects, it's actually somewhat satisfying. After all, you're expending a lot of energy and if anyone were to catch you in the act, you could say, "Look at me, look at everything I'm handling." On top of the loss of productivity, however, you're increasing your stress level unnecessarily.

Is it likely that back in the office she tackles tasks one at a time? Management sage Dr. Peter Drucker conducted his own survey of top executives and found that they too attempted to do too much, resulting in a loss of productivity and an increase of stress.

The Paper Chase

I find that the mere volume of paper confronting many professionals today is, in itself, a key form of distraction. The personal computer, fax machines, laser printers, and personal copiers have resulted in an outpouring of more paper in your life than anyone could have predicted 15 to 20 years ago. Paper gluts the offices of industry, government, professionals, retailers, you name it.

Warning
American offices, in particular, are plagued by paper because we have the greatest distribution of the aforementioned technologies of any place in the world. Far more than Germany, Japan, or any other country.

I heard a telling anecdote, the veracity of which I cannot verify, attributed to Franklin Delano Roosevelt, U.S. president from 1933 to 1945. The lesson, however, is clear.

FDR, it seems, had commissioned a special task force to determine the answer to a question critical to his administration. The task force met for a period of eight days and generated a voluminous report. The spokesperson brought the report to FDR, who was busy at the time and told the messenger to, "Please, boil it down."

The spokesperson left, returning in a couple hours with a slimmer version of the report. FDR looked at it and said, "No, I mean *boil it down.*" Once again the spokesperson left, this time returning in about an hour, with a concise, executive summary of eight pages. Two more times, FDR asked for greater summary. When the aide returned with a single paragraph, FDR finally said, "Can you give it to me in a sentence?"

➤ Immediately reduce books to their essence by scanning the entire book. Then, copy the key pages you wish to retain along with the title page and table of contents. Recycle the book when you're done.

➤ With other printed information such as catalogs, fliers, and brochures, scan and break it down to the few scraps of relevant information. Recycle the rest.

➤ Establish a drawer to temporarily house whatever you want out of sight (where it's out of mind). When you have the strength, go back to the drawer, take out the items, and use the recommendations above.

➤ For each item that crosses your desk, ask yourself:

What is the issue behind the document?

Should I have received this at all?

How else can this be handled? Can I delegate this?

Will it matter if I don't handle it at all?

Can I file it under "Things to Review Next Month"?

Timing Isn't Everything, But It's a Lot

If the distractions you face in your workplace seem insurmountable and you've taken the words here and in Chapter 7, you may want to examine the timing of what you do and when you do it.

Is it possible for you to go to bed earlier, wake up earlier, and get to the office before everyone else? Many top executives do, and they remark that this is one of the bright spots of their day, when they get the most done. This is before the phones start ringing, before anyone even knows they're in the office.

If you're like most professionals today, however, adjusting your schedule to earlier hours may require a concerted effort to change a long-standing habit. You're probably staying up too late (I'll discuss the role of sleep in Chapter 13). Before the 1960s, the concept of staying up late to catch the 11:00 news and the late-night talk shows was unheard of. Jack Paar was the first of a long line of talk show hosts, the most famous obviously being Johnny Carson, who induced an entire nation to stay up later than it was accustomed to.

Go!
If you arrive at work earlier, what you accomplish in that extra hour or two before everyone else comes in can affect your productivity and perspective for the entire day, because you begin with a feeling of accomplishment.

Today, with Leno and Letterman battling it out each night, and millions of people tuning in, is it any wonder that so many people drag themselves into the office in the morning? This doesn't have to be you, and turning in earlier could make a difference in your stress level.

In addition to the time of your arrival, you may also want to consider the time of your departure. If you leave at 4:30, 5:00, or 5:30 in the afternoon, and fight your way home in that moving parking lot they call a "freeway," perhaps it would be better to leave at 6:00 or 6:30, after everyone else has taken off.

Now, let's not confuse issues. In the early chapters, I discussed the vital importance of not overworking. What I'm saying here is that in your particular instance, based on where you live, with whom you live, your job, and so on, it may make sense for you to work a later shift—that is, 10:00 a.m. to 6:00 p.m. or 10:00 a.m. to 7:00 p.m. in the evening.

Shake It Up, Baby

Here is a potpourri of other ways to shake up your routine and whip distractions so that you can work productively, with less stress, and feel good about yourself and your career:

Work on the porch of your house instead of in the office. When you change your scenery, you open up new vistas and escape interruptions. When you do this for some tasks (especially tasks that require creative thinking), you'll be more productive than ever. I can proofread much better on the porch than at my desk. Identify places that are welcome retreats where you can go and work—a library, a park, even a shopping center. When you change where you work, you can benefit immensely and immediately.

If possible, don't get your mail until Friday. Postpone tearing through all your mail. Most things are not so urgent that you need to attend to them that day. We tend to place an immediacy upon things that often is unnecessary.

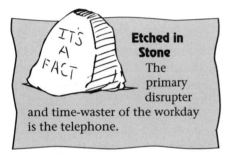

Etched in Stone
The primary disrupter and time-waster of the workday is the telephone.

If possible, hold all calls for two days. Think of it as if you were on vacation and were unable to be reached for a couple of days. You don't have to respond immediately to every call. When you hold your calls for a few hours—or a day—you open up time so that you can get things done in a way that is impossible when you are preoccupied with answering calls. You don't want to be totally inaccessible all the time, but you can coach those who may call you to adapt to your schedule (see Chapter 7).

Mental Methods for Reducing Distractions

Dr. Wayne Dyer, author or *Your Erroneous Zones*, *Pulling Your Own Strings*, and a variety of other self-help books, recalls an instance when he was tranquilly looking out at the scenery, when a gentleman on the next property began using a power mower with a particularly wicked engine noise. Each time the power mower came close to where Dyer was sitting, he became upset. The noise was disrupting his quiet contemplation.

Etched in Stone
What you resist persists.

After a while, however, Dyer managed to incorporate the noise of the mower as a part of his environment. It no longer was a distraction, nor did it diminish his feelings of tranquility. How did he get to this hallowed state? He accepted that people cutting grass is part of the overall environment and that there was a rhythm and hum to the power mower, much like that of a gurgling brook or other phenomenon of nature.

If you're trying to read and somebody three rows back in the airplane is coughing, and you're dreading the next time he or she coughs, sure enough, you won't get any reading done. Alternatively, if you accept that coughs happen, even loud, obnoxious coughs, and continue to focus on the task at hand, guess what? More often than not, the distraction diminishes, sometimes to the point where you don't even think about it.

I Do So Affirm

You can use affirmations to creatively employ potential distractions as triggers to help you concentrate more deeply. Say *what?!* Suppose you're in your office and someone in the office suite upstairs is banging on the wall a couple of times every three or four minutes. Obviously, some type of equipment installation or office renovation is going on. How do you take such potential disruption and turn it to your favor? Mentally, you say to yourself that "With each bang on the wall or screech, I will become even more focused on the task at hand."

Thereafter, with each bang on the wall, you allow your concentration to get more focused and more intense. This won't happen automatically. At first, each outside disturbance will continue to be a disturbance. You'll hear each one and think to yourself, how is this helping me? If you stick with the process, however, miraculously, subsequent incidents begin to diminish in amplitude and, seemingly, frequency.

If you get really good at this process, after a while, you won't even "hear" the external noise. This is analogous to people who buy property under the flight path of a major airport. How could they possibly live with planes flying overhead all day long? After a few weeks and in some cases a few days, the noise of the flights overhead becomes part of the overall environment. Neither disruptive, nor stress inducing, nor particularly worth noting.

This is not to say that all background and environmental noise eventually becomes benign. Indeed, the decibel level of a particular noise, or of noise in general, can be debilitating. See Chapter 7.

The Sacred Hoops Approach

With the success of the Chicago Bulls of the National Basketball Association in the 1990s, the coaching methods and philosophies of Phil Jackson have become of interest to many people, not just basketball fans. Jackson's book, *Sacred Hoops,* discusses his approach to the game and to life in general.

"Basketball is a game, a journey, a dance. I emphasize to the players that when they work together, good things happen." The press notes that Jackson has been meditating for more than 20 years. Jackson says that "basketball requires shifting from one objective to another at lightning speed. To excel, you need to act with a clear mind and be totally focused. The secret is not thinking. This means quieting the endless jabbering of thoughts so that your body can act instinctively."

> **What a Concept!**
>
> When you think about external disrupters, you're not likely to be very productive. When you focus on what you're trying to accomplish, the disrupters simply can't have the same impact.

What happens when Jackson encounters a particularly intense moment? Instead of focusing on a mistake or disruption, he focuses on recovering from the disruption and moving on to the next challenge in the game.

Similarly, your ability to recover from interruptions, distractions, and all the other malarkey that goes on in the contemporary office will enable you to get more work done each day, feel less stress, and feel better about the whole deal.

How Do You Spell Relief?

Here are a variety of other short-term maneuvers that may bring relief from office interruptions:

➤ Take a walk; whatever is distracting you may be gone by the time you return, or if not, perhaps it'll be less of a distraction.

➤ Take a look at Chapter 16, "Becoming the Master of Your Environment."

➤ Turn on a fan, air conditioning system, or office equipment so its hum can help serve as a noise mask.

➤ Continually look for distraction-free sanctuaries, wherever they may be. This could include the lunchroom after the line closes down, the chairs in your building's lobby, or a rooftop overlook.

➤ Coach others to support you in your quest by asking them not to interrupt you at certain times of day, for example.

The Least You Need to Know

➤ An interruption-management system can reduce your daily disruptions by half or more.

➤ Multitasking is fine for office equipment, but a bad idea for you.

➤ Maybe you need to get into the office much earlier or stay later.

➤ Mental methods for reducing distractions can be the most powerful of all.

Chapter 9

Workplace Violence: Stress Boiling Over the Top

In This Chapter

➤ Violence at work is much like violence away from work

➤ Workplace stress can reach dangerous levels

➤ How to deal with an abusive manager

➤ Becoming Mr. or Ms. Congeniality

If you're in a stressful but relatively tolerable work environment, you may want to skip this chapter. Please, at least skim through it once.

I'm assuming that you personally are not prone to violence, regardless of how much stress you experience professionally or personally. This chapter gives you what you need to know if someone you work with, work for, or who works for you is a candidate for workplace violence.

Violence at Work Mirrors the Larger Society

A Centers for Disease Control study reveals that within a 30-day period, "more than one in three high school boys admitted to carrying a gun, knife, or club." As the level of violence in society rises, so does the level of violence at work. In a 12-month period, more than two million hostile attacks at work on bosses or coworkers occurred in America. More than 1,000 employees murdered their bosses.

Alcohol and other drugs are associated with 50 percent of spouse abuse cases, 68 percent of manslaughter charges, and 52 percent of rapes. Chemical and substance abuse in one's personal life obviously has ramifications to one's performance and behavior in the workplace.

Sabotage is also present in the workplace. Deliberate damage to computer hardware and software occurs with alarming regularity. These are not signs of a well-functioning society or harmonious workplaces.

Warning
By the year 2000, the information you're exposed to will increase to 60 times more than you encountered in 1990! That alone, even without terrible bosses, unfair working conditions, and impossible demands, would be a recipe for stress.

Although I don't condone such violence, I'm beginning to understand it. The volume of information, the number of responsibilities, and the competition for the time and attention of the typical employee rises beyond anyone's capacity. You already know that the volume of information you encounter is increasing exponentially.

More people are feeling more stress more often at work. A majority of managers say their jobs are more stressful than a decade ago—no surprise there. Many predict that their jobs will be even more stressful in the next three to four years. By some estimates, at least half of American managers suffer too much stress and are becoming abusive, intolerant, and dictatorial.

Tell me these aren't signs of stress bubbling over the top:

➤ When General Motors gave a manager in his mid-fifties the option of early retirement, he had to think about it carefully. Four of his colleagues in similar situations accepted the offer, but shortly thereafter, they killed themselves.

➤ When J.C. Penney moved its corporate headquarters from New York to Plano, Texas, many employees were so despondent that the company ended up increasing its professional counseling staff from one person to 12.

➤ Mental health experts estimate that as much as 15 percent of executives and managers suffer from depression or critical levels of stress.

When Workplace Stress Is at Dangerous Levels

Far too many companies, however, don't understand the problems confronting their workforce. Few corporations want to address the reality that their policies and procedures contribute to high stress—high enough to result in workplace violence. Sometimes they offer programs, but such programs don't address the needs of seriously stressed or depressed employees.

The odds are slim that you have the ability to change your corporate or organizational culture. Still, it's best to take a defensive posture—arm yourself with some basic facts about workplace violence and basic tips on what you can do to help yourself and others.

The Society for Human Resources Management surveyed its members on workplace violence and found that one-third of respondents reported that their workplace had experienced a violent incident in the past five years, and that the frequency of such incidents is on the rise. Forty-four percent of respondents said that the most recent incident of work place violence occurred in the current year.

Respondents indicated that the motivation for the most recent violent incident was a personality conflict. A majority said they couldn't have identified the assailants' potential for violence; however, anger, aggressiveness, and threatening behavior were the most common traits of assailants who could be identified. Other common traits included apparent emotional or mental disorders, loner status, sullen behavior, obsessiveness, overly quiet, or morose.

Following a violent incident in the workplace, many organizations may rely on a professional employee assistance program; other resources include counseling for employees, training, increased security, more thorough security and reference checks among new hires, and installation of new security systems.

> **Warning**
> On average, more violent acts occur in June, July, August, and September. Watch for signs of violence during these months. Fewer violent acts occur in November, December, and January.

Neither Rain Nor Snow Nor Gunpoint...

In recent years, the U.S. Postal Service has been gripped by workplace violence. The Postal Service employed more than three-quarters of a million people in 1992, and that same year endured more than 2,000 cases of workplace violence. In his book, *Ticking Bombs: Defusing Violence in the Work Place*, author Michael Mantell says, "Workplace violence has never been a prominent business or social issue until now." Workplace violence has grown and evolved from an "underground problem for business into a substantial hazard, not only for the nineties, but well into the next century."

Although it would be easy to dismiss many incidents as simply another "nut with a gun at work" story, the problem is far more complex. As of the mid-90s, the situation is getting worse. *Murder on the job is now the third leading cause of occupational death.*

> **Warning**
> Despite alarming statistics, countless incidents occur in the workplace that are not reported. Hence, the number of serious acts of violence—punching, pushing, and kicking—that take place on the job may be far greater than anyone imagines.

Workplace Subversion

Perhaps your organization, department, or division has been lucky enough not to encounter overt acts of violence like one individual striking or attacking another. What about acts of subversion? Consider the following questions:

➤ Has anyone damaged a PC, printer, or fax machine?

➤ Has anyone tampered with the postage meter?

➤ Has anyone vandalized a vending machine?

➤ Are the public phones in and around your grounds operable?

➤ Are electric doors, escalators, or elevators frequently and mysteriously breaking down?

➤ Are appliances in your kitchen in good working order?

➤ Does the plumbing in your washrooms get backed up often?

➤ Are any cars in employee parking lots vandalized?

➤ Are any pictures, posters, display windows, bulletin boards, and the like vandalized?

➤ Are office furnishings breaking with increased regularity?

➤ Is the landscaping outside being vandalized?

➤ Are objects frequently missing from the waiting room?

If the answer to any of the preceding questions is "yes," subversion is occurring, and since that could lead to overt violence, the subversion and anyone suspected should be reported as quickly as possible.

Treating Termination Carefully

Downsizing continues to be prevalent among organizations—not that downsizing itself is the cause for increased violence. Kevin Flynn, a Ph.D. based in Los Angeles, says a key problem with downsizing is that management is often "ill-prepared to deal with the turmoil and anguish to employees. Instead of dealing compassionately with it, they ignore it." Too many employees are hired with the message, "Yes, we value loyalty," only to be let go with the message, "Sorry, things have changed; your services are no longer necessary."

Professionals who work with people who are newly unemployed find that approximately 10 percent experience problems, including severe anxiety or depression, sufficient enough to warrant professional help. When weeks and months go by without finding new work, the strain on their family and themselves can lead to undesirable behavior. In thousands of cases each year, ex-workers show up months after being terminated to seek vengeance on the former boss or supervisor, or someone who they identify as the source of their misfortune.

So, if you suspend a worker for breaking rules, he or she may come after you? Maybe. If you need to fire someone for gross incompetence, do you also need to worry about them coming back with a gun? Possibly.

Employees who lose their jobs can react with furious anger. More than a few have outwardly destructive outbursts in exit interviews with departing staff. In one instance, a supervisor was about to put a problem worker on probation and soon thereafter terminate the employee. In this instance, there would be no severance pay or benefits forthcoming. A coworker who knew of the situation told the supervisor to watch out because the employee, about to be put on probation, had expressed his desire to kill the supervisor should he lose his job.

The supervisor was shaken and called his boss, who brought in a specialist in handling workplace violence. In this case, things worked out for the best. The specialist devised a plan whereby the employee was not only fired, but eventually rehabilitated. This doesn't usually happen.

The supervisor, his boss, and the specialist met with the problem employee and presented the plan in a calm, even-handed manner. The employee realized the gravity of the situation and agreed to accept counseling, as well as additional job training so he could retain his position in the company. The plan worked because the problem employee wasn't dangerous, according to the specialist. He simply was suffering from emotional distress in his domestic life that spilled over to his work life, and predictably, treatment would work.

Many specialists advocate that problem employees be dealt with as early as possible, while there's still real potential for improvement. In addition, here are other steps for dealing with problem employees:

> **Warning**
> The obviously disgruntled employee represents perhaps the most recognizable scenario in which violence may follow a layoff. If you're worried about the possibility, make sure your company's Human Resources department is taking steps to protect you.

> **Warning**
> Supervisors often handle termination in a heartless manner, hoping to conclude things quickly. Some books say to terminate an employee on Friday afternoon, to minimize workplace disruption. The problem is that the employee's support system is placed in a stranglehold—everything is suddenly cut off. For those on the borderline, hostilities can be triggered.

➤ When confronting such an employee, be firm, listen as much as you speak, and visibly show empathy.

➤ Create a threat-management team, which can consist of a psychologist, someone from your legal department, someone from human resources, some security, some labor, and perhaps an outside specialist.

➤ Devise an organizational policy to let employees know how and where to report threats, violence, and subversive behavior.

➤ Give supervisors at least an hour's worth of training each month on recognizing trouble signs.

➤ Instruct supervisors as to when and how to refer a problem employee to a specialist.

In most cases where violence occurred, the violent party's immediate boss didn't recognize the potential threat. Often, coworkers are aware of problems, but aren't informed how or when or to whom to report them.

Some organizations dispense confidential employee surveys on a regular basis to take the pulse of the organization, a department, or division. If your organization does, make sure you have the assistance of an impartial third party who is skilled in dispensing such surveys. Otherwise, you may simply be coaching employees to report what you want to hear as opposed to how the climate really is.

Warning
After violent incidents, an organization is not the same. People are paranoid, less trusting, and more defensive. A violent incident can be highly traumatic even for those who weren't involved. Just knowing that an incident took place can cause trauma for some.

Progressive organizations are also putting more time and attention into the firing process. They recognize that someone who's been laid off or terminated has to be treated with respect and compassion. The longer someone has been with the organization, the more time they need to adjust.

Organizations that have already invested significantly in their people need to recognize the importance of ensuring that these valuable assets continue to work in an environment in which they feel free to be productive and relaxed.

Dealing with an Abusive Manager

In Chapter 5, you saw how to keep stress under control even when you work for a bad boss. What about when you work for a boss who borders on the psychopathic?

Monstrous behavior—sexual harassment of the crudest sort, physical and verbal threats, and all manner of inhumane acts—is unfortunately too prevalent in the workplace.

Bosses who engage in such practices can trigger violent behavior in someone who might not have otherwise engaged in it. Employees victimized by brutal bosses can suffer from anxiety, depression, heart problems, gastrointestinal disorders, headaches, skin rashes, insomnia, and sexual dysfunction.

Etched in Stone

Violence begets violence.

In some organizations, electronic surveillance systems monitor and control behavior in ways that cross the boundaries of reason and respect.

➤ If you get overly anxious from working for a harsh boss or anything else, you have to recognize that they can't get to you unless you let them.

➤ Be alert for unwarranted behavior from the top and band together with others who are being abused.

➤ If you're being victimized, make sure you're not victimizing your own subordinates.

Dr. Victor Frankl, a World War II concentration camp survivor, observed that some people, while imprisoned in the camps, died quickly because they could not live in confinement, with harsh treatment from guards, not knowing what would happen next, and having no larger purpose in life.

Others, including himself, were able to survive and ultimately flourish. He observes that such people had a larger purpose in life—perhaps there was someone they wanted to see should the camp ever be freed and the war be over. Some simply waited until they could get revenge on the guards. In his classic book, *Man's Search for Meaning*, Frankl says that regardless of the treatment he received, he resolved that the guards and the setting would have no effect on how he chose to feel internally—his regard for his fellow prisoners, loved ones he wanted to see again, or his faith in humanity.

I'm not asking you to be a saint. I'm not. These are certainly important words to ponder, however, particularly if you're in a setting where the potential for workplace violence exists.

A Coworker Whom Others Respect

Regardless of your situation and the level of stress in your workplace, you can do things to be a boss, coworker, or subordinate whom others respect. Having good relations with others can reduce the stress of everyone involved, let alone keep you from being someone's target. Your behavior can set the example and diffuse tense situations. Here are some tips to help you be the kind of person others want to be around:

Go!
To be a better listener, look directly at others when they speak, offer your undivided attention, nod to show you're listening, don't interrupt, and if the setting warrants it, take notes!

Avoid making promises you can't keep. It's better to under-promise and over-deliver than to over-promise and under-deliver. You already know this.

As much as possible, maintain a cheerful disposition—even smile at people. They don't have to do anything for you, and you don't have to be seeking anything. A smile is simply a smile.

Be as good a listener as you can. The typical person, when polled, thinks he or she is a good listener. The reality is that most people aren't. I'm not, and you probably have room for improvement, too.

Strive to treat others in your workplace with respect, regardless of their position. Treat employees who just started with the same respect you show your CEO. After all, the self-worth of an individual can't be determined by rank. People are worthy simply for being human beings.

Look for the best in others. Everyone does something in which you can find approval. Look for the good in others, and they'll look for the good in you.

Avoid participating in the rumor mill. Nothing dampens the morale and spirit of an organization faster than spreading stories about others, few of which are entirely true. Yes, it's titillating to talk about others, particularly higher-ups in the organization.

Take responsibility for your own mistakes rather than passing out blame. The truth wins out most of the time, anyway, and people know who was responsible when things don't go according to plan. Conversely, seek to give credit to your group when some major success is achieved, rather than seeking to get credit for yourself.

Go!
The people who are promoted most readily are those who seek credit for achievements by the group rather than grabbing the glory as an individual.

Avoid making decisions in anger. The chances are great that a decision made in anger won't be a wise one.

Try not to get upset about things people say about you, particularly when they're untrue. Demonstrate through your actions that such comments are not correct. Let negative comments fall away, like water off the proverbial duck's back.

Last, and perhaps most important, control your emotions. Be known as one who makes decisions after having first thought them through.

The Least You Need to Know

➤ Although workplace stress is at dangerous levels, too many companies don't understand the nature of the problems confronting their employees and are loathe to admit it.

➤ Employees who lose their jobs can react with furious anger. The longer a person has been with the organization, the more time he or she needs to adjust to the change in status.

➤ Problem employees need to be dealt with as early as possible, while there's still real potential for improved performance.

➤ Good relations with others can reduce everyone's job-related stress, let alone keep you from being someone else's target.

Part 3
External Stressors

Now we come to a different, but highly significant, set of stressors. My goal is not to freak you out, but more and more people are going to populate this planet for the rest of your life. And more news, information, sound bites, and drivel than you can imagine will be competing for your attention. All this is likely to exacerbate the stress you already experience.

In terms of population, some "experts" tell us that everyone could comfortably fit in Texas. If we used our resources perfectly, they say, the increasing human population would not be a problem. If that is true, why are we doing so poorly spread out across the globe? Let me guess—could it be that human beings are rather imperfect and make lots of mistakes? Sure, everyone could fit in Texas. You could also live to be 120 years old—but you probably won't.

In terms of information, a tidal wave is about to hit—and you thought you'd already been hit! Everyone is being hit with more data than we can fathom. More information is generated in one hour than you could take in for the rest of your life—and the true Information Age is just beginning!

Over-population and over-information are not reasons to forsake humanity, but they're definitely external stressors over which no one has much control. In an increasingly crowded and complex world, you need some time out.

Chapter 10

The Stress of Population Density

In This Chapter

➤ Overcrowding of the planet—and your life

➤ Taking the anthropological view

➤ Why contrarian lifestyles make sense

➤ How to stay calm even during a Manhattan rush hour

➤ Advanced strategies in an overpopulated world

The unrelenting stress you may experience getting to work, finding an empty park bench, or simply jockeying for a corner office, can be attributed in part to an increasing world population density! Sounds wild, huh? In a few minutes, you're going to be a believer.

There aren't a plethora of tips in this chapter, and most of the warnings are of a "macro" nature. I'd just like you to absorb the reality of how increases in global population ultimately infiltrate your life and heap oodles of stress on you. Coming on the heels of Chapter 9 on workplace violence, this isn't going to be fun reading, either. But hey, somebody's got to tackle these issues, particularly in a book on stress, and I guess it has to be me.

The Planet and Your Life

Sometime during 1995, world population passed 5.8 billion people. I find this notable, when juxtaposed (a ten-penny word if I ever used one) with the fact that there are 58 million square miles of land on earth. In other words, human population density, on average, of every single square mile on earth is now at 100 people. In 1960, human population density was 50 people per square mile, meaning that population density has doubled in less than a lifetime.

Some places are a little more crowded than others. According to *Escape Magazine*, the most densely populated places on earth are Macau and Monaco, with 54,782 and 40,666 people per square mile, respectively. At the low end, Greenland has 0.1 person per square mile, and the Western Sahara has 2.2 persons per square mile.

If you live in America, you'll be pleased to know that population density in the U.S. is only 70.5 people per square mile, but an increasing percentage of the population lives closer to each other, namely in urban areas (see Table 10.1). Escalating global population growth contributes to rapid urbanization, which consumes the valuable arable land needed to sustain communities and exacerbates environmental problems such as deforestation and pollution.

Table 10.1 Urbanization Across the Globe

Area or Country	Population (Millions) –1995–	Projected Population (Millions) –2025–	Urban Population –1995–	Urban Growth –1995–	Projected Urban Population –2025–
World	5,716	8,294	45%	2.5%	58%
United States	263	331	76%	1.2%	85%
Mexico	93	137	75%	2.4%	86%
India	936	1,392	27%	3.0%	45%
China	1,222	1,526	30%	3.6%	55%

Source: The State of World Population 1995, United Nations

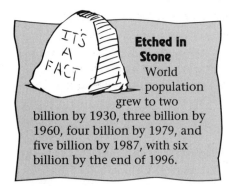

Etched in Stone

World population grew to two billion by 1930, three billion by 1960, four billion by 1979, and five billion by 1987, with six billion by the end of 1996.

World population impacts the quality of your life everyday. Every three years, world population grows by more than the current population of the United States—268,000,000 people. Every decade, world population grows by more than a billion people. Yet, it took from the beginning of creation to 1850 AD for world population to reach its first billion.

Some people believe that via overpopulation, we have, as a species, created an environment that in itself is highly stressful and ultimately destructive to society, the economy, and individuals' health and well-being.

With each additional person, population density increases as literal and figurative space per person decreases. The world of your parents' childhood, and of your own, is gone. Forever.

What Scarcity Is All About

The geometric growth in human population now permeates and dominates every aspect of the planet, its resources, the environment, and the life of each person. It also results in more of each day, yours and mine, being consumed to maintain standards of living. The more everyone wants to enjoy personal freedoms, the lower the population must be. Here are just two examples:

➤ The 13 million people of Los Angeles are being told that they must give up backyard barbecues and reliance on their automobiles.

➤ Ethnic hostilities around the world grab their share of headlines, as members of different ethnic groups compete for territory and control of resources like fuels, mineral deposits, seaports, and more. Each winning group leaves the losing group with the same number of people to support, but fewer resources to get the job done.

An economics professor of mine in college defined economics as the allocation of scarce resources. Only when a society has to manage limited resources is it an "economic" society. The population explosion has transformed our world into an economic society only in the last 10 or 15 years, and we haven't yet understood true economics—that there's a cost for our overuse of resources and that as the resources become more scarce, that cost will rise—and that's part of the problem.

Resources Vanishing Before Your Eyes

Increasing populations don't inherently mean mismanagement of resources and more stress, yet that has been the norm. A statement signed by 1,575 scientists from 69 countries was sent to 160 national leaders, as reported by The Union of Concerned Scientists in Washington, D.C. Signers included 99 of the 196 living Nobel laureates at the time, as well as senior officers from many of the most prestigious scientific academies in the world.

What was in the letter? It warned that, "Human beings in the natural world are on a collision course." Population stress is apparent in the atmosphere, water resources, oceans, soil, tropical and tempered forests, and living species. The scientists lamented that, "Much of this damage is irreversible on a scale of centuries or permanent." They went on to say, "We are fast approaching many of the earth's limits."

Go! Action usually invigorates. Your ability to make a real difference will help you feel better. Do something, even if it's a small thing like recycling, to feel like you're having a positive impact and have control.

The following are examples of the kinds of resource scarcity we're facing throughout the world:

➤ In 1990, 1.2 billion of 5.4 billion people had no access to clean drinking water.

➤ One in 15 people live in areas defined as water-stressed or water-scarce. By 2025, this number could rise to one in three people.

➤ Chronic fresh-water shortages are expected in Africa, the Middle East, Northern China, parts of India, Mexico, Brazil, several former Soviet republics, and the western United States.

➤ Theoretically, humanity has the ability to feed everyone on the planet. In reality, starvation is a way of life and death in vast areas of the planet.

➤ The earth has lost 3 percent of its protective stratospheric ozone, resulting in a 6 percent increase in ultraviolet radiation. Greater losses are expected.

➤ More people imperil many other species. The World Wildlife Federation's endangered species list includes tigers, rhinos, and the giant panda.

The Ever-Critical Masses

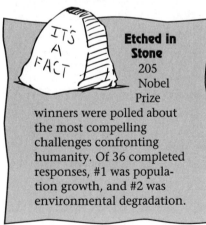

It's A Fact

Etched in Stone 205 Nobel Prize winners were polled about the most compelling challenges confronting humanity. Of 36 completed responses, #1 was population growth, and #2 was environmental degradation.

Some people think that war, famine, and pestilence all reduce population. "Doesn't nature manage things?" they ask. There is no war, no starvation—even in Somalia or Ethiopia—that can compete with a million new people every four days.

I'm not arguing to reduce the number of people already living. I'm concerned about the generations coming and the quality of life for everyone, including you. The key is keeping population at a *replacement level* (the number of births equal to the number of deaths).

What About Declining Fertility Rates?

Even with fertility declining worldwide, the fertility in developing countries still averages 4.4 children per family. Thirty percent of Latin American women, 40 percent of Asian women, and 50 percent of African women are married by age 18.

According to the World Watch Institute, of all 14-year-old girls alive today, 40 percent will be pregnant by the time they are 20.

About 40 percent of the population of developing countries is under the age of 15. With so many entering their reproductive years, population is destined to increase for many decades. Swelling populations across the globe will invariably lead to more strain on the planet, and ultimately to more stress on everyone.

Wanted: Hundreds of Millions of Jobs

Some 500 million people are already unemployed or underemployed in developing countries, and 30 million more are entering the job market each year. Hence, 800 million jobs will have to be created in less developed countries during the 1990s alone.

One political leader in Mexico says that the consequences of not creating at least 15 million jobs in the next 15 years are unthinkable. Mexicans who cannot find jobs will have three options: The United States, the streets, or revolution.

As you saw in Table 10.1, difficult economic conditions, exacerbated by rapid population growth, have prompted millions of rural poor to migrate to cities and millions more—at a rate of 10,000 per day—to cross international borders in search of a better life.

What a Concept!

New York, which in 1950 topped the list of the 10 largest cities in the world, at its present growth rate is not likely to make the list by the year 2025.

Ben Wattenberg, an economist at the American Enterprise Institute, in an all-time short-sighted observation, said "Why should we worry? We've gone from one billion to five billion while living standards have gone up exponentially. There's no evidence that population growth diminishes or dilutes development."

The Long Waits Scare Me

As if the preceding data weren't enough, signs of overpopulation show up in other ways all over the globe; they aren't necessarily as life threatening, but are nevertheless bothersome.

The highways in Asia's biggest cities are starting to resemble parking lots. In Bangkok, the average speed on the city streets has slowed to less than six miles an hour (on average, over a full 24-hour time period). Traffic has become so slow that people now sell newspapers, magazines, flowers, soft drinks, or chewing gum to captive stuck motorists.

Perhaps we'll get population under control. Perhaps we're at the dawn of achieving a sustainable environment. However, there's no indication of this. If you can't manage your resources with six billion people, how can you expect to do it with eight, or ten?

Back in the USA

Of course, all this stuff is going on too far afield to impact you. Or is it?

The U.S. population was a mere 186 million in 1968, and now it's more than 268 million. In other words, we have grown by 50 percent in about a generation. By the middle of the next century, U.S. population is projected to increase to 400 million people. This is equivalent to adding 38 cities the size of Los Angeles. However, the 400 million estimate might be low.

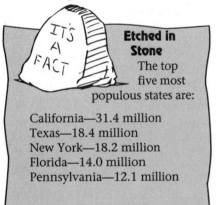

Etched in Stone

The top five most populous states are:

California—31.4 million
Texas—18.4 million
New York—18.2 million
Florida—14.0 million
Pennsylvania—12.1 million

Some "experts" tell us that our national population could all fit in Texas. If we perfectly used our resources, they say, and set up an infrastructure, our entire current population could live comfortably there. If that is true, why are we doing so poorly, spread out across the nation? Human beings as a species are rather imperfect and make lots of mistakes.

The next time you head out on the highway, for example, (regardless of whether you're in a gas guzzler) and notice that traffic is moving at a crawl, remember it's not just your city or state; it's happening across the U.S. and across the globe.

The anger and hostility people feel toward one another when they get behind the wheel is a mirror of the overall feelings that increasing numbers of people are beginning to experience with living in a society that is getting too crowded, moving too fast, is too congested, and may be inherently stressful.

Today, rather than the saber-toothed tiger, your stress comes from endless miles of chugging along at five miles an hour, or ridiculously slow supermarket checkout counters. The repeated release of stress hormones can accelerate the development of clogged arteries.

Strategies to Reduce Stress from Overcrowding

My hat is off to you—you've made it through the worst part of another tough chapter!

To avoid being stuck in traffic, waiting in line, and scrambling with the masses for goods and services, some obvious strategies begin to appear.

Live closer to your office. If you can afford it, I can't think of anything that makes more sense. If you work for an organization, regardless of the metro or suburban area in which you work, undoubtedly there are good neighborhoods a reasonable distance away. When you live closer to your office, you benefit in many, many ways:

> ➤ Less commuting time, less gasoline cost

> ➤ Less wear and tear on your car

> ➤ More flexibility coming and going

Telecommute. If you can work at home as little as one day per week, perhaps a Wednesday, you cut your week of commuting in half. The equipment you need to telecommute from home is highly affordable these days, with good modems dropping under the $150 price range.

Become a contrarian. If everyone vacations on holidays, use that day to work. Take your time off when everyone else is working.

Do more of your shopping by phone, fax, and modem. Rather than fight with all the other people for parking spaces at the super regional mall, order by catalog. Increasingly, catalog vendors offer an 800 number, an 800 fax line, and even 24-hour customer service.

Word Power!
A **contrarian** is someone who does things in opposite ways or at opposite times from the masses.

Go!
If everyone heads into the city between 7:00 and 9:00 a.m., you could head in between 5:00 and 6:00, or 10:00 and 11:00. People who arrange their schedules to avoid competing with the masses in terms of travel and leisure feel good about it. If this sounds too stark for you, experiment with it a little at a time.

What a Concept!
I've been ordering by catalog for several years now because I can sit and think about what I'm doing, whereas in a mall, for example, I frequently get jostled, overwhelmed, and unfocused.

Be more selective as to what information you take in. Remember, in a world of six billion people, there will be more books, articles, movies, plays, commentaries, opinions, and points of view. Unless you actively limit what you allow to compete for your time and attention, your days will race by faster than you care to live them.

Give yourself a recurring sanctuary. Everybody needs some time for themselves, if only to "zone out." In a world with 269,000 more people each day, this could become harder to do. Undoubtedly, there are places you've already carved out—your rec room, study, backyard, or favorite vacation spot. The key is to use them and get some of the rest and relaxation you so fervently need.

Forsake day-to-day tuning in. Instead of trying to ingest everything that the media has to offer, seek summaries of news and information, perhaps on a weekly or biweekly basis. As you'll see in Chapters 11 and 12, much of what's presented to you is not news anyway.

The Least You Need to Know

➤ Growing populations result in loss of individual freedom and an increase in individual stress.

➤ Become a contrarian—take your time off when everyone else is working.

➤ Everybody needs to have some time for themselves, if only to "zone out."

Chapter 11

The Information Industry

Much of the stress you feel today can be traced to monolithic purveyors of news and information. The U.S. government, believe it or not, is the world's largest publisher by far, and the information impacting your life that it spews out on a daily basis is beyond comprehension. At the same time, too much of the news media, bent on highlighting the latest gore to explore and piously deplore, convolutes society on a daily basis, offering unbalanced coverage of the absurd, the titillating, and the sensational (covered in Chapter 12). If only these two institutions were the only over-information culprits.

Unfortunately, society is beset with purveyors of news and information. I could fill a whole book on how too much information adds to your stress level, but I won't. Instead, I'll just fill this chapter.

The Great Age of Information Hasn't Arrived

Chances are, you are besieged by all kinds of information competing for your time and attention. Is this merely a lucky guess?

What is the origin of this information buildup? Was it predictable? Can you look to the past to see why there's so much information today? It turns out you can. There have been three great ages of humanity, with a fourth about to emerge.

➤ The first was the Age of Hunting and Gathering, where people principally lived by hunting animals and collecting berries. Your ancestors apparently did a pretty good job at this. You're here today, aren't you?

➤ The Age of Agriculture followed, when people learned they didn't have to be nomads, wandering around looking for their next meal. Instead, they could cultivate the soil, predict when crops would grow, and forecast what their yield would be. This was a great leap forward in some respects; it allowed for an understanding of how to work with nature and the seasons. It also prompted people to have unprecedented numbers of children. Many died at birth, and all who survived were needed to work the fields as soon as they could.

➤ Next was the great Age of Industry, in which all manner of capital were put together so that consumers, as a class, would be served by producers. Producers learned countless ways to turn out products through mass production capabilities. Improved printing and publishing processes were among the key developments of this age.

Etched in Stone
Given the way society is progressing, everyone who holds a position of responsibility is besieged by too much competition for their time and attention.

➤ The next age that will emerge—but is not here in full swing—is the Information Age. In the Information Age, information will *serve* you, and you will not be abused by an *excess* of information. The present, pre-Information Age is an era of over-information, an idea to which you can probably relate.

Flip the Switch, Man

In the Industrial Age, when people needed to achieve something rather ordinary, did they have to go through a series of motions, read manuals, or become experts at the task? Not at all. Consider turning on the lights in your room. You flip a switch (or clap your hands or whatever). To start your car, you turn the key. To take care of other tasks, you push a button, flip a switch, or turn a dial. These are Industrial-Age processes at their best; you don't have to become an electrical engineer or physicist to function effectively.

Breathing Space and The Four Economic Ages				
Characteristic	Hunting and Gathering Age	Agriculture Age	Industry Age	Information Age
Principle Goods:	Prey, roots, berries	Crops, livestock	Raw material	Knowledge
Dependent Upon...	Luck, instinct, game available	Timing, weather, location	Capital, labor	System configuration
Knowledge Base:	Oral history, observation	Oral history, almanacs	Training, manuals	Overabundance of all data
Location:	Wilderness near water/refuge	Rural, on fertile soil	Urban, near labor supply	Anywhere
Lifestyle:	Nomadic patterns	Settled, plots of land	Commuting	Telecommuting
Mobility:	Necessarily mobile	Necessarily stationary	Necessarily mobile	Stationary or mobile
Social Unit:	Tribe, clan	Extended family	Family	Self/family
The Elite:	Biggest, strongest, fastest	Most efficient	Capitalists, politicians	Anyone, entrepreneurs
Success Traits:	Agility, cunning	Strength	Distribution	Application

An Overabundance

Consider what it takes to function effectively in these early days of the Information Age. To get the information you need, you have to go online or open a manual, make several calls, consult an expert, or buy the latest issue of something. Unfortunately, right now—particularly in the workplace—you undertake a series of activities to get the precise information you need.

Often, your problem is not a lack of information. Frequently, the problem is an *abundance* of information, or too much *general* information.

In the coming Information Age, you'll instantaneously receive answers to your questions. Before the great age is fully in swing, you'll be besieged by more information than all previous generations combined. For example, I received a flyer in the mail about a new "superstore" book seller opening near me. The store would feature more than 150,000 titles; stock more than 2,500 domestic and international newspapers, periodicals, and magazines; and have the capability to order an additional 200,000 book titles from national distributors.

The children's section would include 15,000 titles, and the music section, 25,000 CDs and cassettes. And this was simply an outlet for producers and publishers who were probably generating 10 times those numbers of products.

Publish and Perish

I knew the amount and nature of information our society was generating had gone beyond absurdity when I was flipping through a publisher's catalog. There it was: a book on manhole covers. The description said the book "catalogs an often-ignored yet singular form of urban industrial art and its place in American culture."

A reviewer of the book—how do you find an expert on manhole covers who can write reviews as well?—said that the book "occupies a rather indeterminate genre category: part history of material culture, part exercise in obsessive photographic cataloging of related objects, part Crypto-Pop artists book. There's a crisp and even elegant matter-of-factness to their writing and their pictures, a spare functionalist precision."

With books on manhole covers (or should they now be called personhole covers?), and a legion of books on cats, is it any wonder that at least 3,000 books are published in the U.S. alone, every week, and at least 2,000 books a day worldwide? The real question is, how many of them need to be published in the first place? (If less of other people's books were published, mine would sell more!)

When you understand the true nature and volume of information confronting you, you can see how important it is to become more selective than ever.

Information by the Boatload

No bookstore chain and no commercial publisher, however, can equal the onslaught of information generated and disseminated by the federal government.

One of the chief collectors of over-information is a little-known office of the federal government called the Washington National Record Center located in Suitland, Maryland. Nineteen rooms comprise the government's sprawling warehouse, which contains 8 billion of the federal government's old policy papers, budget projections, meeting minutes, and research reports. Eight billion?

"Can't some of this be destroyed?" you ask. Yes, some of it is; yet every day truckloads of new boxes arrive, at a rate 50 percent faster than the older boxes are destroyed.

It seems every government agency generates paper and information like it's going out of style. The Office of Thrift Supervision has 440 cubic feet of documents just relating to the Lincoln Federal Savings and Loan scandal of several years back. This would fill 55 four-drawer filing cabinets. The U.S. Department of Justice has 160 cubic feet of paperwork just on the Exxon Valdez oil spill.

It makes you wonder: Has more paper been spilled than oil?

"Can't all this stuff be put on disk?" you ask. Theoretically, yes, because even a simple 3.5-inch floppy can hold about 240 sheets of paper, so the amount of actual printed documents ought to decline. However, just the opposite seems to be occurring.

Federal regulations, and you knew there were a lot of them, now exceed 200 volumes, numbering more than 130,000 pages. To give you some perspective, current federal regulations are 15 times greater than in 1950 and 4 times greater than in 1965. In agriculture alone, there are 19 volumes. In environment, 16 volumes.

Government regulations impose more than $5 billion in costs annually. Spread out over a population of 200,000,000 people over age 16, this translates to $2,500 per person per year, $25,000 per decade. In your life, it shows up in the form of more cumbersome tax forms; higher prices, because retailers must pass on the cost to someone (and it's always you); and a variety of other hidden charges—wherever you go, whatever you do.

The IRS single-handedly loses more than 2,000,000 pieces of paper annually. I'm still hoping for the day that my tax returns are among them.

Warning

Your life is more stressful because society is governed by elected officials who have no idea what havoc they wreak by generating more regulations, more paper, and more things that stifle creativity and imagination and glut the very lifeblood of our existence.

Today's Additions

At the Library of Congress (L.O.C.), 7,000 new items are procured, organized, and cataloged *every day*. Although the numbers change by the minute, the library's current holdings require more than 500 miles of shelf space and include such gargantuan numbers as 14,000,000 prints, posters, and photographs; 4,000,000 maps; 500,000 reels of film; 3,500,000 pieces of music; 39,000,000 pages of personal papers and manuscripts; and, if you can believe it, 5,600 volumes printed before the year 1500.

Society is engulfing us with too much information, and the preoccupation is catalogued and supported by the government.

> **What a Concept!**
>
> Contrary to semipopular belief, the L.O.C. does not house every book, or English-language book, or American book ever published, or even published within a year. It retains about a third of each year's new American books. (Hmm, wonder if they have *Vanna Speaks*?)

Last year, the Smithsonian Institution in Washington added nearly one million new items to its collection—despite the fact that they've been in existence for a century and a half. That's 4,000 items a day! They'll probably have 1.1 million next year.

Soon, more information will be generated in one minute than you could ingest in the rest of your life. Humanity has never experienced anything like this, and the effects are incalculable.

More Than You Bargained For

Do you wake up already feeling behind for the day? It is a socially pervasive phenomenon for people to feel stress upon awakening, in the absence of direct stimuli, simply because they anticipate another day wherein more transpires than they can comfortably ingest.

You can't keep up with the flow of information, and hereafter, you don't need to take it as something personal.

Knowing More, but Falling Behind

Why is it that events of the last 20 to 25 years are becoming more difficult to recall? It's because everything has gone by like one big blur. When many things compete for your time and attention, it's difficult to keep things in context.

I routinely give quizzes when I give presentations, and I find that it's often easier for groups to cite dates in the distant past than to recall something in the last 20 to 25 years. A surprising number of people know that the Vikings landed in Newfoundland around A.D. 1000 to 1002, to be exact.

Etched in Stone

When you're hit by too much information, it goes by in one big blur.

What about the Norman invasion of England? Every time I ask for this date, somebody correctly says 1066. When was the Magna Carta signed? Many people know the answer: 1215. When did the Pilgrims land on Plymouth Rock? 1620.

As sophisticated and knowledgeable as you are, how well would you do on a quiz of cultural knowledge? Did you know that Cambodia's principal language is Khmer?

Or that Belgium's principal language is Flemish? What about Portuguese in Brazil, or Persian in Iran? The people of these countries share the planet with us, but most of us have no idea what language they speak.

What do the following items have in common: Surabeya, Port Alegra, Harbin, Pune, Changdu, Huan, Yangdong, Tiago, Tashkent, and Kanpur? They are all cities of several million people. Have you even *heard* of any of them? They probably exceed the population of your city.

There's no need to worry: Everyone is being hit with more data than anyone can fathom.

> ➤ Be more selective than ever about what you take in.

> ➤ Decide what information is truly important to you.

Etched in Stone

More information in your life means that you'll know *less and less* of the total available information. Any time you are *inundated* with information, you will be less effective than you would be with a few thin files of potent information designed *specifically* for the task.

I Didn't Know That, and I Feel Fine

I used to feel the anxiety of being in an era of over-information when I walked into a magazine store containing hundreds of newspapers and magazines. I also felt it when I went into a bookstore with thousands of books including dozens on the very topics about which I write.

Lynn Lively, author of *Managing Information Overload*, observes that at work or elsewhere, many people feel a twinge when someone presents important information that they had no clue was coming.

Here are the kind of response statements that Lively suggests are worth adopting:

> ➤ "I really hadn't given that much thought."

> ➤ "Considering the situation, what do you think is best?"

> ➤ "I think Mike in Accounting knows the answer."

> ➤ "I appreciate you bringing this to my attention."

> ➤ "It's not currently an area of interest to me, although it is interesting."

> ➤ "I'm under deadline now and can't give it any attention."

Is No Information Sacred?

You may think that everyone should know the dates of the Civil War in the United States (1861 to 1865). But if someone came to America within the last half decade, and he's been learning English and learning the culture, he may not know the dates of the Civil War, and it may not have as much importance to him.

If you're a manager or supervisor, your challenge in explaining things to people is greater today than it was to your counterpart of years ago. You can't make assumptions that managers made years ago.

Certainly there's no need to take in information because you feel you "ought to," or you "must." Do you feel anxiety, however, when you can't respond to all the promotions, discounts, and bonus offers in the mail? You know you can't read, absorb, or take advantage of all of them.

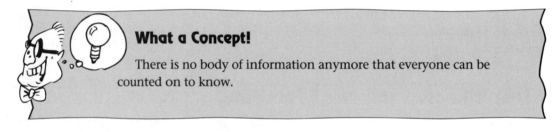

What a Concept!

There is no body of information anymore that everyone can be counted on to know.

Reducing Your Information Intake

When you're continually besieged by information, you begin to feel overwhelmed, which leads to feeling overworked and stressed. If you can eliminate much of that extraneous information, you actually won't feel overwhelmed as often, and you won't feel as overworked. I am off of mailing lists and have dropped most of my subscriptions.

Go!
You control your space, and this will allow you to stay in control of your information.

➤ Control the spaces in your life, because information is stored in spaces—tables shelves, desks, disks, web sites, and so on.

➤ If your desk is a mess, with piles that are growing higher, you *can* take control of that space.

➤ The same principle applies to your filing cabinet, your shelves, the top of your dining room table, your kitchen counter, your glove compartment, or your back seat.

Organize the Information You Do Want to Keep

If you're facing volumes of information, divide and conquer. Let's say you're facing a ten-inch pile of information...

➤ Put it into file folders.

➤ Group similar items together.

➤ Eliminate duplicates.

➤ Prioritize the important items in a given file.

Etched in Stone
It's harmful to ingest too much information at once.

At least half of dealing with most information is simply dividing it into piles, categorizing, or putting it into various directories on your hard drive.

A key question when evaluating any item is, "Where does this go?" The answer is finding an appropriate file where you can find the material easily. You may need to re-label files, but that's OK. This is *your* system, designed for *you*—never mind what it looks like to others. Re-labeling files indicates that you're getting good at filing.

Even students or your spouse at home could benefit from more effective filing and better organization. Oh, you don't think you have time to get organized? The reality is that you're already taking time from other things if you're not organized. At the least, it takes you longer to find things.

➤ You're also expending mental and emotional energy because you're not organized. Anxiety, worry, and frustration eat into your productivity and your day.

➤ You're in an era that will continue to dump more information than you can respond to. Setting up personal systems to become and remain organized is a solid investment in your career and long-term well-being.

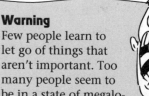

Warning
Few people learn to let go of things that aren't important. Too many people seem to be in a state of megalomania, grabbing every bit of information available and surrendering almost nothing.

Tickler Files

It's worth considering the benefits of having a file folder for each month of the year and a file folder for each day of the month. This idea, the *tickler file*, has been in practice for years. Create a file for days 1 to 31 of the month, and place it at the front of one of your file drawers. Behind that, have a file for each month of the year.

If it's the second day of the month, for example, but you receive something that you won't need to deal with until the 15th, put it in the file for, say, the 13th (to allow yourself some slack). If anything comes in that you don't need to handle now, put it in your tickler file. This yields immediate benefits: It keeps your desk clear and eliminates a lot of worry about where things go.

As the days and months pass, you continually move files that were in front and put them in the back. Once you get this system in place, you'll find that many of the things you file may not need to be acted on later. The benefits of this system are immediate.

Letting Go of Excess

Look at your system and determine how you can pare down. I suggest opening your mail over the waste basket; it's much easier to throw things out with the waste basket below you. If you get a magazine or journal, go through it rapidly and take out the articles or items that look like they'll be of interest. Recycle the rest of the publication.

Go! I don't need to keep the physical hard copy of a book. Thirty or forty books take up an entire shelf; a dossier of these books is, at most, two inches thick.

Often, there's no need to hang on to the back issues of a publication. These days, much of the information is also online. Pare down to only what you need—get the volume down as quickly and easily as possible. See if you can use the copier to assemble key facts on a single sheet.

The same applies to books. I receive books from people all the time. I quickly scan the entire book. I read the table of contents and index and find the pages that contain information of value to me. I photocopy those pages, along with the cover and publishing information, and create a dossier of the information from that book that's important to me.

I then give that book away to an associate, a friend, a library—wherever.

Often, I don't even keep the dossier; I'll dictate the key points and have a typist transcribe the tape. I have hundreds of books on my hard disk and can find them easily. There's no accumulation, no pile. With the word search ability of word processing software, I can find the information I need immediately.

Handle It Like a Pro

Hereafter, when information crosses your desk, ask yourself some key questions to determine whether to keep and file, place in a tickler file, create a dossier, or immediately toss the information:

➤ Should I have received this?

➤ What is the issue behind this document?

➤ Is the information of marginal value that I could easily skip and suffer no loss in my career for not retaining it? If so, then let it go!

➤ Will it matter if I don't handle it?

➤ What am I saving it for?

➤ Do I need it, or do I fear that if I don't have it, I'll somehow be deficient?

➤ Does it support what I already know or believe?

➤ Can I delegate the information in the document?

If you have set up a tickler file, can you file the new information as something to review next month? Most of what crosses your desk doesn't need to linger; it can go elsewhere.

When you're in control of your information, you can more easily retrieve and use it. Information is power, but if you can't find what you retain, it's of no value. It's only of value when you *can* find it and combine it with other things.

A Lifetime Guarantee

You are part of the pioneer generation, moving into a rapidly changing future, and you can handle it. You have the intelligence and the capability. Every day, for the rest of your life, you are likely to be besieged by more information, not less. When you understand what you're up against, you're in a better position to take control.

The Least You Need to Know

➤ Information overkill is stressing out nearly everyone; be more selective than you've ever been.

➤ There's no need to take in information because you feel you "ought" to or you "must."

➤ You control your space and hence you can stay in control of information you encounter by organizing that space.

➤ It's harmful to ingest too much information at once.

➤ When information crosses your desk ask yourself, "Did I need to receive this at all?" and then handle the information accordingly: file, condense, or toss.

Chapter 12

Overexposure to Unreality

In This Chapter

➤ The reality of unreality

➤ If it bleeds, it leads

➤ Discerning what's news

➤ Blabgate

➤ Media-fueled anxiety

In the mid 1980s, a study by the Louis Harris Organization found that two out of every three adults in the United States report that they "fidget, fuss, take furtive glances in windows and mirrors, and study other people's reactions to the way they look." Harris concluded that a solid majority of Americans are almost "obsessed with their physical appearance." All indications since then—cosmetic sales, cosmetic operations, the rise of the image industry—are that this obsession has reached new heights.

Nearly 96 percent of respondents in the Harris poll said they would change their appearance if they could. For example, about half of all men would like to change their weight or waistline. Women are worried about their waistlines, thighs, and aging, among other things.

"To have others admire one's looks," says Harris, "ranks high on the list of both men and women, especially the young, even if those looks are only superficial and wildly deceiving." Even the most revered Hollywood sex symbols have undergone considerable cosmetic and surgical alterations to increase their chances of adulation from fans who might otherwise ignore them.

Etched in Stone
Vast numbers of Americans have become **other-directed**—more concerned "with what others think of them than what they think of themselves."

If you're a reasonably attractive single woman, how many guys do you suppose don't call because you don't measure up to their Hollywood fantasy woman? If you're an average Joe, how many women do you suppose give you the cold shoulder because you don't measure up to Brad Pitt?

The reality of unreality is that decades of watching how other people supposedly look and live (from *Charlie's Angels* to *Baywatch*) have resulted in mass discontent with self-image, a form of social stress unknown in previous times.

Pervasive and Unrecognized

What television and movies have done to society is profound, yet so intrusive that it is nearly unrecognized. It's made us discontent with ourselves and with others. TV is not simply an electronic box in the corner, but an actual member of the family, with all rights and privileges accorded to family members.

While TV characters don't raid the refrigerator or tie up the bathroom, if they appear regularly they have a profound influence over the family. People walk like them, talk like them, dress like them, smoke like them, and yearn to look like them.

Undermining Your Town

A growing number of people believe that popular culture, particularly as transmitted by electronic media, is undermining the character of society. Regardless of your politics, when eight-year-olds can buy CDs with lyrics that speak in vulgarities, and of rape, incest, murder, and horrible mistreatment of women, you don't have to have a Ph.D. in psychology to understand that over a prolonged period, some of it seeps in.

The president of the American Medical Association observed that the typical child today sees at least 8,000 murders and 10,000 acts of violence in the media before the seventh grade.

As it is, most American children begin watching television before they can talk. By the time they are six, many children have invested more hours watching TV than they will spend speaking with their fathers in an entire lifetime.

A World Apart

Sneak Previews cohost Michael Medved observes that the Hollywood perspective on the American family reflects novelty-seeking, eccentricity, and nonconformity. It highlights people running to sperm banks, single mothers, and absent, hostile fathers.

When leading academics and media researchers gathered for a conference on "The Impact of the Media on Children and the Family," one of the organizers was surprised to find so much agreement given the diversity of participants. The group reached a consensus that values in much of the mass media, especially in violent and sexually explicit materials, are on a collision course with traditional family values and the protection of children.

So, You Know Better?

Among adults, who supposedly can discern fact from fiction, polls show that otherwise rational people in large percentages believe one or more of the following:

➤ Alien visitors walk among us.

➤ Aliens helped build the pyramids.

➤ Homo sapiens and dinosaurs appeared on earth at the same time.

➤ Elvis may still be alive.

➤ Six million Jews didn't perish in Nazi concentration camps during World War II.

➤ Wolves attack people in droves.

➤ The Loch Ness Monster lives.

➤ The Bermuda Triangle swallows up ships and planes.

➤ JFK's assassination was a conspiracy.

In his 1993 book, *Case Closed*, Gerald Posner walks the reader through every conceivable detail of the case and shows conclusively why it was definitely Lee Harvey Oswald who fired the gun and how the "magic bullets" indeed did take the angles they were supposed to. The analysis was so thorough that *U.S. News and World Report* concluded that *Case Closed* would be the *last* book reviewed on the JFK assassination. Currently, the "who shot JFK?" industry earns $200 million a year, with the potential to go higher, constantly fed by more TV news magazine "investigations," authors, books, and tours.

I don't regard the misinformation surrounding JFK's death lightly. The nature of society changed as nearly an entire generation suspected that a conspiracy, perhaps government-led, may have brought down the leader of the free world in broad daylight. Who knows what cynicism about government, the press, truth itself, ensued?

I submit to you, gentle reader, that the nature of your life has changed as a result of the misinformation that glutted society's information channels. I submit to you that the base of what it means to be a citizen in a democracy has eroded since 1963, for you and everyone you know.

Violence, Cigarettes, and Drugs—They're not Just for Breakfast Anymore

You know there's a lot of violence on TV, but did you know that violence on television is far more pervasive than in real life by a factor of 1,000 times? One study showed that

Warning
"What we think of now as the excess of the Roman circuses, where in the end hundreds of thousands of people died, didn't start out that way," says Bill Moyers. They started out as legitimate circuses, but the demand for more and more resulted in more bloody and grotesque forms of entertainment.

since 1955, television characters have been murdered at a rate 1,000 times higher than real-world victims. Also, businessmen and businesswomen are twice as likely to represent villains and three times as likely to commit crimes as are characters in other professions. Three out of four programs that show business dealings portray business as dishonest or corrupt.

The National Coalition on Television Violence in Washington D.C. has undertaken many studies that show a substantial increase in playground violence among otherwise normal children immediately after they watch programs that emphasize combat.

It does not surprise me that many countries around the globe are legislating limits to how much American television they will allow to be broadcast in their countries. Some countries have levied an outright ban on American television programs.

Winding Down or Cranking Up?

Too many people, you included, rely on the tube to wind down at the end of a day. Since the early 1980s, television viewing has had the opposite effect to reducing your stress. In their book *Television and the Quality of Life*, authors Mihaly Csikszentmihalyi and Robert Kubey, after conducting a 13-year study of 1,200 people, found that most people are now more rattled after having watched some prime time or late night television and then turning in for bed.

What a Concept!
"It is important that the people who make films have ethics classes, philosophy classes, and history classes. Otherwise, we are witch doctors."
—George Lucas

The evidence is clear: If you've been experiencing any significant level of stress, you are more likely to feel worse after having viewed an hour or two of television.

Sucked into the Vortex of Entertainment

To be sure, entertainment has a necessary function in your life: It stimulates thinking. It can be liberating to your soul. It can give you a break from the drudgery or monotony of daily living. More important, entertainment can free you to explore new ways of thinking, new ideas, and new possibilities.

The harm in being over-entertained—which we all now face—is that your own life pales by comparison. Consider how much time and energy you're willing to spend with your favorite characters on a TV drama or sitcom. Now contrast this with how much time you actually spend with anyone in your community.

What a Concept!

When compared to what you see on the screen, your own life may seem dull, boring, and plastic; in fact, it is real and holds rich potential.

In the end, the quality of your life and the memories in your life will depend on what you actively did, not what you passively ingested (that is, watching *Star Wars* for the sixth time).

If It Bleeds, It Leads

Most of the news you receive is convoluted.

"And that's the way it is..." No, Mr. Cronkite, that's the way a handful of news executives, producers, and writers decided it would be conveyed to the public. What gets broadcast, at best, is a subset of a fraction of a sliver of what's occurring in the world.

CNN keeps blaring away in the airport, making everything sound as if it's important, the latest, and vital. Magazines and newspapers shout out their headlines. Television news flashes major features of 45 seconds or less, followed by titillating television news magazines that don't always check their "facts."

It's increasingly difficult to identify what you need to know versus what's nice to know. Consider the following stories:

- ➤ U.S. invasion of Panama
- ➤ U.S. invasion of Persian Gulf
- ➤ Menendez brothers' trial
- ➤ Clarence Thomas hearings
- ➤ William Kennedy Smith trial
- ➤ Whitewater investigation
- ➤ FBI shoot-out in Waco
- ➤ U.S. deployment in Somalia
- ➤ Unrest in Checheznia

- ➤ Attack on Nancy Kerrigan
- ➤ Baseball strike
- ➤ World Trade Center bombing
- ➤ O.J. Simpson trial
- ➤ U.S. redeployment in Persian Gulf
- ➤ Saudi Arabia bombing
- ➤ NYC subway mass murders
- ➤ Nerve gas attack, Japan
- ➤ Next week's attack

139

Unless you've had a friend or loved one in the military or directly involved in something listed above, chances are that few of these stories have had any impact on you whatsoever.

It's curious that "news" largely originates from a mere handful of "news centers": New York, Los Angeles, London, Paris, Moscow, Tokyo, and so on. News is routinely packaged nationally as economic vicissitudes, hostilities, or drug wars and locally as floods, crime, fires, and scandals.

Do you hear much about positive developments in other countries, real scientific break-throughs, human triumphs, and other such news?

Local television news, in particular, has become a cesspool that portrays in living color—usually blood red—personal tragedies, mayhem, and tabloid violence. It seems as if journalists, or perhaps their assignment editors, revel in creating what some call a dra-matic tension that conveniently is never resolved.

Few reporters, certainly on the local level, have an in-depth understanding of what they're actually covering. Many are assigned beats for which they have no experience; many stories are covered by whomever the station can dispatch. The assignment is completed, the story aired, and tomorrow they'll do it again, with different names and faces—but they'll fill those 22 minutes. Meanwhile, turnover of personnel is high, so new hires are pressed into service—knowledgeable or not.

Warning

The negativity that pervades local news and the media in general impacts our beliefs, emotions, and opinions by adding community and social stress to our personal lives and personal stress.

Those award-winning local news teams, at their best, might be engaged in a three- or a five-day feature, to run three to four minutes each night. Although with seemingly redeem-ing efforts and worthy topics, the gesture represents no more than throwing the public a "bone." If you received a constant barrage of positive stories starting from your infancy, your whole life would be different.

Is It "News"?

It's time to redefine what is news. "News" is a derivative of "new." Here are some news items that I don't consider new:

➤ Ethnic clashes that have been going on for thousands of years aren't news—there would have to be a breakthrough for them to be "news."

➤ Ancient hostilities, the death of communism, political corruption, government blundering—not news unless there's a different nature to them.

➤ Unsubstantiated allegations against politicians or celebrities aren't news.

➤ Last night's fire, inner-city crime, and the plight of the homeless are all undesirable situations, but they're not news.

News would be *new* developments:

➤ Ways that some ethnic groups have made substantial progress in resolving their differences.

➤ New forms of cooperation or political integrity.

➤ In-depth analysis of good deeds, service, and sacrifice on the part of public figures.

➤ Innovative strategies that communities are exploring to reduce the incidence of fire, crime, and homelessness.

Go!
If you surf the chan- nels and intellectually resonate with all the world's problems, who are you helping? No one—least of all, yourself. Pay attention and take action only in a couple of key areas. You do not need to be subject to a whirlpool of informa- tion that is not digestible.

When nearly every TV station gives you the same type of information night after night, they are simulta- neously ignoring the breakthroughs in human potential and the fact that most people went to bed happy last night. This convolutes your view of society; you're deluged with news that says things aren't going so well. Certainly, we have problems, but this constant barrage of what's going wrong shapes perceptions.

The Wrath of Rather

In 1993, Dan Rather blasted fellow news broadcasters at the annual Radio and Television News Directors Association convention. Rather delivered a scathing attack on current news industry trends that were more concerned with dead bodies, mayhem, and terror than with giving viewers any semblance of balance in reporting.

Some 25 years earlier, the now-revered Edward R. Murrow blistered the same Radio and Television News Directors Association about the current state of affairs in the news industry. Yet, by comparison, the standards then, if not the morals of the industry, were exemplary by today's standards.

Rather's stance, perhaps no less valiant, unfortunately, was simply lost among the megadoses of information that everyone takes in daily. Yesterday's news might as well be ancient history.

Express Yourself

If you're concerned about television content or programming or would like to express your views in writing, here are some key addresses:

ABC Entertainment President
2040 Avenue of the Stars
Los Angeles, CA 90067

CBS Audience Services
524 West 57th Street
New York, NY 10019

NBC Entertainment President
3000 W. Alameda
Burbank, CA 91523

Public Broadcasting Service
1320 Braddock Place
Alexandria, VA 22314

Federal Communications Commission
Complaints & Investigations
Branch Enforcement Division
2025 M Street, NW Room 8210
Washington DC 20554

The Tabloid Mentality

As you stand in line at your supermarket checkout counter, even if you dislike them, you can't help but notice the shouting headlines on the tabloids. Starting in the 1960s, it was Burton and Taylor; in the '70s, lurid tales inside the Nixon White House; in the '80s, all the dirt on Burt and Loni you could take; and in the '90s, take your pick. If the attacks on the well-known or well-to-do aren't enough for you, there are also stories about miracle diets, alien visitors, chainsaw massacres, and little known facts about the Pope.

When I'm in checkout lines, I routinely ask cashiers why they carry publications with such lurid headlines, in full view of children and other gentle creatures. None seems to know. One of them responded that the tabloids probably pay a lot of money to be placed in such a prominent position.

Amazing as it may seem, the unreality spread by tabloid news pales by comparison to that spread by the supposedly "legitimate press."

About Me, Placed By Me

Pick up your local newspaper and flip to the business, outlook, lifestyle, or health section. Every issue carries an interview with or a feature on some executive or entrepreneur. The majority of these stories are placed by public relations firms who have been paid by the person for whom the story is about.

The features and profiles you see are part of a coordinated public relations effort, undertaken and funded by the company or individual. Publishers, magazine publishers in particular, know that executives and entrepreneurs in their community want to be written about, and have the funds to commission an article, so publishers often get material for free.

The next time you see an item in print about a company or individual with whom you compete, consider how it got there. The next time you read about some movie star who has it all (including a photographer with a fabulous airbrush), some book that topped the bestseller list in eight days, or who knows what else, think, "Is this part of the unreality industry?"

Warning

It may seem like others in your industry or profession generate spontaneous press coverage. That's a stressor for people who *don't* get interviewed. Unreality strikes again.

Fueling Anxiety

Subscribe now! Sign up today! Free trial demo!

You've seen the endless parade of articles on how important it is to jump on the information highway. Do these messages seem to have a familiar ring? They should; they mirror what happened 12 to 14 years ago as the PC was introduced in America.

Vendors advertised heavily on television. One showed a Charlie Chaplin-type figure who sat down at a keyboard. With the greatest of ease and hardly cracking a software manual, he effortlessly and efficiently ran a business. The trouble with the ads is that it took another three to five years before even progressive businesses had a majority of their employees working with a PC.

In the years ahead, you will be flooded with as many articles on the information superhighway as you saw on PCs in the early 1980s or on AIDS during 1986 and 1987. Articles on the information superhighway will begin to diminish just when it becomes more important, just as there are fewer articles on AIDS now that it's ravaging segments of our society and other societies. Why so much coverage six to eight years ago (albeit it was a good public service) when by comparison, the problem is 15- to 20-fold today?

What a Concept!

If the information you can acquire over the information highway is crucial to your business, chances are that you're already a subscriber, or making plans to be. If not, it's time to cautiously begin looking at the possibilities.

Oversaturation in the early years is the norm, and undercoverage in the years when it takes full effect, sadly, is also the norm. Hype regarding technology results in much stress and gnashing of teeth.

If the high technology available today readily enhances your position in the minds of those whom you serve, by all means, proceed with the wiring process. If you're unsure, proceed at a moderate pace. Please don't get caught up, however, in the media induced hysteria of the moment.

Stop the Media Insanity!

Instead of using the media as the bellwether of what merits your time and attention, it's time to make profound personal choices as to where you'll seek information and advice. Strive for objectivity, despite the unreality all around you. Don't let reporters, journalists, and the industry vendors who influence them add undue stress to your life or make you feel inadequate. Don't let them set your agenda or timetables. They're not qualified.

➤ Watch only one news program per day.

➤ If you read the paper, don't watch the TV news.

➤ Limit your viewing to one to two hours of entertainment TV per week—spend the new free time exercising to eliminate stress.

➤ Once you cut your TV viewing to three to four hours per week, stop your cable subscription to save money.

➤ Check out movies for free from your library, which will limit your selection and offer more non-violent choices.

The Least You Need to Know

➤ If you've been experiencing stress, you are more likely to feel worse after having viewed an hour or two of television.

➤ Become more discriminating about your attention to news, information, and entertainment.

➤ At least 75 percent of all the optional features and profile pieces (not "hard" or late-breaking news) in smaller local newspapers and magazines have been "placed" by agents representing those parties featured.

➤ Don't let reporters, journalists, and industry vendors who influence them add undue stress to your life.

Part 4
Self-Induced Stressors

The external stressors of population density, the news and information industry, and overexposure to unreality have a combined effect that is staggering. But remember that in Chapter 1, you learned that most stress is self-induced—you invite or allow it into your life. This section examines three critical areas where stress you experience is clearly self-induced:

➤ *Not getting enough sleep*

➤ *Having an unconditioned personal environment*

➤ *Not achieving completions*

The first one is something you understand. The next two might contain unfamiliar terminology, but they'll become clear soon enough.

If you're fatigued right now, go right to Chapter 13, "Shortchanging Your Sleep." If you're well-rested and fit, perhaps you need to work a few 12-hour days, get as little sleep as you can, and then tackle it. Either way, struggling through the chapter, barely able to give it your full attention, you'll understand firsthand what I mean.

Shortchanging Your Sleep

In This Chapter

➤ A society of thoroughly tired people

➤ The link between sleep and stress

➤ How much sleep do you need?

➤ Getting rest in general

You're not getting enough sleep, and it's contributing to the accumulating stress you feel in your life.

If it seems that all around you people are showing symptoms of fatigue, you've probably heard or said:

> "I feel so fatigued, I often worry about how I'll be able to make it through the work week. Sometimes, it's a miracle I don't get in a car accident on the way home."

> "I feel as if I've used up my reserve of energy. When I put in a decent day's work there's not much left by the end of the day. My family and friends haven't seen the real me for a long time."

These statements, which I'm guessing could have been said by you, reflect the thoughts of many people today. This chapter covers fatigue and its relationship to stress.

A Long-Term Trend in the Making

According to experts:

➤ Americans' average sleep time per night has dropped by 20 percent during the last century.

➤ Americans have added 158 hours to their yearly working and commuting time since 1969.

➤ Businesses lose as much as $1,000 a year per employee in lost productivity due to fatigued employees.

➤ Doctors' offices are flooded with people wondering why they simply feel exhausted.

Doctors, nurses, and others in the medical community used to be among the most likely to experience fatigue. Now, the exhaustion has spread to all parts of society. Stress, as well as a few medical conditions, may be at work.

No one knows how many people suffer from *insomnia* (difficulty sleeping), but estimates range between 36 and 62 million people in the United States. Second- and third-shift workers are particularly prone to insomnia, as are older adults. Women, more than men, also seem to be susceptible. If you're like most stressed-out adults, you've probably endured mild insomnia (sleepless nights) brought on by your stress.

About 250,000 to 300,000 others are affected by *narcolepsy*, a malfunction of the central nervous system that causes daytime sleepiness including sudden, temporary losses of muscle control, and brief paralysis when falling asleep or waking. A narcoleptic's sleep attacks may occur while driving, operating dangerous equipment, or simply in the middle of a conversation.

Warning

Fatigue is now one of the top five reasons that people make doctor appointments.

Sleep apnea is another fatigue-causing affliction that causes a person to stop breathing during sleep, usually because of some type of obstruction. Usually the person is aroused from sleep by an automatic breathing reflex, so he or she may end up getting very little sleep at all.

Hard to Stay Awake

A survey commissioned by the Better Sleep Council found that of 1,000 adults, one in three surveyed admitted to sleeplessness affecting their work. Among observations about sleep:

➤ Twice as many men as women confessed to dozing at their desks on company time.

➤ About one out of two people believe that long work hours keep them from getting all the sleep they need (which, I'll discuss, is not true).

➤ About 20 percent of people calling in sick or being tardy for work say they didn't sleep well the night before.

➤ One out of three adults say they are not well rested when they wake up for work.

What a Concept!

Stress can cause a lack of sleep. A lack of sleep can contribute to stress. It's pretty vicious!

Nothing New but Definitely of Concern

Exhaustion is nothing new and nothing to take lightly. George Washington, it is said, used to retreat for days if not weeks on end to get precious rest, and restore his faculties, while he was President.

Okay, so you don't get enough sleep, but why is that potentially dangerous? Remember, you respond to stressful situations by working at a higher gear. Your heart pumps blood faster; your muscles contract; and your blood thickens. You're ready for fight or flight. If you did fight or fly, the condition largely would take care of itself.

Instead of that old saber-tooth, you're confronting the challenges of the hectic, work-a-day world. So your engine is revving for eight, maybe ten, hours straight. You get home, and as you learned in Chapter 3, there are potentially more stressors there. You don't sleep as many hours as your body needs, or if you do, it's not very good sleep, it's fitful. The net result:

➤ You're being worn down.

➤ Your immune system is weakened.

➤ You're much more susceptible to illness.

Some experts believe that getting too little sleep on a consistent basis may undermine your entire being—impacting your entire life to your detriment. Any illness that you do contract, combined with too little sleep, will be more severe.

The Danger Signals

You feel tired, but when is the tired feeling that you have bordering on danger? There are many signs, among them these:

Your fatigue is prolonged. Getting several nights of extra sleep in a row or sleeping for an entire weekend doesn't seem to put a dent in your feeling of fatigue. Perhaps worse, you feel as if you "will never catch up."

You experience indigestion or lack of appetite. You normally look forward to meals, but when highly fatigued, you have trouble swallowing. Maybe you're eating less.

You experience loss of sex drive. This isn't as obvious as you might think. Loss of your libido can occur gradually. Your partner will notice.

You begin to experience trouble getting to sleep, if not outright insomnia. During the night, you find yourself waking more often and then to exacerbate the situation, you spend the rest of the night worrying that you're not getting good sleep.

You feel tired in the morning even after a full night's sleep. Realistically, there's little reason for this. If by 9:30 or 10:00 in the morning, you can hardly keep your head up, it's time to take heed.

You feel that you're no longer in control. In many ways, this is the most insidious of the signs. You doze at inopportune moments, such as in an important meeting or when driving (more on this later in the chapter).

Not Dangerous, but Not Desirable Either

Here's a second list of indicators that you're not getting enough sleep, but perhaps you're not at the danger level:

➤ Your eyes are red.

➤ You avoid tasks that involve adding up numbers.

➤ In situations with others you simply go through the motions.

➤ You don't want to handle any phone calls if you can help it.

➤ You watch the clock frequently throughout the day, hoping time will go by more quickly.

Comparest Thou Not with Others

Why do some high achiever types often feel that they can shortchange sleep without penalty? Some believe that by working longer or harder now, perhaps getting less sleep, the potential payoffs can be larger.

Some people knowingly take less sleep as part of a calculated plot to become prosperous younger or sooner. Paradoxically, the most successful people I know tend to have regular, sufficient sleep patterns. Whether they retire early or late, they get ample sleep daily and weekly, to keep themselves vibrant and moving forward.

Now and then, you read about some ultra-high achiever who only sleeps an average of four or five hours a night. You have to remember:

➤ Your need for sleep differs from others. Don't compare yourself.

➤ Unless a longitudinal study of their sleep patterns is undertaken, no one knows the long-term effects. Maybe such people will develop acute disorders. Who can say?

Go!
Your quest is to get the amount of sleep you need to feel and perform at your best.

Driving and Dozing

You're a danger to yourself and others when you try to function with consistently too little sleep. Simply too many transportation mishaps today are a direct result of someone being fatigued at the wheel. Vast numbers of people in society engage in micro-sleep, which is a form of trying to compensate for under-sleeping.

School bus drivers, with 40 children in tow may be engaging in micro-sleep. Train conductors responsible for hundreds of passengers engage in micro-sleep.

The National Highway Transportation Safety Administration estimates that each year at least 1,500 deaths and 32,000 injuries can be attributed to vehicle crashes associated with driver drowsiness, as illustrated in Table 13.1.

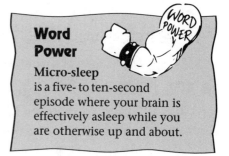

Word Power

Micro-sleep is a five- to ten-second episode where your brain is effectively asleep while you are otherwise up and about.

Table 13.1 Dreaming and Driving: Auto Accidents Where Sleeping at the Wheel Was a Factor

Year	Crashes	Injuries	Deaths
1990	57,000	40,000	1,596
1991	59,000	45,000	1,579
1992	50,000	33,000	1,440
1993	43,000	32,000	1,557

Source: Fatal Accident Reporting System of the NHTSA

Some people mistakenly believe that the act of driving is sleep inducing. However, if you weren't sleepy to begin with, you wouldn't nod off while driving.

The incidence of drowsy driver crashes may be highly understated. Because many drowsy driver crashes only involve the driver, many go unreported. Or, in the case of a fatal accident, many accidents are misclassified.

Although auto manufacturers hunt for driver warning systems that will reduce the number of drowsy driver accidents, and even if your car is so equipped or equipped in the future, it's no excuse for you to ever get behind the wheel *if you even suspect* that your level of fatigue will impair your driving ability.

If you can't do much about completely overcoming your fatigue right now, then please consider the following:

➤ Use public transportation as often as possible.

➤ Become part of a ride-share system, and at least be well rested when it's your turn to drive.

➤ Avoid taking any long trips, where the probability of a mishap increases markedly.

➤ For short trips, consider a taxi, bike, or walking.

It's a Female Thing, You Wouldn't Understand

Based on findings of the National Commission on Sleep Disorders Research, as well as several other groups, women often have a more difficult time getting good sleep than men. Particularly among women who work outside the home and raise children, the effects can be pronounced.

Out of any group of working women, as many as half may routinely experience a sudden awakening in the wee hours of the night. There are many reasons why women may have sleep related problems, including the following:

➤ Women usually spend more hours on domestic tasks in addition to occupations outside the home.

➤ Society's expectations regarding their appearance prompts them to spend more time getting dressed, groomed, and so on.

➤ Historically, women have had lower levels of income, which means they must work longer or harder to achieve the same level of income as men. Thus they have a difficult time meeting household expenses and are prone to fatigue.

➤ Many women are involved in their children's education, attending PTA meetings, participating in school events, reading to the child at night, and so forth. (This is not to slight any men—your section is coming up.)

As more women share or assume the full economic role (single mothers), they may find themselves as sole caretakers of the emotional and spiritual well being of family members. All of the above and the following new pressures (from the Women's Bureau of the U.S. Department of Labor) ultimately impact the amount and quality of women's sleep.

➤ Sixty-three percent of women with children work outside the home.

➤ Fifty percent of working women return to work within a year of having a baby. An additional 30 percent return to work after more than a year.

➤ Ninety percent of elderly parents needing care are cared for directly by their families. Sixty-seven percent of the primary care givers are working women.

An increasing number of women who work do not have the time to advance their careers because of dual home and family responsibilities. By some estimates, women still do about 80 percent of all work associated with housekeeping and raising the children. By the time they get to bed, they are all but exhausted. You would think that would be a scenario for deep sleep, but the more wired and agitated you are mentally throughout the day, the less likely you are to sleep through the entire night.

Women aren't the only people with tremendous demands on their days, which in turn impact their nights.

A Man's World?

Within the last decade, an increasing percentage of men have found themselves candidates for exhaustion. After all, trying to be a good father, responsive husband, champion breadwinner, enlightened manager, on-call handyman, and pillar of the community takes its toll. Consider too, these little bonus tasks:

➤ Men do most of the driving on family related trips, particularly long trips.

➤ Men spend more time working around the yard and on other physically strenuous tasks.

➤ Men spend more time working on family finances and in particular income taxes.

➤ Men are more likely to be little league coaches; officers of social, civic, and charitable organizations; volunteer fire fighters; or part of the National Guard.

You could say that men have it pretty tough.

Etched in Stone
In his book, *The Myth of Male Power*, Dr. Warren Farrel points out that men are far more likely to die on the job than they are in war.

The gap in life expectancy between men and women in America today is an astounding seven years. Lest you believe this is attributed to genetics, guess again. In 1920, the gap between the expected life spans of men and women was only one year. Many men face increasing responsibilities at work, and far more men face potential health hazards on the job than women. *Hazardous occupations are virtually men's domains.*

Whether you're a woman or a man, if I can get some agreement here, many factors contribute to the feeling of fatigue on the part of both sexes.

Sleep and Recover

Suppose that you are the President of the United States of America. You have foreign dignitaries coming to a lavish dinner in the White House. You're going to get up and say a few words, and dance with the First Lady (or First Gentlemen, if that be the case—I'm assuming that this book has a long shelf life!). You're going to be charming, powerful, and witty.

The evening comes, the guests arrive, and the affair comes off without a hitch. You are dashing, the center of attention, a suitable symbol for all that's right with the Western world.

Obviously, no one maintains this level of performance consistently. Most days, even as President, you drop back to a lower level of operation. You sign executive orders, handle important phone calls, and meet with your staff, but you don't have to be "beaming."

Back to reality—in your everyday life, in whatever your occupation, you alternate between periods of performance and recovery. You're not hibernating during recovery, rather, you're regrouping your physical and mental resources and replenishing your spirit and emotions for those times when you may be called upon again to "perform."

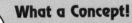

What a Concept!
Deep REM sleep enables you to more fully engage in conceptual, first-time, and breakthrough thinking. If you have to learn a new routine, new instructions, or new equipment, the amount and quality of REM sleep you get the night before will decidedly impact your abilities.

Sufficient sleep on a regular basis enables your body to recover from the stresses and strains you experience during the day.

Although recovery also comes as a result of being mentally and physically relaxed, getting deep sleep is critical for the challenging tasks you face daily.

Paradoxically, you're most likely to resist allowing yourself a recovery period of good sleep precisely at that time when you're most in need of it. If you're among the multitudes at war with themselves when it comes to getting the sleep you need, perhaps these suggestions on restructuring your sleeping environment will help:

➤ Have you checked your mattress lately? A bad mattress engages your muscles all night, as if you've been *working* all night.

➤ Particularly in the summer, make sure that the room you sleep in is cool and refreshed. You would be better off sleeping in a slightly chilled atmosphere with an additional blanket than a warmer one with less blankets.

➤ Make sure that you have a bed sufficiently large enough to allow you and your partner the freedom of movement. If you're afraid of clunking into one another, you'll restrict your movements, and unknowingly, diminish the quality of your sleep.

➤ Turn off the ringer on your phone, or if you have an answering machine attached, switch the appropriate lever to silent. As I pointed out in Chapter 7, too many people sleep with their heads by the phone because they have an aged loved one far away, or they worry about the one call in 15 years that might haul them out of bed at 3:00 a.m. Realistically, you can't do much at 3:00 a.m., anyway. You would be better off getting 15 years of sound sleep.

Word Power

REMs are **rapid eye movements** that are a crucial part of your overall cycle. If your REM pattern is disrupted, even eight hours of sleep may not yield the benefits you need to be effective.

➤ Keep your room dark or wear a night blindfold.

➤ Buy a snore control device if a sleep partner keeps you awake or to simply improve the quality of your own sleep.

Developing Good Sleep Habits

If it's been months, or years, since you've engaged in the habit of regular, sufficient, sound sleep, you've got an unfamiliar, but pleasant task ahead of you.

Here are some ideas for redeveloping the personal habit of having good sleep every night:

➤ Don't work out too hard before retiring, it may keep you too keyed up.

➤ Avoid caffeine at least six hours before retiring and alcohol altogether if you're interested in having good sleep that night. Alcohol, in particular, is sleep disrupting. Yes, you'll fall asleep quickly, but invariably you'll arise too early. Then, you'll likely have trouble getting back to sleep.

155

Go!
Most sleep researchers agree that getting sufficient sleep is a habit that you can develop. Conversely, not getting enough sleep is a bad habit that you developed over the years but never considered it as such.

➤ If you're so disposed, take a glass of milk before you sleep. It can help.

➤ Go to sleep when you're tired, not because the clock happens to say a particular time.

➤ Let others around you know when you want quiet because you are going to sleep!

Sleeping Away from Home

Suppose that you're traveling for work or vacation and will be staying in a hotel room. Use these techniques to help keep your sleep routine on track:

➤ Specifically ask for a room where you'll have peace and quiet. Explain that you have a huge presentation to deliver in the morning and that sleep is crucial. That might prompt them to give you a room in a quiet section of the hotel.

➤ Ask for a room without a door adjoining another room, where the guest from hell is likely to be staying.

Investigate getting ear plugs, which will reduce about 70 percent of the sounds you might hear from your external environment. Or buy a sound screen, which creates a blanket of "white noise" sound around you to drone out the effects of the more obtrusive sounds outside your door:

Noise Filter®
Cabot Safety Corporation
5457 West 79th Street
Indianapolis, IN 46268

Sound Screen® and **Sleep Mate**®
Marpac Corporation
P.O. Box 3098
Wilmington, NC 28406-0098

About Napping

What effect, you may ponder, does napping have on your ability to sleep soundly during the night? If you take a nap between the hours of 1:00 and 3:00 p.m. you'll be fine. Your body temperature takes a natural dip at this time, allowing you to nod off quickly. If you nap for less than 20 minutes, you don't incur REM sleep and can wake from your nap refreshed and alert.

Warning

Your nap needs to be short and sweet and offer quick refreshment. Avoid taking naps as a substitute to not getting enough sleep the night before. If you rely on naps to make it through the day, you could shortchange your sleep at night.

Have You Had Enough Sleep?

Sound sleep gives you the recovery time you need from the stress you experience during the day, keeps you sharp and alert, and maybe even restores your sex life. Here are some signs that you're getting the sleep that you need:

➤ You spring out of bed upon awakening.

➤ Your voice is clear and strong.

➤ You experience no fatigue during the morning.

➤ You have enough energy to have a life after the workday.

➤ You find yourself whistling or humming.

➤ You actually have the energy to be nice to people.

➤ You think to yourself that your boss or spouse is not so bad after all.

➤ You have sex on your mind.

It may take you a few weeks, or months, but you can get back into the groove when it comes to having good sleep!

The Least You Need to Know

➤ Lack of sleep is endemic to our society, and is both the result of and a contributor to stress.

➤ You need to proactively ensure the probability of sound sleep for the whole night.

➤ Don't compare the amount of sleep you need to that of others. Your needs are unique.

➤ Sleep provides an element of recovery from the day's stresses. This is crucial.

➤ If you're going to nap, the best times are between 1:00 and 3:00 p.m.

Chapter 14

Unconditioned Personal Environments

In This Chapter

➤ Making your home your castle

➤ Solicitors and other uninvited guests

➤ All about phone calls

➤ God bless this space

As you saw in preceding chapters, it's getting hard to defend your turf from outside noise, information, interruptions, distractions, solicitors, and other disturbances as well as self-generated clutter. It has been said that your home is your castle (unless you fall into the moat or get eaten by crocodiles).

If you've ever traveled the intercoastal highway in Florida and seen the hundreds of luxury condominiums that line the road, what I am about to describe will be familiar. Virtually every community is sealed off from the main street. A fence or gate surrounds the property and there's a guard house with at least one guard on duty, and often two. The guards stop all visitors, ask them who they will be visiting, and obtain clearance for the visitor. Residents often have their own gate pass, sticker, or some other identifying insignia that enables them to breeze right through. Somewhere near the entrance, usually prominently posted, is a sign that reads, "No Soliciting."

Although it may seem that such communities are obsessed with the notion of privacy, consider that the residents are usually elderly people who want privacy, fear crime, and are willing to pay for the protection. I'm not saying this is the environment in which everyone should live. Increasingly, however, people are taking it upon themselves to secure privacy or are moving to places that enable them to keep others from "invading their space."

Some days, their quest seems perfectly reasonable. I live smack dab in the middle of semirural North Carolina, in the posh community of Chapel Hill, an ultra-liberal bastion where no crime is too heinous to be forgiven.

Every so often, people come to the door, offering magazine subscriptions, opportunities to make donations to the police officers' benevolent fund, scout cookies, or tree-cutting services—I kid you not. On occasion, I have been greeted by members of various religious sects, people campaigning for political office, telephone repair people who never seem to get the job done right, and a host of others.

Ensuring that your home and other spaces are pleasant calls for specific measures. I am happy to report in this chapter that none are arduous.

Making Your Home Your Castle

An occasional unsolicited ring at my door is not stress inducing in itself—far from it. However, added to the phone calls from people selling newspaper subscriptions, broker-age services, and long-distance services; or seeking charitable contributions, survey information, and who knows what else, the situation begins to intensify.

Add in all the junk mail you receive—including faxes and e-mail if you have a PC—and my guess is you will soon have the makings of an *unconditioned personal environment*. In other words, anyone or anything is likely to beg for your attention at any time. Think back to what you learned in Chapter 3, on how the direction of stress has changed—it flows from home to office instead of vice versa—and you begin to understand why it becomes increasingly important to reclaim your castle.

Now add some clutter and noise for good measure—if you've lived at your current residence for any length of time, you have undoubtedly begun to accumulate things. The closets that looked so big when you first moved in are probably inadequate now. You're thinking that you could probably use more shelves. Kitchen cabinets seem woefully inadequate. The linen closet is too small. In short, your place is becoming cluttered. Plus, the TV is probably on a little bit too often; stereos or CD players might be blaring out music that you don't want to hear; or people on the radio might be jabbering away, saying nothing, for hours on end.

I am not suggesting that keeping your home at the level of quiet that you desire and clutter-free equates with a happy home life. Certainly, there are relationship issues of greater magnitude. However, having a conditioned personal environment certainly can't hurt.

To help you reclaim your castle, this chapter discusses five issues starting with the most intrusive, solicitors and other uninvited guests, and working down to the less intrusive, self-generated clutter and noise.

Solicitors and Other Uninvited Guests

Like the luxury condominiums in Florida, you could put up a sign that says "No Soliciting" and that would fend off about 90 percent of the solicitors who knock on your door.

Some people use security system signage for the dual purpose of providing security and keeping away solicitors. You have seen the signs; they say things like:

"Premises secured by XYZ systems"

or

"Warning, alarm will sound if you XYZ."

I have a friend in Great Falls, Virginia, who has a strategically placed sticker that says, "Premises secured by Smith and Wesson." I don't know that I would post such a message myself, but he seems happy with the results.

Go!
You could put up signs that say HUGE DOG ON PREMISES or something similar. These cut down on unwanted solicitors as well.

The Uninvited

When it comes to neighbors and other acquaintances who call at inopportune moments, courtesy mixed with firmness is the rule. Try these approaches:

"I'd invite you to come in, but I'm updating my tax log now, and I don't want to lose my place."

"Hey, nice to see you. Can I take a rain check? This was the evening that I promised Bill I would complete the XYZ."

"Glad you stopped by. But as it turns out, I'm expecting a phone call from XYZ. Perhaps we could get together another evening."

You always have the option of not responding to a knock on the door or the ring of the bell. If your car is in the garage and not clearly visible, this strategy offends no one. If your car is visible, or if it's obvious that someone is home by the lights or sounds in the house, it's still your option not to answer the door.

Go! Where is it written that every time the phone rings you have to answer it? Where is it written that every time there is a knock on the door you have to open it?

Somehow, the pervasive notion has gripped society that you and I, like good little soldiers, must respond to the beck and, specifically, call of others. Not so. This is probably a holdover from Colonial days when people didn't have phones or fax machines, received but one letter per month, and had a whole different orientation toward visitors.

In the days of yore, a visitor meant a chance to interact with humanity. News. Even entertainment. When you couldn't switch on a radio, channel surf, cruise the Internet, or get on the phone and chat, a real, live in-your-face visitor gave you a chance to reconnect with the outside world. You only have to watch *The Age of Innocence* or *Sense and Sensibility* to see this phenomenon at play.

From Whence Comest Thou, Stranger?

If, out of the blue, somebody pops over and you have to be "on" (see Chapter 13) at a moment's notice—let alone bathed, dressed, and otherwise presentable—this disruption in your evening is likely to have its effect.

In the 1968 movie *Rosemary's Baby*, we see Mia Farrow as Rosemary curled up on her couch about to dive into a big, thick book. There is a knock at the door; it is Minnie, her elderly neighbor. Unbeknownst to Rosemary, Minnie is a broom-carrying officer of the local witches coven.

Minnie barges in, sits down on the couch, and takes out her knitting. All of a sudden, Rosemary's evening is disrupted. She'll be the gracious host and participate in bland conversation that kills her evening.

I don't surmise that this scenario plays out well today, in movies or in real life. Human nature, at least in this society, has changed.

No Extremes

You don't want to send the message that you never want anyone to call or drop by, because soon enough that's what will happen—no one will. There are ways, however, to convey when is a good time to visit and when isn't, like these:

➤ If you can keep your front door open without concern in your community (and there are fewer and fewer of these every year) that's a sign that a quick chat or drop-in visit would be welcomed.

➤ If you're actually on your front or back porch or working in the yard, all the more so. Of course, that's assuming that you want to be accessible to neighbors, have friends, and be approachable.

When you are besieged by the unexpected visitor, someone you like and want to see, but the time is not so convenient, you have options at your disposal:

➤ Invite him/her in, but preface the invitation with, "I only have a few minutes, and then I have to get ready for XYZ."

➤ "Um, I was just about to take a nap, but why don't you come in for a few minutes? I apologize if I seem a little tired, I've just been running around so much." Then, if they had intended to stay for 30 minutes, you've effectively conveyed that 10 would be more like it.

➤ Step out and meet with them on the front steps, walkway, or porch. This tells them you're glad to see them, but you're not going to let them in on this particular visit. This also gives you the opportunity to head back in when the time is right. At least a good 10 minutes is polite; a little longer is generous.

Go!
Your goal is to not eliminate drop-in visitors, but rather to have more control over the process.

➤ Reverse the tables. Announce some important task that you were going to tackle at that moment, but ask if you could drop by their house when convenient for you.

Dealing with Unwanted Phone Solicitations

If you're getting too many unsolicited sales phone calls, it might be time to consider getting an unlisted number. More than 20 million homes in America already have. At a minimum, you can count on 20 to 40 fewer solicitations per year. You can always distribute your number to those people you want to have it. If an unlisted phone number is too drastic for you or you already have one, here are a few more strategies:

➤ Get an answering machine. This enables you to screen calls. There's no reason you should get up during dinner to listen to someone's

Etched in Stone
The "do not call" provision within the Telemarketing and Consumer Fraud and Abuse Prevention Act means you have the right to not receive calls! A telemarketer may not call you again if you say that you do not want any more calls from or on behalf of a particular seller whose goods or services are being offered.

pitch about newspaper subscriptions, financial services, or the latest poll that the person is taking.

➤ When confronted by a telephone solicitor, be polite, but firm. My typical response is, "I'm sorry, but I am just not interested," and then I hang up. Jerry Seinfeld's is, "I'll tell you what, why don't you give me your home phone number, and I'll call you back tomorrow night while *you're* having dinner."

➤ If someone asks if the man or the woman of the house is in, you could say, "No, and I don't know when they will be returning."

➤ Inform the telemarketer that you no longer want to receive solicitation calls regarding the organization she or he is representing.

A Quick 10k (and I Don't Mean a Road Race)

Are you ready for the next part? Calling a consumer who has requested not to be called is a rule violation by a telemarketer, risking a $10,000 civil penalty per violation.

Please note, there are exceptions to the situation, such as when the seller or telemarketer has implemented "Do not call" procedures, but the consumer is called in error. Shucks! If there is a high instance of errors, it may be determined that the procedures are inadequate and thus, it is a rule violation. If there is a low instance of errors, it may not be a rule violation.

The rule is enforced by the Federal Trade Commission. If you have a complaint or want to air any other grievance, send your written information to:

Office of the Director
Bureau of Consumer Protection
Federal Trade Commission
6th & Pennsylvania Avenue, NW
Washington, DC 20580

If you want a complete copy of the telemarketing sales rules that all telemarketers must adhere to, write to:

The Direct Marketing Association
1120 Avenue of the Americas
New York, NY 10036-6700

Dealing with Junk Mailers

Do you realize that the Direct Marketing Association tells its own members that consumers who provide data that may be rented, sold, or exchanged for direct marketing purposes periodically should be informed of the potential for the rental, sale, or exchange of such data, and that list compilers should suppress names from lists when requested by the individual.

To receive fewer national advertiser junk mailings, send your name, address, and phone number to:

> DMA Mail Preference Service
> P.O. Box 9014
> Farmingdale, NY 11735-9014

To resolve a problem with a direct mail company, send your name, address, and phone number; the company's name, address, and phone number; copies of any canceled checks, order forms, or other documents; and a letter summarizing the facts of the complaint to:

> Mail Order Action Line
> Direct Marketing Association
> 1101 17th Street NW, Suite 705
> Washington, DC 20036-4704

The mail order action line will refer the letter to the company on the consumer's behalf and ask that the company resolve the matter. Most complaints are resolved within 30 days.

Here are some additional, little-known tips you can use to ensure that offending parties get your message:

➤ If an item comes to you by first-class mail, currently more than 32 cents or more for letters and 20 cents or more for postcards, you can simply write "Refused" on the outside of the envelope and put it back in your mailbox with the flag up. Your postal carrier will return it to the sender at no cost to you.

➤ If an item comes to you as presorted first-class mail, it means that the item has come to you for a price of 26 cents or more per item. You could also write "Refused" on the outside of the envelope and, again, the postal carrier will return it at no cost to you. The sender got a reduced rate because they did some zip code sorting themselves.

➤ If you receive mail at the true bulk rates, less than 26 cents per item, unfortunately, you can't refuse the mail in the sense of having the postal carrier take it and send it back to the sender. In that case, you'll have to throw it out yourself or pay to have it returned. The Post Office won't return it at no cost.

Much of your junk mail, mercifully, comes at the two higher rates, meaning that you are only seconds away from having it zipped back to the offending party. If it strikes your fancy, you can even get a red rubber stamp that shouts out "Refused" in huge, unmistakable letters.

God Bless This Space

The last way in which you may "lose" control of your home environment comes from within—the clutter that you allow to build up. One of the easiest ways to control your space is to pay homage to what I call the replacement principle. Here's how it works.

Suppose you have accumulated a collection of videos over the years. Some are copies of your favorite movies; others are presidential speeches, sports contests, the Olympics, or maybe—ooh boy—an hour-long Barbara Walters special.

Studies show that 60 percent of what people videotape is never viewed again. That means that out of every 25 tapes that you have, on average, you won't even look at 15 of them again.

I'm not saying you should throw away 15 of your videotapes, I'm just suggesting that when you tape a program, you might copy over one of your existing tapes. When you want to tape a second and third program, you will find a second or third video to tape over. As long as you keep your collection at whatever you deem to be a reasonable number, you'll be able to:

➤ Not spend another dime on a video

➤ Keep in control of the spaces in your life

➤ Demonstrate to yourself that you are capable of restraint

➤ Be a positive example to others in your household who are becoming overrun by their "collections"

When my little girl was three years old, the number of coloring books in her collection reached 18. She had some tough decisions to make. Was it *Pinocchio, Smokey the Bear, Sesame Street,* or *Mother Goose*? I say with all pride, it was surprising to see how she grasped the concept and made intelligent choices even then.

I am not the parent of the year, but hey, the principle spread into other categories in her life. She no longer needed to have 18 of these things, 14 of those, 26 of that, and so forth. She realized that a reasonable amount of cassette tapes, toys, and dolls was more than enough.

Then, every December 20th, we'd go to the Ronald McDonald House and give the excess of her gifts in excellent condition to less fortunate children. The Goodwill, the Salvation Army, and various causes around town also are regular haunts. I only wish that as a child, such practices had been instilled in me.

Retaining Versus Tossing

Sometimes, replacing things simply isn't enough. You have to make a retain/toss decision. This is not easy for many people; after all, tossing can be permanent. Still, to be the master of your castle, you have to acknowledge that on occasion—and in your case, bucko, on frequent occasions—you hold onto too much.

If you don't muster the will to toss all the stuff that you are hanging onto, who will? You and you alone, unless you have a vociferous spouse, must be the self-appointed bearer of clean hallways, closets with excess capacity, and bureau drawers that can still hold more.

The following chart is as succinct as I can get it, covering all manner of items that you may have at home as well as in your office.

When to Retain and When to Toss

Item	Feel Free to Toss or Recycle If...	Feel Free to Retain If...
Business cards, assorted notes:	You have many cards and never call anyone, you can't recall the person, or his goods or services.	You already have a card holder, can scan it, know you'll use it, or feel you will.
Paper, files, documents:	It's old, outdated, uninformative, it's been transferred to disk, or it no longer covers your derriere.	It's your duty to retain, you refer to it often, it has future value, or it comforts you.
Reports, magazines:	It's old, outdated, stacking up, your think you have to retain to "keep up," you fear a quiz on it.	It's vital to your career or well being, you choose to retain it, or there will be quiz on it.
Books, guides, directories:	You've copied, scanned or made notes on the pages of interest, it is obsolete or just became updated.	It's part of your life's collections, you refer to it monthly, it has sentimental value, or you want it.
CDs, cassettes, videos, and A/V:	You never play it, and if you do, it doesn't evoke any feelings or memories. It plays poorly.	You play it, you like it, you couldn't bear to not have it in your collection. It's your keepsake.
Outdated office equipment:	You know who would like it as a donation, you can sell it, it's collecting dust, or it's in the way.	It serves a specific purpose, it adds to the decor, or it can be overhauled or revitalized.
Mementos, memorabilia:	It no longer holds meaning, you have many similar items, you do not have room, you've changed.	It still evokes strong memories, you will hand it down someday, or it looks good on display.
Gifts, cards, presents:	It's never in use, not wanted, and the provider won't know or be concerned that you tossed it.	You use it often, are glad you have it, or are saving it for some special reason.

The Least You Need to Know

➤ An increasing percentage of people have unlisted phone numbers—maybe you need one.

➤ A simple sign that says "No Soliciting" can work wonders.

➤ Because people drop by doesn't mean that you have to entertain them. Make it clear when you will and won't receive visitors.

➤ Be polite but firm when fielding unsolicited phone calls or visitors.

➤ Replace some items and toss others when your collections begin to overrun your home.

Lack of Completions

In This Chapter

➤ Incompletions and why they occur

➤ Stress attached to incompletions

➤ What is incomplete in your life and in your career

➤ Getting complete now and again

➤ Finding completions everywhere

One of the most ineffective stress-management techniques is *worrying*. Worrying occupies your mind, sometimes to a great extent, chews up minutes and hours of the day, and provides nothing. It's analogous to the wheel of a car spinning in the mud while the car goes nowhere.

Worries can be short- or long-term, nagging, insidious forms of stress. What do they have to do with what I call the lack of completions? Plenty. If you consider what you worry about in the course of a day, month, or year, invariably they are issues, no matter how big or small, that are *incomplete*. Suppose that an aging loved one is gravely ill, as a dramatic example, and you worry for weeks or months whether he or she will make it. Then, this person dies. You attend the funeral, grieve deeply, and mourn for months thereafter. However, in regard to this person's health, is there anything more to worry about?

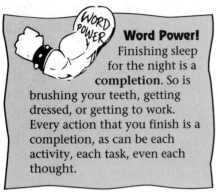

Word Power!
Finishing sleep for the night is a **completion**. So is brushing your teeth, getting dressed, or getting to work. Every action that you finish is a completion, as can be each activity, each task, even each thought.

Here is a second, lesser example. You are a solo entrepreneur, and several clients have been slow to pay. The mortgage on your home is, as always, due on the first of the month, a mere eight days away. No one appears to be moving quickly in response to your invoices. It looks like you are not going to be able to make your mortgage payment on time.

Is the preceding scenario a cause for worry? Perhaps. If you receive the money and make your payment on time, will you have anything more to worry about? Certainly not.

Mentally survey your office, your home, and your life. Equipment that you bought and haven't used, projects that you started but haven't finished, and personal relationships that are a little frayed at the edges—incompletions all—are also potential topics for worry or stress. This chapter shows you how to deal with the incompletions that surround you.

What a Concept!

When a situation is largely resolved (not necessarily 100 percent), it's difficult to drum up any more worry over it, although you can always find other issues to fill the gap.

From Incompletion to Death

I know a psychologist who believes that every incompletion you let build up around you is a stepping stone to a major heart attack. Certainly, people who are chronic worriers can be more susceptible to illness and even major disease. Mounting piles are a highly visible form of incompletions. Incompletions, however, come in many forms:

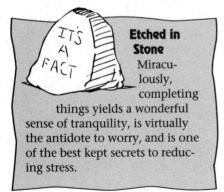

Etched in Stone
Miraculously, completing things yields a wonderful sense of tranquility, is virtually the antidote to worry, and is one of the best kept secrets to reducing stress.

➤ Files left undone

➤ Drawers open

➤ Items purchased but not used

➤ Plans established but not acted upon

In your personal life, the list is endless.

A good way to get complete about a situation over which you're worrying is to say to yourself, "I'm going to give myself five minutes to fret over this, and then I'm going to move on." This works enough of the time to be worthwhile. In essence, you are *getting complete about your excessive concern* over an issue.

You may still be concerned about an issue. Eliminating the *excessive* concern, however, can be a major boon to your day.

> **Word Power!**
> Getting complete is synonymous with coming to terms with an issue, or perhaps actually achieving resolution or closure. It is a mental state that frees you to move on.

In a Sped-up World, Incompletions Proliferate

There is a direct relationship between the speed at which your life unfolds and the potential for incompletions. Look around your office. There are copiers, PCs, fax machines, modems, laser printers, answering machines, dictating equipment, electronic postage meters, scanners, paper shredders, and a variety of other equipment. How many do you know how to fully operate? How many come with thick instruction books?

As you saw in Chapter 6, regardless of your industry or profession, expectations about your performance are at an all-time high. Bosses, coworkers, and customers, in particular, expect a speedy, accurate, and *complete* response.

Concurrently, in an environment where you can both send and receive messages in a millisecond, the potential for incompletions arises. How many e-mail messages received in the last month or more are sitting in your various in-baskets, but you haven't taken any action on them?

Whether it is e-mail or snail mail, equipment or software instruction manuals, or a pile of stuff accumulating in the corner of your office, they all represent an incompletion. And, one incompletion leads to another.

And another.

And another.

The fact that you have much incomplete in your career or life is not, in itself, debilitating. Most people have much incomplete in their lives.

When you are under continual stress, fatigued (see Chapter 13), and have mounting incompletions, the situation feeds on itself. One task merges into the next and the next. You never get true mental relief from the tasks that face you. What occurs is an

> **Warning**
> The introduction of ever-more sophisticated technology ensures that there will be equipment around you that you don't know how to use or use for its fully intended functions.

unending series of incompletions that perceptually make your hours run into days, your days run into weeks, your weeks run into months, your months run into years, your years run into decades.

So, you ask with baited breath, is there a way to get "complete" about the mounting incompletions in your life? But of course! Read on.

Getting Complete Now and Again

On your path to understanding about completions, your primary step is understanding that ultimately, everything reaches completion. Every single pile in your office will, one way or the other, cease to exist in time. Your piles will diminish either because you've acted on them; an earthquake occurs and the building collapses; or you move on, are replaced, or die, and someone takes over your office.

The light bulbs in your fixtures will burn out in 700 to 800 hours, just as your car's water pump will give out in 3.5 years. Jupiter will complete a revolution around the sun in 11.9 years, A tortoise on the Galapagos Islands will draw its last breath, on average, in about 100 years.

Cro-Magnon man lasted about 30,000 years; dinosaurs ruled the earth for a couple hundred million years; the sun's remaining life is about five billion years. Even human-kind will come to a completion at some point.

Your Daily Completions

As simple as it seems, when you wake each morning, you have completed sleep for that night. When you turn in a big report at work and you know it's ready, that is a completion. If you gain nothing from this book but guidance on using completions, you will have benefited greatly.

Go!
Achieving completions is energizing because it offers a clean end to activities or even thoughts and a good beginning for what's next. Be aware of even small completions to give yourself this mental boost.

Large or small, completions provide a mental and emotional break. They help you feel better. Simply putting away the dishes or taking out the garbage are completions that yield benefits. You can continually gain completions in every area of your life. You can achieve them on multi-year projects or activities that only last a few seconds.

To achieve more completions...

➤ Break down tasks to subtasks.

➤ Acknowledge yourself finishing each subtask.

➤ Move on to what's next.

➤ Keep seeking completions.

➤ Keep acknowledging yourself.

Completions All Around

Megan was a systems consultant to several organizations. To complete each engagement, she had to prepare and deliver a final report.

In the past, Megan thought it was enough to write, proof, and e-mail the entire report to the client by the due date. Previously, Megan would tie up loose ends several days or weeks after sending the report while in the midst of other activities.

Recognizing the power of completions, however, Megan...

➤ Built proofing and formatting her report into her schedule.

➤ Updated her files.

➤ Completed project logs.

➤ Calculated cost data.

➤ Prepared invoices.

➤ Streamlined her working notes file.

By viewing all aspects of the engagement as a unit, Megan was able to finish up all related activities. By the time the report was transmitted, Megan was clear mentally and emotionally. She felt good about her accomplishment and was energized to start what came next.

Completions with a Loved One

My father passed away suddenly on February 17, 1977. He experienced his first, and last, heart attack that Thursday morning in Hartford, Connecticut, my birthplace. I was a management consultant in Vernon, Connecticut. I had last seen him on Monday of the same week.

I have come to believe that the sudden death of loved ones, particularly when you didn't get a chance to talk to them again, is doubly upsetting, because:

1. You have lost someone dear.

2. You weren't able to get complete.

The phone call from my brother, Richard, came at about 9:30 a.m. "Father stopped breathing. It doesn't look good. I've called the ambulance, and they're taking him to Mount Sinai Hospital." I raced from my office in Vernon with dread. Hoping against hope, I sped into Hartford and pulled over as the very ambulance carrying my father passed me. Thirty seconds later, I trailed him into the emergency ward.

Shortly after hearing the doctor's cushioned blow, I asked one of the nurses if I could be with my father. Then I faced the physical shell of what had been to me a force larger than life.

He "stared" blankly at the ceiling. It was as if a light switch, a life switch, had simply been turned off. Yet, his massive frame was everything it had been.

I felt sad for all the simple pleasures that he would never experience again. Then and there, I told him of the deep sorrow I had for the experiences he would never realize—grandchildren, retirement, travel. I had no regrets for the relationship between us. Somehow, years before I knew about completions, I had to see my father one last time, talk to him, and tell him everything would be all right. I have since learned that some people are able to get complete with a departed one even years afterward.

The passing of my mother 14 years later was somewhat "easier to take," as if those words can be used to describe a profound loss. My mother's health was rapidly deteriorating. One Monday in February, she entered the hospital, and we knew that she would not be exiting.

We got to visit her on the tenth floor of the Hartford Hospital several times. We were able to reflect on our times and relationships. Other people came to pay their respects. When I left her hospital room one Wednesday morning, I sensed that it was the last time I would see her on this earthly plane.

Her death wasn't as sorrowful as I thought it would be. Knowingly or unknowingly, my mother had enabled each of us to be complete about her passing.

Today, 20 years after my father's departure, and 5 years after my mother's, I still wish I could have had more time to be with my father, as I experienced with my mother. Death cares not.

When someone you love dies suddenly, this may help:

➤ Talk to them as if they were still alive.

➤ Tell them how you feel.

➤ Feel their energy still present.

➤ Leave after you compose yourself.

Completions in the Face of Chaos

It is fundamental to your existence and well-being to continually have completions of whatever magnitude in your life, even if you have to look for the completion in the face of a stressful situation that seems beyond your control.

Here's a career-related example of completion thinking. The only time I've ever been late in my 14-year speaking career occurred in November, 1992. I had booked the first flight out of the Raleigh-Durham International airport on my trip to Washington, D.C. I was to speak to the U.S. Treasury Executives Institute at 9:00 a.m. I was scheduled to fly at 6:50 a.m., and the flight time was only 35 minutes. There were several other flights to D.C. leaving soon after mine on other airlines. Thus, I felt reasonably assured that I would be there on time.

As we rolled onto the runway, the pilot announced that there would be a delay. "No problem," I thought. "I'll still be there with plenty of time." After ten minutes, I became concerned. Finally, another announcement came. We would have to go back to the gate because something was wrong with the plane. Now I was steamed. We were a half-hour behind schedule, and even if I could get on another plane within 10 or 15 minutes, I would arrive at Washington National Airport at 8:15 or 8:20 a.m., and that would be pushing it to arrive at the site with grace and ease before 9:00.

Why do the airlines wait until you are in the plane, seated, and ready to roll, before announcing a delay? If I had known, I could have quickly gotten on one of several other flights. In this case, the pilot did not actually know that there was going to be a problem until he got to the runway.

I finally did get a flight up to D.C. and landed at about 8:40 a.m. I called the client from the airport. Then I quickly jumped into a cab and prayed that this driver could get through the D.C. morning rush hour and get me to the site somewhere close to 9:00. In the back of the cab, I had a choice to make: I could be totally stressed out over being late on so momentous an occasion, or I could seek completion of the morning's events and be free to direct my energy more appropriately.

Here's how my thoughts unfolded:

"OK, I'm late. I accept that."

"There are a dozen things I could have done differently, such as depart the night before, but all other scenarios are simply moot at this point."

"I am in the back of a cab, on my way to the client's site."

"I feel complete about my career."

"I feel complete about the plane ride."

"I feel complete about my capabilities."

"I choose to feel relaxed."

"I'll get the cab fare ready in advance and pay the driver the moment we stop."

Upon arriving at the building, now 9:12 a. m., I thought:

"I am complete about this cab ride."

"I am walking purposefully but not hurriedly into the building."

"I am walking purposefully to the elevator."

"I am complete about reaching the fourth floor."

"I am entering the room with poise and confidence."

"I am greeting the client."

"I am assuring him that I am ready to go."

"I feel complete about my entrance."

"I am starting the session with energy."

Consequently, I started the session at 9:16 a.m. Not a catastrophe. It was a late start, but one I could make up by the noon ending time.

During that 2 hour and 44 minute presentation, I was at my best. I wove in anecdotes and stories to make my session come alive. About an hour into my presentation, when we got to the section on completions, I used the morning's incident as part of the session. That helped everyone in the room become complete about my not being there on time and about how each of us, on occasion, runs into similar circumstances.

The client was thrilled with the presentation and soon hired me back for seven more. When I left Washington that day, I gave myself mental completions about my performance, about exiting the building, about making my way back to the airport, about the flight home, and so on.

I also got complete about taking flights the same morning as a scheduled presentation. I don't do it anymore.

Getting Complete in the Face of Too Much Data

Suppose that you face a daily deluge of information (which, based on Chapter 11, you know to be true).

Let's look at what you can do in a situation where much of the information you take in comes as a result of downloading from the Internet or other sources. Before you encounter mounds of new information, eliminate what is not useful to you.

➤ Create a default "download" directory on your hard drive or on the network and specify this directory in the "preferences" section of your favorite Internet software. This way, you will always know where to find freshly downloaded files instead of having to search your computer system.

➤ Create directories into which you'll transfer important files from your default download directory—after you confirm their long-term usefulness.

➤ Download only the information that will truly support you. Instead of downloading a file you might use only occasionally, bookmark its address and leave the information on the Internet.

➤ Knowing that you'll be saving Internet addresses, create a computer file for storing and organizing them.

It takes preparation to get complete. Once you begin striving for completion, though, the payoffs are so tremendous that you won't avoid the preparation. Sure, you're already inundated with rules, guidelines, and checklists. Seeking completion, however, isn't a bunch of rules, *it's a way of being.*

Letting Others Get Complete

Completion thinking helps you (and, potentially, others) deal with this very moment, and the next, and the next. Suppose that you are in a business where you distribute goods to customers, and they expect very high performance standards. Sometimes, no matter how well your system is functioning, things are bound to go awry.

When your customers are counting on you for timely delivery, but something is temporarily out of your control, the best that you can do for both you and them is to get complete about the situation. The moment you are aware of any problems, I suggest that you inform the customer. That enables him to get complete about the situation as well.

I know people who, when due to arrive at 6:00, call at 6:00 to say that they will be 30 minutes late. They think as long as they call by 6:00 that they have temporarily met their responsibilities. They haven't. If you are expected at a certain time and you know

Go!
Invariably, you will find that customers are understanding about tough situations and your attempts to resolve them. This beats withholding information, and keeping you and the customer from being complete about what is transpiring. The sooner you inform a customer about a situation, the more content the customer will be.

you cannot make it, the onus is on you to be complete about your lateness and let the other party know as soon as possible.

If you know at 5:40 that you are not going to make it by 6:00, call at 5:40. This lets the other party readjust and get complete about the fact that you will not be meeting at 6:00.

Completion in the Face of Procrastination

In many ways, procrastination is the antithesis of completion. I am not condoning procrastination, but I understand why it happens. The more things competing for your time and attention, the more stressors impacting you during the day, the greater the probability that you are going to put off some things. The problem is that when you begin to have piles and piles of minor tasks, perceptibly they all begin to loom larger, and your stress level goes up.

If the lack of completions is chronic, such as when there are piles all over your desk and all the other flat surfaces in your life, you may be approaching the danger level that I discussed at the beginning of this chapter. Certainly, your life and career have reached points of immobility on several fronts.

Go! Often, the key to getting started is *to not look for the logical beginning* and not even wait until the time is right.

One woman claimed that she became paralyzed and always had a difficult time writing anything—whether letters to friends or reports for top management. Her solution came when she decided to merely begin writing and not be concerned about how well she was doing or even if she had started at the beginning.

Here are some other suggestions to break through procrastination and achieve completions:

➤ Line up all the project materials the night before with the intention of starting tomorrow. Then sleep on it.

➤ Develop a clear vision of how you'll feel once you achieve completion.

➤ Look for three to five small tasks that you can initiate quickly and easily. The momentum from handling these may prompt you to stay on track.

➤ Promise yourself that you'll only work on an activity for five minutes. Thereafter, you may not want to stop.

➤ Find a partner who will help you get started and stay with it long enough so that you are fully immersed in the project.

The Art of Doing One Thing at a Time

When I am bouncing from one project to another, it can be somewhat psychologically satisfying. After all, one could say to the world, "Look at me; look how busy I am," or "Look at how important I am. I've got these multiple demands on my time."

Here are some tips for getting back to that sweet mind-set where you are able to tackle one thing at a time:

➤ Determine which tasks you can complete entirely on your own, versus those that require the input of others. Then schedule accordingly. If you know that you cannot meet with John until Tuesday, complete all the tasks that you can on your own on Monday.

➤ Give yourself quiet time throughout the day. Set aside 5, 10, or 15 minutes to close your eyes and let some of the tension wind down. Take some deep breaths. Let your forehead relax, your neck relax, and your shoulders relax.

➤ Get complete about where you are, what you have accomplished, and what you will tackle next. As you saw earlier, getting complete about the present energizes you for tackling what's next.

When you face a challenging situation, define for yourself, mentally or on paper, the precise steps that you need to take to be successful. When I was in graduate school, I had a professor I will never forget. Zenon Malinowski taught statistics to the MBA class at the University of Connecticut.

Dr. Malinowski's major premise was that until you precisely define a problem, you cannot solve it. Week after week, he threw questions at us that could be solved using statistics, but only if we were able to first accurately determine what was being asked. Then, our solutions, no less, had to be couched in careful terms that precisely described the statistical probability of an event occurring.

> **Warning**
> The temporary psychic satisfaction of "balancing several tasks" is more than offset by long-term stress and dissatisfaction of having too many things left undone and piling up. Don't let juggling become procrastination.

When 90 Percent Is Complete

Some tasks that you face do not require a 100 percent effort on your part for you to achieve completion. Let me explain. A study showed that many projects submitted within a company were 90 to 95 percent "correct" as originally submitted.

When such projects were returned to the project managers, it took them another 50 percent of the original project time to reach "perfection." In other words, if you spent two hours on XYZ and were able to get it 90 to 95 percent correct, it would take you another hour to finish the last 5 to 10 percent.

Go! For projects that don't require 100 percent precision, and in the course of your day and week there undoubtedly are many, you will save hours, if not days, by *not* reworking the project. Turn your attention, instead, to completing another project—which will help reduce your stress!

That last 5 to 10 percent is often the more stressful, as you try to get every i dotted and t crossed. Some projects demand 100 percent precision; many others like these don't, so don't stress yourself out by working on them unless you're specifically asked to:

➤ Internal project notes

➤ Memos between staffs

➤ Rough prototypes

➤ Draft reports

➤ Research on inconsequential items

The Least You Need to Know

➤ New technology, increased expectations, and change in general, all potentially contribute to more incompletions in your life.

➤ The more incompletions in your life, the more stress tends to accumulate.

➤ Completions are mental partitions between tasks, activities, or even thoughts.

➤ The art of doing one thing at a time enhances your ability to achieve completions.

➤ Many tasks that you face don't require 100 percent "correctness" for you to move on.

Part 5
Getting Your Stress Level Back Down

By now you know that the deck is stacked against anyone trying to live with a minimum of stress. Part 5 contains five chapters that specifically address techniques that you can use when stressors crop up.

In Chapter 16, "Becoming the Master of Your Environment," I discuss how to reduce stress levels and recharge your batteries by knowing how and when to pause throughout the day. Some of the best times and places to pause will surprise you. One step further, Chapter 17, "Perfecting the Strategic Pause," takes you into the world of meditation, guided imagery, yoga, and other techniques that people use successfully to stay in control of stress.

Chapter 18, "Asking the Magic Question," offers questions you can ask yourself to dislodge maladaptive behaviors. We all play a part in creating the stress we encounter, and these powerful, profound questions will help you get to the root of what may be stressing you.

Chapter 19, "Choosing When It's Confusing," discusses how you can flourish despite an overabundance of choices, the importance of narrowing your parameters, and making effective purchase decisions.

Chapter 20, "Choosing to Have Less Stress," offers you simple, but deceptively powerful, choices about your day, week, career, and life that will have a profound impact.

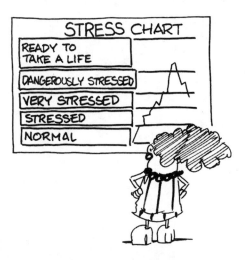

Chapter 16

Becoming the Master of Your Environment

In This Chapter

➤ All about the strategic pause

➤ Second, third, and even fourth winds

➤ Haste can waste you

➤ How to control your immediate environment

I moved to Washington, D.C. in 1977. My third week there, I was at a party talking with three women when someone asked the four of us if we would like tickets to the *Westside Waltz*, with Katherine Hepburn, playing at the Kennedy Center. I barely knew one of the women; but the four of us took immediate advantage of the offer.

What I am about to explain accounts for why I can recall the details of this evening so vividly. We got to the seats—and they were good ones—with about eight minutes to spare. We were in the balcony, dead center, about two rows back. It was a thrill to be at the Kennedy Center for the first time, with free tickets, seeing Katherine Hepburn.

Several minutes into the second act, while Miss Hepburn (it is never "Ms." with Miss Hepburn) was delivering a line, someone took a flash picture of her. This, of course, is forbidden in the Kennedy Center and during theatrical plays in general.

Miss Hepburn stopped in her tracks and for a few seconds seemed to be in a trance. Then she broke out of character, walked a couple of paces to the front of the stage, and peered intensely at the perpetrator.

"How rude! How utterly rude," she said in a voice and tone that the offender, let alone I and probably everyone else in the hall, will never forget. I was so embarrassed, *I* wanted to disappear, and I hadn't even done anything! Imagine how the guy felt who had snapped the picture.

Quite magically, she then retreated to her position on stage, metamorphosed before our eyes, and become her character again. She picked up her lines right where she had left them. The rest of the play continued without a hitch.

It took me all these years to understand the phenomenon in its full context. Katherine Hepburn was the master of her environment, certainly on stage, and no boorish, unauthorized, amateur photographer would have the temerity to ever "invade" her space like that again. What's more, Miss Hepburn was able to keep her stress in check by responding to the offending source, in the moment, air her views on the matter, however dramatic, and then move past it.

I've never had the opportunity to speak to Miss Hepburn, and I didn't read any reviews or newspaper columns the following day. I can surmise, however, that she carried no residue of the incident following that performance. Also, it became abundantly clear for me why Katherine Hepburn had endured so long and so prominently on the stage and screen—in an ultra-competitive profession that offers little mercy, you are only as good as your last performance, and your next performance may be your last. All of us need to act with control, which in turn will help reduce the feeling that we're experiencing stress.

All About the Strategic Pause

Who knows if such an incident had happened to Katherine Hepburn previously. Perhaps not. She conveyed to me that she was the master of the *strategic pause*. She dealt with an acute stressor as it arose. What would have happened if she had simply ignored the flash?

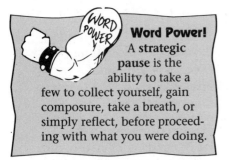

Word Power!
A strategic pause is the ability to take a few to collect yourself, gain composure, take a breath, or simply reflect, before proceeding with what you were doing.

Would the offender have tried it again?

Would others have attempted it?

Would she have been as sharp in portraying her character for the rest of the performance? Would the others in the play have been as sharp?

How would she have felt about herself for having let the perpetrator soil her art?

In your world, you can't read enough books, take enough courses, attend enough seminars, or make enough observations that will provide the "sacred scrolls" for functioning effectively in a world filled with stressors. The major component to keeping your level of stress in check is to become, to the degree that you can, a master of your immediate environment.

This is aided by the ability to pause, even fleetingly, so that you can assess where you are and take action, in the moment, to maintain control. The pause could be merely seconds, or several minutes. In the Katherine Hepburn example, it was a couple of seconds, but clearly, she rapidly undertook some reflection and acted.

You're always getting encouragement to speed up—read more, take in more, do more. Sometimes, however, the best response to a situation is not to proceed rapidly, but take a strategic pause, whereby you give yourself a chance to:

➤ Take a deep breath or get a glass of water.

➤ Compose yourself.

➤ Collect your thoughts.

➤ Creatively address the situation.

At your workplace, unfortunately, motion and activity are probably valued more than thought and reflection. Sometimes, the most important thing to do, when confronted with an issue, is to simply sit and think. I saw a clever book title once that encapsulates my observation: *Don't Just Do Something, Sit There*.

Go!
When you go home at the end of the day, it's easy to use your family as a sounding board for what went wrong, but you're upsetting your home environment. It's better to take a few minutes to sit quietly, allow the tribulations of the workday to dissipate, and then be the spouse or parent you know you can be.

The Strategic Pause Can Be Illusory

Frequently, you see apparent go-getters, people who work around the clock, seemingly never stopping to take a breath, accomplishing all kinds of activities. Be careful in your observations. You are only seeing the proverbial "tip of the iceberg," the top 10 percent, whereas 90 percent of the "iceberg" is submerged in the water.

Etched in Stone
Those who accomplish great things understand the value of taking a strategic pause, resetting their body's clock, reflecting, and getting back in control of their personal environment.

Completely Missing the Point

A major magazine editorial lauded a senior writer who died of a massive heart attack at age 44. They described him as a bright personality, first-rate intellect, and consummate professional. The editorial/obituary said that this fellow did an extraordinary number of things extraordinarily well. He vigorously filled his post and also wrote extensively about politics, social issues, the media, and books. In addition to those things, he frequently appeared on TV panels, ready to express provocative, but well thought-out opinions. This gentleman lectured, wrote books, and freelanced for other publications. Amazingly, they say that he had a wide, varied circle of friends, people at every level.

I was aghast when the editorial/obituary said that this fellow rarely did *fewer than two things at once* (italics mine) and lauded him for doing so. He read his mail while discussing story ideas. When he went to lunch with a coworker, he often took a book. Apparently, he never turned down an assignment, and he attacked the most mundane task as if Heaven and Earth depended on it. The piece concluded by observing that this gentleman had a forthcoming book wherein he decried that it was plainly evident that some individuals are better than others—more intelligent, industrious, hard-working, inquisitive, productive, and harder to replace.

Don't the good people at this magazine understand that cramming everything into your life at hyperspeed leads to an early death?

I wrote to the magazine following this commentary, although I didn't expect them to answer. I asked, "Where was the reflection in his life? When did he pause? When did he ever reset his body clock?" I understood that he was a notable individual, but to praise him publicly for doing two things at once and in the same breath recount that he died of "a massive heart attack at 44" is dripping with irony.

This person was the antithesis of someone who masters his environment. Rather, he allowed all assignments, all intellectual queries, all interests, anything that appeared on his personal radar screen, *to master him.*

Breaking a Problem Down

Here is an example of how one could dissect a situation and formulate a strategy to alleviate the feeling of lack of control.

National moving companies have data indicating that when an employee of a company is transferred, the employee's spouse experiences more stress than the employee. This is understandable for many reasons. The employee…

➤ Knows something about what he or she will be doing in the new job.

➤ Perhaps has visited the new city.

➤ Perhaps had a hand in selecting the new locale.

➤ Perhaps is receiving a promotion or raise that positively reinforces that move.

➤ Will know some people in advance.

➤ Has been mentally gearing up for the move.

The spouse, on the other hand...

➤ May not have visited the city.

➤ May know no one in advance.

➤ May be mentally resisting the move.

If the spouse were to pause strategically sometime weeks or months before the move, what could he or she do to have some control over the new personal environment?

➤ Take a weekend or more to visit the new location in an unhurried manner.

➤ Find out about schools and colleges, places of worship, community groups, and so on.

➤ Subscribe to the local newspaper and any weekly or monthly local or regional publications.

➤ Write to the Chamber of Commerce and request a list of businesses, family support services, and maps.

➤ Write to the Welcome Wagon.

➤ Write to the state office of tourism and request information about resorts, beaches, mountains, lakes, streams, and hiking paths.

What About You?

In your life, what are some general techniques that you could use daily to pause, collect your thoughts, reduce your level of stress, and move on with relative grace and ease? Here are some suggestions:

➤ Close your eyes for as little as 60 seconds and visualize a pleasurable scene. It could be a waterfall, a favorite hiking trail, a mountaintop view, the shoreline, a campfire, or simply the image of a loved one.

➤ As a variation on this theme, with your eyes closed, listen to music with your headphones. When you concentrate solely on music that you like, giving it your undivided attention, time begins to expand. A three- or four-minute song seems to last 10 minutes.

➤ Allow your sense of smell, taste, or touch, to dominate. For the next several minutes, close your eyes and simply explore your immediate environment by touch only. Yes, I know that you already know how these things will feel when you touch them. Make a game out of it. Pretend that your sense of touch is the only vehicle that you have for understanding your environment. When you open your eyes again, the world will look a little different, and things will be a little less intense.

Go! Anytime you can visualize a pleasurable scene, it is like resetting your internal clock. You get an immediate "time out." Think of it as a vacation of the mind. When you return to where you are, invariably, you will be in at least a slightly better frame of mind.

➤ Do the same with your sense of smell. If you are in an office environment, and think that you don't have options, look around you. Perhaps there is a non-toxic smelling magic marker nearby. How about a flower or a lead pencil or a cup of coffee? When have you ever stopped and actually smelled the coffee?

➤ Play with Rover. Interacting with pets enables you to reset your internal clock. A growing body of evidence shows that pets have a calming, tranquil effect on people.

Breathing Is the Key

An increasing body of evidence indicates that panic disorders, in part, are respiration disorders. In other words, the onset of panic is often due to improper breathing on the part of the victim. Doctors observe that panic patients frequently practice chest breathing, which requires the use of more muscles and energy to draw shallower breaths than diaphragmatic breathing. The typical adult uses the diaphragm muscles below the lungs to breathe, which yields a deeper, less taxing, more easily achievable breath.

Go! If you can control your breathing, you can actually control the beat of your heart and most other symptoms of stress that you experience. Such a deal.

Breathing is fundamental to your ability to function optimally and maintain a feeling of ease and control. Phil Jackson, coach of the Chicago Bulls, notes that when he feels anxious or out of control, especially during an intense moment in a game, it's because he is shortchanging his breathing in some way. When he focuses on his breath and gets back to a normal rhythm, he more readily regains control.

Second, Third, and Even Fourth Winds

When you think about it, there are plenty of times throughout the day when you can stop and get a second, third, or even fourth wind by exercising your right to a strategic pause. Unfortunately, all too often, your internal motor is revving a little too high, and you miss the opportunity. Think about the last time that you stood in a bank line that was moving too slowly for you. Did you fidget and fret because you wanted to be out of there? If so, you added to the stresses of the day.

The next time that you are in any line that is moving too slowly for you, may I suggest the following? Use the opportunity to

➤ Take some deep breaths.

➤ Straighten your back.

➤ Envision a pleasant scene.

➤ Get complete about what you have accomplished so far today (see Chapter 15 on completions).

Following are some other opportune places to pause, perhaps where you least expect there to be a pause.

A Plane Seat, Train Seat, Bus Seat, or Back of a Cab

When you are being transported by others, given that there isn't undue concern for your safety, you have a wonderful opportunity to pause and reflect.

The odds of your demise while the passenger of a vehicle are very slim indeed. In fact, they are much lower than when you are driving. Use the opportunity of being in motion but not having to steer to best advantage. The longer the ride, the longer you get to pause.

Before Dinner

Rather than wolf down your food, stop and reflect how great it is that you are about to eat. Think about how the food is going to taste before you actually taste it. Many people recite a prayer (see Chapter 17) for the "bounty which we are about to receive," and if that works for you, splendid.

Before Making Love

Especially if you are in love with your partner, what a wonderful time to momentarily dwell upon where you are in life. You are about to partake of some of the essence of another person.

During Athletic Contests

Have you ever noticed that the best foul shooters in basketball take an extra couple of seconds before releasing their shot? The best hitters in baseball stare into the field, get firmly set, and then look at the pitcher. In all sports, there is an advantage in taking a strategic pause at opportune moments to maintain a higher level of personal control.

When Getting Chewed Out

This may seem like the least likely time to pause, but if you do, you are in a better position to defuse inflammatory situations.

Much of the anger that other people direct at you is self-correcting; that is, later they will apologize for overstepping their boundaries or for blowing their stack. Moreover, your most appropriate response is not likely to come if you respond in anger. When you pause and rather matter-of-factly reflect on the situation, you have a much better chance of responding in a way that is helpful to both parties.

What a Concept!

When a boss, or spouse for that matter, is incensed and you are the object of their wrath you can gain insights by pausing that you might not gain if you simply jump into the fray.

There is a compelling scene in the movie *Crimson Tide* where Gene Hackman smacks Denzel Washington on the jaw twice. It is a dramatic moment in which the two men's differences on whether to launch a nuclear missile towards Russia come to a head. Part of the drama is that Washington's character is much younger, bigger, and more physically fit than Hackman's, and it would be no sweat to take Hackman out with one punch.

Washington would be justified in striking back. After both blows, instead, he puts his hand to his jaw as if to survey the damage and to relieve some of the pain, and then looks back at his attacker with an almost curious detachment. Washington is pausing and reflecting on an issue of importance to humankind. There are three minutes left before the decision to launch the missile has to be made. The men are awaiting crucial information that will affect the decision.

Washington's ability to reflect on the potential for global thermonuclear war greatly outweighed the momentary pain and discomfort of being struck.

Mastering Your Space

Just as mastering the strategic pause gives you a sense of control in your interactions with others, becoming a master of your environment can improve your ability to control stress.

Your thoughts, feelings, and actions are shaped to a great extent by your surroundings. In her book, *The Power of Place: How Our Surroundings Shape Our Thoughts, Emotions, and Actions*, Winifred Gallagher says that the reason "we work so hard to keep our surroundings predictable is that we rely on them to help us move smoothly from role to role throughout the day."

The right furnishings, enough space, and the proper tools make a considerable difference in your output and frame of mind.

The power of arranging one's surroundings to achieve harmony and prosperity has long been known in the Far East, and only recently in the West. The Asians call it *feng shui*. At the corporate level, it might involve designing a landscape around a building in a specific way to nurture employees as they enter or exit. Or, as Motorola did in its office in Phoenix, constructing two waterfalls at the entrance so that employees will resonate in favorable ways.

There are many ways to master your environment:

➤ Set up your desk for the way that you actually work (see Chapter 7).

➤ Minimize disruptions. Let people know when it's best to call, best to visit, best to leave you alone (see Chapter 8).

➤ Create a quiet environment. Employ a room divider or sound barrier, if needed, or a white noise machine (see Chapter 14).

➤ Find alternative quiet locations (see Chapter 8).

➤ Control the room atmospherics. Ensure that you have the right temperature, adjusted to your liking, and the right lighting.

➤ Have amenities on hand. This might include having tissues, light snacks, a bottle of water, or breath mints.

Go!
Curiously, unless you work for yourself, you're probably never consulted about the design of the place where you work. That's why it's fundamental that you take it upon yourself to control your personal environment.

All of this requires you to strategically pause, reflect on your work situation, and then take action. You may have heard the old joke about the construction worker who opens his lunch box at noon each day, and complains that it's always a bologna sandwich. After several days of this, a coworker asks, "Why don't you ask your wife to make you something else?" The first fellow replies, "What do you mean? I make my own lunch."

So it is with your office and other environments. You create your own environment, although there are extenuating influences and impediments to your having total control.

In your home environment, as you saw in Chapter 14, there are many strategies for dealing with solicitors, uninvited guests, phone calls, mail, and other factors that may converge and contribute to your being anything but a master of your personal environment.

Go!
Becoming a master of your personal environment will enable you to become more productive, and you will experience less stress than if you resign to accepting things as you found them.

A Nice Place to Visit

When I was a teenager, my mother redecorated our upstairs bathroom with snazzy wallpaper, a new shower curtain, pictures on the wall, and some flower arrangements—even a bowl of those multicolored, circular, aromatic mini-soaps that nobody uses. I didn't understand why she went to all that trouble. After all, it was only a bathroom, and everybody knows what you do there. Yet, in retrospect, I understand it perfectly. She was conditioning an environment in which she knew that she would spend at least 30 minutes out of every day of her life. (Of course, today, designer bathrooms are all the rage in California.)

Expanding this concept a little further, what do you see the moment you walk into your house? Is it simply a hallway, with a coat rack, a side table, a closet door half open, and a well-worn rug runner on a well-worn rug? How many times over the next 12 months do you want to have that as your opening environment upon your return? 365 times? With a little imagination and hardly any expense, you could convert your first view upon returning home to something more pleasant, upbeat, need I say it, inspiring! Paint costs very little; so do rug runners. A simple portrait or a silk flower arrangement won't even set you back $20. A new improved light fixture or higher wattage bulbs, can immeasurably brighten the cavern.

How about the view when you enter your bedroom. Is your supposed sanctuary cluttered with more furniture than you need or use? Are any shelves, tables, or night stands strewn with clutter? How about the decor? Has it been the same since 1988? Do you even notice?

Extending the concept once more, what about when you step into your kitchen, living room, or den? How about your garage, what about your closets?

Do you control the spaces of your life, or do they control you?

The Least You Need to Know

- ➤ Take a deep breath and collect your thoughts as often as you need to throughout the day.
- ➤ Anytime that you can visualize a pleasurable scene, you get an immediate "time out."
- ➤ Breathing deeply is the key to life and can help you control your reaction to the current situation that confronts.
- ➤ Your thoughts, feelings, and actions are shaped by your surroundings.
- ➤ Mastery of your personal environment will enable you to become more productive, and you will experience less stress.

Cleansing breath...

Perfecting the Strategic Pause

Chapter 17

In This Chapter

➤ Stuff you don't need

➤ Popular techniques worth a try

➤ You, too, can relax in minutes

Taking a few minutes out of a hectic day can spell the difference between frenzy and tranquillity, and if you have been experiencing severe stress, it might mean the difference between a long life and checking out early.

People throughout the ages have engaged in all manners of behavior to reduce stress. In this chapter, I am going to focus on what consistently works for people, what is safe, and what you can practice with confidence.

First, What You Don't Need

People have long used drugs (prescribed and otherwise!) and medications to achieve certain effects (see Chapter 21). I'm not knocking all these substances—some of them probably live up to their mystique.

Warning
Heating pads and all other devices run by electricity emit electro-magnetic waves, which could be harmful to cell reproduction.

However, I would say that for many people, there is no need to take drugs because there are so many other ways to effectively reduce stress.

Amidst the flurry of reports from medical researchers, many people also rely on a glass or two of wine each day to relax. Who am I to argue with medical researchers? I'm concerned, however, about the long-term effects of having, say, two glasses of wine, 365 days a year, for 10 or 20 years. Still, if this is your habit, and it works for you, you're on reasonably safe ground.

Heatin' Up

If you've been in a hot tub, you know that it does offer the sensation of relaxation.

For some people, elevating their body's temperature for longer than 20 minutes could be doing more harm than good, especially pregnant women and anyone with a history of heart disease.

Heating pads have also been popular for several decades. For one night, for an adult, you're probably okay.

Forget Bio Dots and Stress Cards

You may have seen a device sometimes referred to as a *stress control card*, or a *biofeedback card*, about the size and shape of a credit card. Don't bother with these. Variations in your skin's temperature render them highly misleading.

Stuff That Works

The rest of this chapter focuses on combatting stress in ways that are completely safe, not habit forming, and not likely to give you false information. There are hundreds of techniques for reducing stress, but you're busy, so I've chosen a select group, starting with what may already be easy and familiar to you and working up to what may be less familiar and a little more involved. You'll need on-site guidance with the more involved techniques such as centering and yoga.

You may recall that in the introduction I said that the changes you implement should come most readily without too much pain, be subtle, and even be natural and easy. Otherwise, you won't stick with them. Lasting and effective change can come from small incremental change. So as you read, keep in mind that not every technique will strike your fancy. That's okay. Enough of them will fit your lifestyle and will work for you enough of the time for you to stay with them and to ultimately exercise control in ways that you have always wanted to.

Prayer and Spirituality

Since people first believed in gods, prayer or any similar form of reflection or contemplation of things larger than one's self has been an effective method of soothing the soul. For some people, the payoff comes with sitting still and being quiet. Many feel a direct connection with their god, which in itself is calming. Those who attend a place of worship every week find that praying with others is comforting.

Go!
Reverence to a higher power, fellowship, and familiar chants and hymns can all aid in reducing stress and bringing inner contentment.

If you haven't prayed in a while, in addition to the religious aspects, the stress reduction can be magnificent. Even if you never attend a formal prayer service, some informal prayer, by your bedside, in a comfortable chair, or somewhere in nature can work just as well.

Talking to Someone

The act of talking to someone about issues confronting you can reduce stress, and is certainly more effective than mentally stewing over things alone. In *The Psychological Society*, author Martin L. Gross concludes that "the modern industry of psychology in America was no more effective in treating patients than witch doctors in Africa were in treating people who came to them." The key was whether *the patient believed the doctor had healing powers*. Hence, if you believe that a witch doctor can help you, then a witch doctor can be as effective as a psychiatrist.

What a Concept!

A trusted friend or relative, with whom you can discuss your problems, can be effective.

The idea of talking to someone about what is stressing you is not so much that you will find a solution, but that *the mere act of discussing the stressor moves you closer to resolution*, perhaps using one of the techniques discussed in this chapter.

Using Humor

Throughout the ages, humor has also been a primary tool in helping to reduce stress. Please don't discount the power of humor before trying it. If it's been awhile, or forever, since you engaged in humor to reduce stress, you're in for a treat. I'm not talking about jokes or side-splitting belly laughs, but rather, a gleeful, playful acceptance of the inane and absurd situations that you encounter. Most, but certainly not all, of the trials and tribulations that you face have a flip side to them, something that's weird, wild, witty, or wacky enough for you to crack a grin.

What a Concept!

The ability to laugh at yourself or to laugh at your situation may spell the difference between people who show resilience in the face of hard times and those who face nervous breakdowns.

Visualization

I refer to *visualization* throughout the book without explanation because you engage in visualization all the time. The examples and suggestions that I offer are designed to get you to focus on positive, pleasant, stress reducing scenes.

Go!
If you only have a few minutes alone at home or at work, visualization can be just your cup of tea.

The supreme benefit of visualization, like prayer, talking to someone, and using humor, is that your time investment to get a good return is minimal.

Visualization, also called *imaging*, is a simple process where you conjure up a mental image of something that conveys happiness, warmth, or peaceful feelings for you. For example, you might remember a meadow or farm from your childhood, a waterfall, a picnic site, a scene from a movie, a favorite cousin, or a lover. By focusing on the image for even as little as a minute or two, you can achieve a drop in pulse, heart rate, and even blood pressure.

Some people suggest closing your eyes and placing your hand on your chest, cheek, or forehead while visualizing a pleasant scene because this helps to connect your body with the image that you conjure up.

Visualizing the Future

Visualization can help you sail more easily through things that have *not yet happened*. For example, basketball players attempting to get better at foul shooting found that by visualizing themselves stepping up to the line and having the shot go in, over and over, the actual foul shot percentage rose in game situations.

Likewise, many Olympic performers on all levels visualize themselves going through their routines, be it speed skating, gymnastics, or throwing the javelin, and actually improve performance once they step into the competitive arena.

Suppose you fear making presentations or confronting your boss about an issue. If you will first visualize yourself successfully handling the situation, you will increase the probability of success. You can even write a short statement about your visualization or a whole article about what you did and how it worked. In this respect, you "live into your visualization."

What a Concept!

Visualization works well because your brain can recall anything that it has ever experienced and particularly pleasurable things that it has experienced.

Chicken Soup for Success

My friend Mark Victor Hanson had written several books since the mid 1980s, none best sellers. When he and his pal, Jack Canfield, thought about the idea for what eventually would become *Chicken Soup for the Soul*, before they ever came up with the title, they envisioned coming up with what Mark called a "million dollar title." After many weeks, the title *Chicken Soup for the Soul* emerged.

When the book was first published, however, there was little fanfare. So Mark took a copy of the *New York Times* bestseller list and, using the same font and point size, he pasted over *Chicken Soup for the Soul* by Mark Victor Hanson and Jack Canfield, in the #1 position for nonfiction books. He put the altered bestseller list on his wall, where he could see it everyday. He drew dynamic energy from it.

After the book's success, I wrote to Mark and told him, "You are the best example of someone who clearly envisioned himself to spectacular success."

Guided Imagery

Guided imagery is much like visualization except that you employ the services of another person, who takes you through a series of steps designed to bring you to a more relaxed state. The instructor or group leader may first ask you to close your eyes, sit erect but comfortably, and perhaps concentrate on some part of your body or your breathing.

Go! In nearly every city, you can enroll in adult education programs taught by instructors skilled in guided imagery, progressive relaxation, visualization, and virtually every technique addressed in this chapter.

Depending on the purpose of the session, it may help you to achieve progressive relaxation—a stress reduction technique. This involves tensing each muscle of the body, for example, your shoulders, and then letting go. Then tensing them again and then letting go. If you'll try this right now, you'll see that after the third time that you ease up, your shoulders feel more relaxed, perhaps even warm.

A guided imagery session may start with your forehead and work down to your feet, or vice versa. Guided imagery works well because you simply respond to the voice instructions. This helps you to diminish any internal mental chatter that could otherwise impede your quest to achieve relaxation.

Self-Talk

Did you know that 80 percent or more of your internal dialogue focuses on your shortcomings? Most of what people say to themselves is negative.

> "What a dummy. I can't believe that I just said that."

> "I know that I could've done better; I'm always messing things up."

> "I'd like to meet that person over there, but I'll probably blow it."

Don't beat yourself up if you have ever said anything like this to yourself. The key in making self-talk work for you, particularly in regards to reducing stress, is to be more conscious of what you say to yourself. Perhaps you can generate a list of positive statements that you can use and write them down, or tape them on cassette. Such a list will help you to replace the negative statements that you more routinely offer yourself.

Pretend that you have to learn to operate some new equipment at work. You're finding the going slow and getting totally stressed out. What message are you probably giving to yourself internally?

> "I can't stand this."

> "I'd rather be any place else."

> "I don't think that I'm going to do well at this."

What could you be saying to yourself?

> "I easily accept this challenge."

"I've mastered things harder than this."

"I am going to more productive because I know how to use this to the best advantage."

By letting positive, self-boosting statements into your internal dialogue, you enhance the learning process, experience less stress, and feel far better about yourself.

Aroma Therapy

Women know that a hot bath can be highly sooth-ing. If you add oil of malacia, lavender, or other bath oils, your weary soul and fatigued body will receive a treat that many people never discover.

Many natural substances help you feel calm and serene. For some people, the smell of pine works wonders; for others, it's lemon. Do you remember your last trip to a shopping mall where you got a strong whiff of the chocolate chip cookies baking around the corner? Or how about a whiff of pizza as the dough was rising in your favorite pizzeria? These smells stimulate your olfactory sensors and help take your mind in the opposite direction of whatever was concerning it.

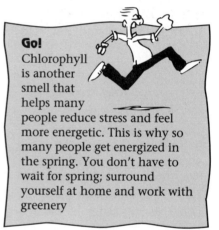

Go!
Chlorophyll is another smell that helps many people reduce stress and feel more energetic. This is why so many people get energized in the spring. You don't have to wait for spring; surround yourself at home and work with greenery

Massage

Open the yellow pages to Massage and undoubtedly you'll see several people listed. You're looking for a certified massage therapist (CMT) as opposed to the kind that works out of a seedy parlor on the second floor of some downtown building. Of course, the latter can reduce stress another way....

A certified massage therapist can do wonders for you in just a one-hour session. At the end of a particu-larly stressful day, there's nothing like it. The mas-seuse knows how to get at toxic buildups in your lymphatic system (in English—they work the kinks out of your back). Many CMTs are skilled in a variety of massage techniques including bipolar, deep muscle, and Swedish massage.

Etched in Stone
You'll feel calmer before a massage session is over and certainly by the time you walk out the door. That night, you'll probably sleep like a baby. You'll feel better the next morning, and perhaps the whole next day. Have I sold you on this yet?

The cost ranges from $40 to $90 an hour, generally higher in major metropolitan areas, and much higher for same-day scheduling. Many people swear by their masseuses and keep regular appointments on a weekly or biweekly basis.

Even if you only schedule yourself once every couple of months, the benefits will be immediate.

Taking Vitamins

So much has been written about vitamins, and so much of it contradictory, that I would just as soon leave out this topic. I routinely take several vitamins, however, and know from firsthand, long-term experience, that vitamins can be a major factor in keeping stress in check.

Because everyone's chemistry is different, I'm not going to attempt to prescribe to you what you "need" to take. Here are a few parameters so that you'll have a running lead if you decide to pursue this further.

Vitamins B and C help to nourish the adrenal glands, which release stress hormones as your body prepares for fight, flight, or the long-term, but low level, insidious stress so prevalent today.

Calcium and magnesium help to fortify your nervous system. Most multiple vitamins are worth taking, although depending on how much they cost, what doses of which vitamins are included, and what your specific needs are, one brand can be much better for you than another.

Perhaps the most sound approach for you is to visit a good nutritionist or dietitian who will trace your…

➤ Health history.

➤ Current dietary habits.

➤ Frequent illnesses and ailments.

➤ Work situation.

➤ Current stressors.

➤ Typical eating patterns.

From this, the nutritionist or dietitian can help you identify what vitamin supplements at what dosage are right for you.

As a quick and cheap alternative, charts are available at health food stores that portray what parts of the body each vitamin supports, what foods contain those vitamins, and what happens if the body is deficient of each vitamin.

Fresh Air

I kid you not, simply getting a few deep whiffs of fresh air works wonders. Fresh air can help you

➤ Achieve measurably lower levels of stress.

➤ Oxygenate your tissues.

➤ Improve circulation.

➤ Increase alertness.

➤ Diminish muscle tension.

➤ Reduce anxiety.

Go! Fresh air combined with a brisk walk is Valhalla.

If you live in an area where the air quality is poor—there is no other way to say this—*you are missing out.* Your best strategy may be to take frequent trips out of town, away from traffic and away from population centers. Get to the top of a small mountain where the air is clear and clean, but not necessarily thin. Or take a walk in the woods, where trees and plants take in carbon dioxide and return oxygen to the atmosphere.

Deep Breathing

Surrounded by fresh air or not, deep, *diaphragmatic breathing* is an important stress reducer for everyone. Much has been written about this, and it's fairly easy to overcomplicate the process. The simplest metaphor that I can think of is this: Imagine that there is a balloon in your stomach. As you inhale, you fill up the balloon. As you exhale, you deflate the balloon. Inhale; exhale. There's no need to rush. The balloon can fill slowly and empty slowly.

As you achieve deep diaphragmatic breaths, your torso will move, but it is not actively involved in the process.

Another way to understand breathing from the diaphragm, especially if you haven't been doing it, is to simply lie on the floor. Now, breathe as you normally would, while placing one or both hands over your stomach, near your navel.

Do you feel that up-and-down motion? That's it; you're doing diaphragmatic breathing, through your abdomen!

So why don't you do this all the time? Other than when you are lying down, if you are excited, tense, or in a hurry, it's easy to slip into a nonproductive routine, raising your shoulders, expanding your chest, and letting these areas be the driving forces behind your breathing.

Warning
Your upper chest and shoulders do not need to be a part of the breathing process. Moreover, it's much better if they're not.

Human anatomy has been a couple million years in the making, however, and chest breathing is simply not as efficient as diaphragmatic breathing. If you've been engaged in vigorous athletic activity, you may resort to using your chest and upper torso in combination with your abdomen to get oxygen into your lungs faster. This is understandable. At a normal heart rate, however, deep diaphragmatic breathing is best for Homo Sapiens, even for you.

Meditation

Meditation is another stress-reduction technique that has been around since words replaced grunts. It is a way of focusing on deeper thoughts and feelings by turning away from the distractions and tensions of everyday living.

Word Power
To meditate is to focus your mind while in a state of relaxed awareness. Hence, you're not asleep, and you're not in a trance.

It is advisable to be seated in a place where you won't be disturbed. Many people begin meditating by devoting their complete attention to a word or sound. In the 1970s, the Transcendental Meditation movement made the sound "Om" highly popular. This is pronounced "ome," which rhymes with home but is elongated so that it takes several seconds to complete. Other people get into the meditative state by focusing on a candle flame, a mandala, or perhaps a simple image. Advanced practitioners need merely focus on the ebb and flow of their own breath.

If you meditate often, over time, you can get to the point where you don't respond so intensely to potential external stressors. For example, if a project is dropped on your lap with short notice and you only have 45 minutes to get it completed, it's likely to be far less upsetting.

Many people swear by meditation, citing it as the single best method for achieving an improved level of calmness and serenity. Others regard meditation as an important process for the following:

➤ Better knowing one's self

➤ Viewing the world without judgment

➤ Being more accepting of others

➤ Getting closer to God

What a Concept!

By whatever route that you are able to start, the goal of your meditation is to free your mind from accumulated tension, to reach a divine emptiness from which deep concentration and relaxation are possible.

Now, Where Was I Going?

One paradox experienced by highly accomplished people when they first begin meditating is that they expect that something is going to happen. You don't meditate to get from point A to point B. *You meditate to meditate*—the act of meditation itself is the reward (of sorts).

Nothing in particular is supposed to happen. There are no thoughts that you are *supposed* to have or realizations that spring forth. If you have some, fine. If you don't, fine. Perhaps this is why meditation is not for everyone, or why others who initially enjoy it, don't stay with it.

Meditation Variations

Have you ever gone on a strenuous hike, perhaps out for six to eight hours on a single day with a backpack, probably in a group? By the end of the day, you're thoroughly exhausted, but it's the good kind of exhaustion. You jump into the shower to get clean, and as you dry off, you notice that you are *mentally* and physically clean. Other people get the same reaction from a vigorous hour of jogging, soccer, or racquetball. Your muscles may be strained and your body aching, but your mind is at rest.

Slow, purposeful walking, for example, affords many meditation opportunities. You could put all your awareness into the swing of your arms, or your legs. You could feel your heels or your toes as they strike the ground. You could pay attention to your breathing or the curvature of your spine.

Some health clubs are offering alternative meditation classes. Crunch Fitness in New York City offers classes in stationary bike meditation. Participants pedal with their arms hanging by their sides. The room is silent except for the sounds of stationary bike wheels whirring in unison.

Children who learn to get into a meditative state during sports activities report that it helps them in other aspects of life as well. They're better able to handle spats with siblings, stay focused on homework, and even walk away from potential fights.

Go!
There are many ways to meditate while in motion. Some people walk in slow, methodical steps while meditating. Some swim. It all depends on how you approach the activity.

203

It is even possible to meditate while washing dishes. The idea of reducing your stress by washing the dishes may sound like the all-time incredulous statement, yet there are people who are able to achieve this everyday. You can focus on the temperature of the water, how the sponge feels in your hand, what it's like to sponge off each plate, or rinse them, and get them squeaky clean. The key is to *mindfully* engage in something that you otherwise do *mindlessly* to help quiet the mind and put your focus on the activity at hand.

The Stress Inventory

The stress inventory is a little like visualization, guided imagery, progressive relaxation, and meditation. So, what is it? It's a way of listening to your body to see where your stresses lie and then purging yourself of them. It starts with closing your eyes and taking a deep breath. With your eyes closed, you turn inward and focus on various parts of your body, usually starting at the top of your head.

As you bring attention to the top of your head, you notice if there is any stress there. Considering the work that you do, the answer for you is yes, there is. If it helps, you can place one hand at the top of your head so that you can stay focused on it. Many people don't need this, however.

Now, what do you feel at the top of your head? Is there pressure? Do you feel tight or perhaps loose? Is it warm or cold?

While continuing to take deep breaths, you focus on the top of your head and what you're feeling there. If there is stress, you "direct it out of your head with your next exhale." Hence, you take a deep breath and currently send your stress away.

What a Concept!

When you identify an area of tension and associate it with your exhalation, you're really retraining your brain to help specific parts of your body relax more readily.

You then move on to the next place on your body, in this case, your forehead, and repeat the process. To get all the way down to your toes can take quite a while. Sometimes, you'll doze off before you get there, but that's fine because it means that you have reached a relaxed stage. If you don't want to doze off, then get up and move around, shake your arms and legs, and reintroduce yourself to the world.

Centering

To be centered is to be mentally, physically, and emotionally rested, relaxed and balanced, and comfortable where you are. Centering allows you to better direct your attention where you choose to direct it. Although centering seems to be related to meditation, the goal is different—to enable you to be comfortably present prior to taking some specific action.

The rationale is that you will be more effective at something if you are first effective at doing nothing. You learned to sit up before you could stand, stand before you could walk, walk before you could run, and so forth.

Centering involves sitting down in a comfortable place, closing your eyes, and being aware of your surroundings. How do you feel? What do you hear? What are you thinking? There's nothing that you are supposed to do or feel. In time, your body will relax; your mind will get calmer; and you will be better able to simply let things happen.

What a Concept!

The more centered you become, the deeper your understanding of what is going on around you, and ultimately, the better your decision as to what to do next.

As you become more skilled in the process of being centered, you can remain centered while in front of another person, being part of a group, working, or being part of an athletic team. A good illustration of centering is that of health care workers, who in the face of an obviously agitated patient, remain calm and understanding.

Yoga

The practice of yoga goes back some five to seven thousand years. You know it's gone mainstream, however, when Jane Fonda's *Yoga Exercise Workout* hits #1 on Billboard's Health and Exercise Video Chart. By some estimates, more than four million people practice yoga in the United States alone. As the baby boom generation ages, it's likely that these numbers will increase dramatically.

Although yoga exercises can be quite vigorous, among the more than 1,000 different poses, there is something for everyone.

➤ Dancers can practice yoga to increase their energy and to improve their stamina.

➤ Business executives can use it to stay calm and balanced in a hectic environment.

➤ Athletes can use it to improve performance or recover more quickly from an injury.

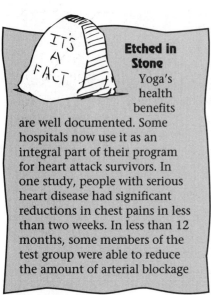

Yoga's health benefits are well documented. Some hospitals now use it as an integral part of their program for heart attack survivors. In one study, people with serious heart disease had significant reductions in chest pains in less than two weeks. In less than 12 months, some members of the test group were able to reduce the amount of arterial blockage

The idea of yoga is to awaken the mind, feed the body, and rekindle the spirit—to create a union between mind and body. Yoga means "union." The masters tell us that 10 to 15 minutes a day of basic yoga exercises can enable you to feel more relaxed at work, concentrate better, have a healthy appetite, have better sex, and sleep more soundly.

Get a Mat

As with many stress-reducing techniques, a yoga exercise begins with a strategic pause. You sit back, take slow deep breaths, and become relaxed. The variety of poses, postures, and stresses helps to keep the body limber. The slowly controlled moves in combination with breathing help to keep the mind calm. The kind of yoga that you might practice at a fitness club or health center is typically 60 or 90 minutes in length. The first 10 or 15 minutes take you through a series of breathing exercises with the primary goal of having you forget about your surroundings.

Thereafter, you might engage in 25 to 50 minutes of various poses, each of which stretch and strengthen muscles. This might include the spinal twist or the upward facing dog. This is like doing a push up except you hold the "up" position for 30 seconds while looking up, and then slowly come down, and then repeat the process. This helps to lengthen your spine and build your back and arm muscles.

In the next 25 or 30 minute section, the typical class would move on to standing postures.

T'ai Chi Ch'aun

T'ai Chi Ch'aun or *T'ai Chi* as it's more popularly called, (pronounced TY-CHEE) is designed to help people have a more even temperament and a more tranquil mind. Unlike other techniques discussed, T'ai Chi is a martial art as well as a philosophy, which in one way or another explains everything in the universe. Basically, there are two parts to T'ai Chi, Yin and Yang. Everything on earth, including you, possesses Yin and Yang. Think of Yin and Yang as two opposing forces that exist both in a material and spiritual state. Now, it really gets complicated. Although they are opposing forces, they work in unity.

In terms of reducing stress, T'ai Chi enables you to concentrate better on routine tasks, make decisions more effectively, and maintain an alert mind for more of the time. As an exercise, it resembles something of a classical dance, although it is actually more like a drill. It is designed to balance the muscles and joints through movement, deep breathing, and manipulation of the diaphragm. These movements impact the central nervous system, which regulates the efficient operation of the organs within your body.

What a Concept!

T'ai Chi can improve your health as well as your disposition. Hence, if you are highly stressed, over time, the practice of T'ai Chi can turn you not into only a less stressed person, but a calm person.

The Least You Need to Know

➤ Taking a few minutes of a hectic day to pause and reflect can spell the difference between frenzy and tranquillity.

➤ Simply talking to a trusted listener about issues confronting you can be stress reducing.

➤ You need to stick with the stress reduction technique of your choice for it to pay off.

➤ Adult education programs in guided imagery, progressive relaxation, visualization, and meditation abound.

Chapter 18

Asking the Magic Question

In This Chapter

➤ Taking responsibility for your stress

➤ Asking the right questions of yourself

➤ Finding solutions more easily

➤ Diminishing stress on the spot

When faced with an undesirable or stressful situation, do you ever stop and consider who created the situation? More times than not, it's likely that you did.

Instead of writing to Eppie Lederer, a 78-year-old woman from Sioux City, Iowa, who receives more than 1,000 letters a day from people seeking her advice even though she has no particular counseling credentials, a faster and more effective way to solve many problems is to ask *yourself*. In this chapter, I am going to discuss key questions that *you pose to yourself*, that enable you to...

➤ Get to the root of challenging issues you face.

➤ Take more responsibility for the stress that you experience.

➤ Achieve resolution more quickly and easily.

Does this sound like it might be of interest to you?

(By the way, Eppie is better known as Ann Landers and she has a full-time staff of seven to handle the mail. Her biggest competitor is her sister, pen name Abigail van Buren, better known by her column, "Dear Abby".)

How Did I Get into This?

This is my favorite question when I've gone down a path that has led to considerable pain and gnashing of teeth. The answer is more involved than you might think.

In the middle of writing this book, for example, I encountered some tough situations involving heavy travel at the same time that chapters were due. While you were watching the in-flight movie on that trip to the coast, I was mulling over notes, organizing pages, creating new passages, and proofreading old ones.

The answer to the question "How did I get into this jam?" can be found in my etymology.

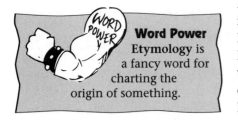

Word Power
Etymology is a fancy word for charting the origin of something.

I'll forego taking you back to the start of humankind and instead start where my parents were born to couples of Byelorussian ancestry and grew up in New England. Because my grandparents were craftsmen (blue-collar workers) who desired that their children go on to higher education, both of my parents graduated college and were highly literate. I suppose that I had good verbal skills at a young age.

My parents met, married, had children, and moved to Bloomfield, Connecticut, which was blessed with good schools at the time. I was placed in the accelerated class. I went on to college and graduate school, majored in marketing, and thereafter, got an MBA. I didn't learn to write until I started my first job as a management consultant.

At the end of each consulting engagement, I had to prepare a consulting report, which was anywhere from 12 to 30 pages. *I learned to write when I had to write for my profession.* After my father's death in 1977, I moved to Washington, D.C. Eighteen months later, my older sister died from a thrombosis—arterial blood clot. This threw me into a mental and emotional tizzy for more than a year. I went on a self-help journey, taking every course on health, nutrition, and stress reduction that I could sign up for.

Along the way, I met an author named Jefferson Bates, who inspired me to join Washington Independent Writers. I became interested in this group and even became an officer. Because of my written articles, I was asked to speak and liked that as well. I then joined the National Speakers Association, where I was exposed to some of the leading thinkers, literally, in the world.

I began to develop higher expectations about myself. That led me to a series of mentors and empowering people, and ultimately to Robert Fritz's book, *The Path of Least Resistance*, wherein I learned about the power of making profound choices.

Getting further into my dual profession of writing and speaking, I noticed that the pace of civilization seemed to be speeding up; more people were in a frenzy, more often. I wrote a book called *Breathing Space: Living and Working at a Comfortable Pace in a Sped-up Society*, and from that, I eventually caught the eye of the publishers at the Alpha Division of Macmillan who asked me to write an earlier book called *The Complete Idiot's Guide to Managing Your Time* and this book.

That, briefly, is precisely how I got into the situation where I had to mix a heavy travel schedule with writing a book, (a stressful activity in itself, without the travel). Note: *I chose to be doing this.*

Go! When you find yourself in a stress-inducing pickle, ask yourself, "How did I get into this?" Then, give yourself time for an extended, thoughtful answer. Most of the time, you got into this because you chose it.

Jot down your own etymology—how you ended up doing what you're doing with your life—to see how your choices led you to your present role. If you accept most of the responsibility for the situation in which you currently find yourself, your quest to reduce stress will be greatly enhanced.

Indeed, consider the alternative: If you don't take responsibility for the situation in which you find yourself, you may have a more difficult time dislodging the stress. After all, if you're not in control, *you are not in control.*

What Would a Calm Person Do?

A group called Overachievers Anonymous annually bestows the "America's Most Overworked Person Award." One winner was described as the most extreme example of someone in the position of power, who has the ability to choose if and how he is going to take care of himself, and yet challenges the limits of human endurance.

Gee, and you thought that you were the only one!

When interviewed by a major newspaper, the award winner said that he wasn't proud of the title and that he knew he needed to make some changes, but he didn't know where to begin.

What a Concept!

The solution to many a dilemma lies in taking the reverse of your situation and making a question out of it.

If you don't know how to slow down, the question to pose to yourself is "What would a calm person do?" or "What would someone who evenly paces himself do in my situation?"

You open yourself up to a world of insights, if you are honest with yourself, merely by posing the question. I suggest writing it at the top of a blank piece of paper so that you will have plenty of room for all the self-generated solutions that you are going to record. Or type it at the top of your PC screen.

No matter how long it's been since you've been in overdrive, posing the question "What would a calm person do?" to yourself opens you up to intriguing insights. Possible answers could include

➤ Do stretches in the morning.

➤ Always have lunch with a friend.

➤ See a therapist.

➤ Read a book on better management.

➤ Delegate!

➤ Concentrate on the most profitable activities.

➤ Schedule more vacation time into your calendar.

➤ Take more frequent walks throughout the day.

➤ Brainstorm with your staff.

➤ Read articles about working at a calm and deliberate pace.

Does This Need to Be Done at All?

Management sage Peter Drucker, in his book, *The Effective Executive*, tells us that 80 percent of what we do at work is dictated by habit and not by need. That means you do much of what you do during the workday because you always do things that way, or that's the way your organization has set it up.

Focusing solely on those things in your control, the question "Does this need to be done at all?" could lead you to greater focus, less time wasted on nonessential tasks, and less stress. So what kind of activities don't need to be done at all by you anymore? Try these on for size:

➤ Checking e-mail three times a day when once is sufficient.

➤ Making a back-up hard copy of documents on your disk.

➤ Sending a fax and then sending a follow-up letter that is the same as the fax.

➤ Reviewing previous policies and procedures that have been updated.

➤ Reviewing training manuals and guides that have been replaced by newer ones.

What Can I Draw from This?

Quiz time! Get out a number two pencil. A century ago, when somebody ate something that didn't agree with them, other than mix a bicarbonate of soda, what did they do? No looking on anyone else's paper—you're only cheating yourself. Answer: They didn't eat that again.

Today, if you eat a pepperoni pizza and get heartburn, but you like pepperoni pizza, chances are you'll keep eating it. As long as you can take some over-the-counter remedy that patches you up, you have little chance of "learning" not to eat it.

What a Concept!

The primary difference between people who achieve spectacular career success and those who don't is that the achievers learn from their failures. The primary difference between those who control stress and those who don't is that those who achieve mastery learn from their failures.

Stress indicates that something is out of balance. Ignoring or medicating your stress may not teach you how to keep it from recurring. The question "What can I draw from this?" in the face of a stressful situation offers many insights. When I sleep for less than seven hours, I'm simply not sharp the next day. What do I draw from this? An extra hour spent on some other activity needs to be directed toward sleep so I can get my full eight hours.

When I sit in front of my computer screen for too long, my eyes lose focus and become red. I can begin to feel zoned out. What can I draw from this?

➤ I should get up from my chair frequently.

➤ I need to buy a screen that covers my PC or a PC monitor that is not high in electro-magnetic waves.

➤ I need fresh air in my office.

➤ I need to sit more than two feet away from my computer screen.

➤ My chair may need readjustment.

➤ I need to look out the window occasionally and focus on something in the distance before looking back at my screen.

➤ I need to work away from the computer screen several times each day.

➤ The lighting needs to be at a level in which I can work comfortably.

➤ I need water nearby to keep me hydrated.

Reframe and Conquer

Suppose that you face a situation at work, such as being passed over for a promotion that you were sure was yours, and it becomes quite stressful for you. What can you draw from this?

➤ Perhaps you didn't have the skills and capabilities desired by top management.

➤ Maybe your organization plays favorites.

➤ Maybe you should take a course to improve your capabilities in some specialized area.

➤ Perhaps you are out of touch with the functioning of your department.

➤ Maybe you need to spend more time greasing the skids personally than simply being functionally superior.

➤ Maybe you're in the wrong organization.

➤ Maybe you're being groomed for something else, more special.

Word Power
When you look at a situation with another perspective, you help **reframe** the situation.

By asking yourself this type of question, you get to *reframe* the situation.

By reframing a situation, you get a new perspective. You're more objective, less emotional, and more likely to derive solutions. In terms of career success, studies show that the most successful people not only fail, but fail often. Surprisingly, they regarded their failures as learning experiences more than anything else.

I know there are many times you would prefer not to have such "learning experiences," but the phrase is more than a platitude. *You get to draw upon the values or critical data that you picked up on the road to where you want to be.* Hence, you get to where you want to be faster.

History is replete with stories of people who maintained their fortitude through one failure after another. Abraham Lincoln, as you may know, lost countless elections for local government, Congress, and the Senate leading up to his election to the presidency in 1860. James Michener didn't get a book published until age 42. Al Pacino won an Oscar the sixth time he was nominated, and Susan Sarandon won at age 50, the fifth time she was nominated. That's a lot of times to sit in the Dorothy Chandler Pavilion and not hear your name when the envelope is opened.

What Experience Do I Want for My Child? For Myself?

Now and then, you attend a Little League game with a parent in the stands who is overly concerned about his or her child's performance. The parent is constantly talking to the manager to ensure that the child is inserted in the right place in the lineup, or berating the umpire as if the umpire were not impartial, or making a major league salary. The parent is so insistent that the child do well, that the child doesn't enjoy participating.

If you feel anxious or stressed when you attend one of your child's sporting events, it's time to ask, "What experience do I want for my child?" You may find that the following answers emerge:

➤ To have my child enjoy himself or herself as a member of the team.

➤ To have my child learn to participate with others.

➤ To have my child appreciate sports and develop a lifelong fitness habit.

➤ To have my child know that I am there in support of him/her.

When you ask the question "What experience do I want for myself?", these answers may emerge:

➤ To enjoy watching my child play.

➤ To relax.

➤ To be sociable with other parents and onlookers.

➤ To show league officials, managers, and coaches that I support them and their efforts.

What Will Happen if I Don't Call?

AT&T surveyed a sampling of its customers and found that 50 percent call in three times or more per week, while on vacation. Three quarters of those 50 percent say that staying in touch does not disrupt their vacations.

The result of this survey surprised even AT&T. A spokesman said, "People always say that they want to get away from work, but they really don't. It doesn't appear to be a sense of fear of what might happen. They just can't break the umbilical cord with the office."

Do you feel compelled to call in every other day or so, even when you're supposed to be taking it easy? After all, you take a vacation so you'll have a different set of experiences than the daily grind.

When you ask yourself, "What will happen if I don't call?", the likely answers are:

➤ Everything is going just fine.

➤ There are some big problems, but other people are taking care of them.

➤ There are some problems, but they can wait until you get back.

➤ Others miss your input, but they can go a week without you.

➤ You're not missed at all.

➤ You can actually rest and relax during your vacation.

What Is This Stress Doing for Me?

Dr. Bernie Seigel routinely ask his patients, "What is your illness doing for you?" This question disarms many people. After all, an illness is something that you get, right? It isn't something that does something *for you*. Same with stress, right?

When you ask the question of yourself, "What is this stress telling me?", here are potential answers:

➤ I am in the wrong job.

➤ I am approaching my job incorrectly.

➤ I need to take breaks more frequently.

➤ I need to drink more water.

➤ I need to learn more about tension relieving techniques that I can self-administer.

➤ I need to let my boss know that I am in over my head right now.

➤ I need to get more sound sleep each night.

By some estimates, stress-induced tension headaches comprise 75 to 80 percent of all headaches people get today. Yet some people don't get headaches at all. They understand what it takes to keep themselves in balance.

Is There Another Way to Proceed?

Sometimes when a situation doesn't seem solvable, the most appropriate solution may be to forsake it and turn your attention to something totally different.

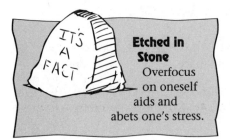

Etched in Stone
Overfocus on oneself aids and abets one's stress.

When you're experiencing considerable stress, it's better to stop what you're doing and decrease your focus on yourself. Look for someone else to help.

In the workplace, maybe there is a junior person who you can help. By delving into his or her problems, you give yourself the kind of break that you can't muster when you're entrenched in your own stuff.

Helping somebody else provides the side benefit of having others regard you in a more positive light. After all, if in the midst of your troubles you're able to turn your attention to someone else, I mean, like, how noble.

What a Concept!

As a by-product of helping others, sometimes you experience the Eureka! effect—the solution to *your* problem jumps out at you when you seemingly weren't attempting to find a solution.

Your mind works in mysterious ways. It's working for you, even when you are not conscious of it. This is why you get great ideas while shaving or putting on makeup, certainly in the shower, and sometimes while resting in the hammock in the backyard.

How Do I Feel Right Now?

This one gets a bit heady. When you ask yourself, "How do I feel right now?" with no other agenda and are accurate and honest with yourself, a strange and wondrous thing happens. Suppose that you're extremely upset, but you have the wherewithal to ask yourself, "How do I feel right now?" The obvious answer is upset. By stopping and noticing how you feel, you actually dissipate some of your feelings about being upset. The same works for being overly stressed or anxious.

I was once embarrassed as all heck. I had done something in full view of dozens of people, and there was no place to hide. (Never mind what it was!) In that moment, I caught myself thinking, "Wow! I am feeling so embarrassed." The next moment, I didn't feel nearly as embarrassed. *The mere act of noticing the undesirable feeling I was experiencing helped to diminish it.*

Go!
Make the leap from the raw feeling of experiencing to the potentially more beneficial one of noticing how you feel.

It's almost as if the act of noticing how you're feeling competes with the actual emotion itself and decreases its intensity. Like Newton's Fourth Law of Thermodynamics, a body cannot be at two places at the same time, perhaps competing energies cannot occupy the same space at the same time. Feeling stressed and noticing that you are feeling stressed compete for the same space.

You're better off noticing that you are feeling stressed as opposed to feeling stressed. In the former, you have the option of doing something, whereas in the later, you tend to be at the mercy of how you feel.

When you notice how you feel, you can engage the key questions raised in this chapter, and many of the other techniques discussed throughout this book.

With Every Stress-Related Problem Comes a Solution

Thomas Kettering, a founder of the Sloan-Kettering Institute, was among the most brilliant inventors in the last hundred years, perhaps on a par with Thomas Edison, but he's barely known today. Kettering perfected the diesel engine, automobile ignition systems, chrome painting procedures, and a host of other innovations that virtually transformed the auto industry in the 1920s and 1930s. His approach to problem solving was unsurpassed. The major distinction between a problem and a solution, according to Kettering, is that people more readily understand a solution.

Kettering said that solutions involve merely a change in perception, because the solution to the problem must have existed all along, within the problem itself. *A problem solver's role is not to master a problem, but to make it generate its own solution.*

In perfecting the diesel locomotive, for example, Kettering once said that his team had little part in it. Instead, the team "offered" the engine six different types of pistons and in essence, let the engine "choose" the one it "liked" best.

When you experience stress as a result of problems, perhaps long-standing problems, there simply has to be a solution. And, as with Kettering's insight, the solution has existed all along in tandem with the problem itself.

From now on, when you exhibit behavior that represents a lack of control, such as lashing out at someone, or when you experience headaches, take comfort in knowing that *the solution does not lag the problem.* You can "ask" the problem—the stressor—key questions, like you've seen in this chapter, and *the answers will generate the solutions you are seeking.*

The Least You Need to Know

➤ Key questions help you discover options to stressful or undesirable situations.

➤ These key questions focus on how to experience the opposite of what you're currently experiencing.

➤ Noticing how you feel diminishes the effect of undesirable feelings.

➤ Solutions to problems come in tandem with the problems themselves. Asking the problem key questions generates solutions.

Choosing When It's Confusing

In This Chapter

➤ The unrelenting task of making choices

➤ The value of making fewer choices

➤ Making effective purchasing decisions

➤ Choosing with less data

➤ Shortcuts to reaching decisions

The unrelenting need to make decisions may be the most imposing stressor of all. Society today is awash with material goods and service options. There are more brands, features, or options than you can fathom. On the job, you face endless decisions regarding equipment, supplies, subscriptions, which calls to return, what to file and where, what to schedule and when, which tasks to tackle, which to delegate, and dozens of others.

On the personal side, it's no easier. Suppose you're trying to buy detergent from the supermarket. The choices you face include Tide with Bleach, Surf, Wisk, Fresh Start, Oxydol, Shaklee, Bold, Era, Fab, Solo, Sears, Dynamo, Arm & Hammer, and so on—it's endless! To buy a tennis racket, you have to choose from different handles, heads, textures, and weights. What kind of bike would you like—a mountain bike, dirt bike, trail bike, 10-speed, 15-speed, or 21-speed?

Warning
People report feeling stressed out even when shopping for children's toys!

You can, however, make decisions without collisions. Even if you're confronted with a bewildering number of alternatives, there's welcome news about how to choose, as you'll learn in this chapter.

The Stress of Too Many Choices

In the mid 1980s, Robin Williams starred in *Moscow on the Hudson.* In one scene, his character is shopping in a Manhattan supermarket with a dazzling coffee display. There's freeze-dried, rich blend, Colombian coffee, coming in cans, pouches, canisters, glass, and cartons with packaging in countless colors.

Williams' character has been brought up in Russia where there were two choices: coffee or no coffee. Now, he's faced with all kinds of choices, and he has an anxiety attack. He faints, pitches forward, and knocks over the whole display.

On a daily basis you experience at least a mild form of the same type of anxiety. The number of choices confounds your ability to choose rather than making it easier. Don't get me wrong, having many choices is a wonderful thing—after all, people fought and died in wars to defend this right. Yet I've turned over every stone, excluding Sharon Stone, and I've never seen a study saying that human beings function effectively when confronted with a profound number of choices.

A colleague of mine went to a restaurant where they asked if he wanted to sit by the window, the balcony, or in the back. For water, he could have it with or without ice, sparkling water, or water with lemon. He was offered a number of appetizers and entrées. A baked potato or french fries? A baked potato with chives, sour cream, butter, plain, with cheese, with broccoli…?

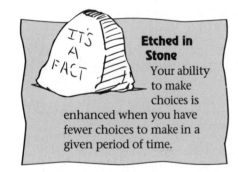

Etched in Stone
Your ability to make choices is enhanced when you have fewer choices to make in a given period of time.

After a while, his enjoyment of the dinner dissipated as he became confounded with the choices he had faced for his evening meal. When the waiter came by several more times offering more inane choices, he got angry and challenged him to a fight, only to be asked if he'd like to fight at the table, in the lobby, or outside!

An Inability to Choose

Think about being single (or when you were single) and imagine this situation. You're 25 years old on a Friday afternoon in the spring. It's a wonderful afternoon, you just got paid, you're looking (and smelling) good, you've got your mojo working, and you're headed for the best pickup spot in town.

Suppose you're a man and you see a few women at a table. What are they talking about (if they don't know you're listening)? More than likely, they're talking about the men in town, and in unflattering terms: "The men in this town are jerks!" (At one convention, regarding what women have to say about eligible men, a lady in my audience from St. Louis responded, "I can't repeat it here!")

Suppose a group of guys is talking. They're probably talking about women, and perhaps in negative terms: "The women in this town are dogs!" In a world of six billion people, what is the reality when it comes to choosing a mate?

There are more choices today than there have ever been, but people *perceive* that there are fewer choices. When you're confronted with too many choices, it confounds your ability to choose, and you proceed as if you have no choices.

Pretend that you're on a jumbo jet from Boston to Los Angeles, which will be in the air for five or six hours. Could you find your future mate on this plane, among the 550 people on board, if you had to? When I speak to groups, many people confess that they could. What if you add the flight attendants and crew? More people confess that they could find a mate.

So if you could find a mate on a jumbo jet plane, or in the next town, which might have "only" 10,000 people, why do you believe there is nobody to meet, or no good movies to see or books to read? Often, the answer is not that there are too *few* choices, but *too many*.

May I suggest that you:

➤ Let go of lower level decisions as often as possible.

➤ Let someone else choose when the choice is of no consequence.

➤ Turn your attention away from the merely titillating or mildly entertaining information that comes your way, lest you drown in it.

What a Concept!

Too many choices leads to the perception of a lack of choices. This perception can be highly stressful, analogous to having little control over a situation.

Beware: Deciding By Not Deciding

I once saw a big poster that read, "Not to decide is to decide." Sometimes, when you're swamped by choices, as you saw above, your ability to make decisions is diminished.

If you don't make a decision, *that* is a decision—a choice not to take action. A strategy for proceeding by indecision only rarely offers desirable results. To keep yourself limber in handling choices throughout the day, draw on some of what you learned in previous chapters.

Set up your desk and office to make decisions. Condition your environment so that you have *space*. All things being equal, if you have a clear desk with one file folder in front of you, you'll have more energy and focus than you would if you had that file folder in addition to 20 other piles. Keep a clear desk if you'll be making big decisions.

Today, where you can come to work and by 10:00 a.m. feel totally out of sorts with everything that's fallen upon you, it's easy to lose track of what's worth deciding.

Where to Begin

What choices are worth making? Unfortunately, this remains highly subjective. Generally, they include the choice of a spouse; the choice of a home; big decisions that affect your business; where you'll live; with whom you'll associate; what course of study you'll pursue; and so on. The key issue is this: Have you identified, in your own life, the handful of choices that are worth making?

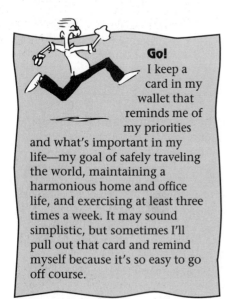

Go!
I keep a card in my wallet that reminds me of my priorities and what's important in my life—my goal of safely traveling the world, maintaining a harmonious home and office life, and exercising at least three times a week. It may sound simplistic, but sometimes I'll pull out that card and remind myself because it's so easy to go off course.

Often, decisions worth making are not always apparent. Is it important to spend time on the color of the next toothbrush you buy? The next movie you see? It may seem important at the time, but of all the movies you've seen, how many have had a profound impact? What about attending the next PTA meeting? If your children are doing well or the school system is strong, you may not need to go.

Although the important decisions in your life may be readily identifiable, a host of decisions of varying degrees of importance will only be briefly important. However, *most decisions you make in life are of no long-term importance*; in many instances, they're not even of short-term importance.

It may be hard to grasp, but how long will it matter what restaurant you went to for lunch? Even with career decisions, you can often go back and change something. Even if you make a bad decision at work, it won't be so bad in the big picture, if you're generally producing good work.

What a Concept!

In retrospect, most decisions you make have no long term or significant impact, however large they may loom right now.

Choosing in the Face of Rapid Change

What about decisions that will have a significant impact, such as which way to take your company or department? In business, it's getting harder to have a monopoly—no one has a lock on a market niche. We experience lucrative micromarkets that explode and then rapidly vanish.

In such a situation, pick a point you want your team or organization to arrive at by a certain time—which means having the strength to let go of other opportunities to ensure that the more important goal is achieved. Then go after what you chose with vigor. Capitalize on the opportunities, realizing that eventually, no matter how sound your plan or how successful your campaign, things will change and you'll have to repeat the process.

Etched in Stone

It's more difficult to make business decisions in a world where nothing stays the same for long.

Narrowing Your Priorities

Organizations that flourish in the face of rapid change are good at identifying priority issues and sticking with them. When it comes to individuals, most people have too many priorities, whereas some seem to have none at all.

Many people can readily list a number of their priorities; it's soon easy to see that they have too many. How is it possible, by definition, to have 18, 20, or 25 things you consider important and consider them all "priorities"? There's no magic number of priorities that you "need" to have, but more than likely, it's smaller than the number of priorities you have now.

If you *do* have many priorities, how much eõme and attention do you give them? A few of them may get the broad measure of your time and attention, while most of them will get next to nothing.

Go!

When you identify core priorities, decision making becomes easier. If you forsake smaller decisions that don't count, you free up mental space for the decisions that do.

When you're clear about your priorities, it reminds you of what you decided is important to your life and your career. When you maintain mental clarity, decisions come faster and easier, with less stress and less energy.

When you're faced with too many decisions, however, *your reflexive action is to try to take them all on.* So, when a coworker asks where you want to go for lunch, your most appropriate response is, "You decide." Of the thousands of times you've gone out to lunch in your career, for example, how many had a lifelong impact? How many can you even recall?

Making Better Purchase Decisions

Within your organization, many decisions have to do with purchases of supplies or services. In many organizations, purchases go through an elaborate procedure to ensure that the vendor meets a set of predetermined guidelines. Hence, your decision is made clearer by the procedure. In smaller organizations, however, those procedures are often not well defined, or may not even exist.

On an individual basis, I rarely see people who follow any kind of procedure. Yet when you seek a product or service, you will have more options than you can possibly entertain, and *it will be that way for the rest of your life.*

The next time you consider a new VCR, fax machine, or other purchase, create your own spec sheet in advance, which you can hand to a vendor. If you're concerned about something better coming out later, look to the future for expandability, portability, or trade-in options. That will ease some of the burden of choosing now. Moreover, if you create your own spec sheet in advance, you eliminate the lack of focus from vendors telling you the other things their products do.

Vendors always introduce new features you may not have considered—you may end up with more items on your list. Afterwards, go back out for round two and see who matches your "must have" list best.

What a Concept!

Any time you make a purchase decision, there will soon be a better, faster, or more economical model. At some point, however, you have to put your stake in the ground.

A Prepared Checklist

When you need to make purchase decisions, it's advisable to have a good set of questions. Ask about quantity discounts or special terms. If you're from an educational or governmental institution, you probably already know if you qualify. If your company buys in large numbers, you might get a corporate discount.

➤ Are there weekly, monthly, or seasonal discounts? I know someone who always buys in August, when many retailers are starving and willing to make deals.

➤ Will they keep your name off of mailing lists? For me, this is becoming a key criterion. I'm not interested in being besieged with more catalogs and information than I need.

There are more items to consider when looking at vendors. Are shipments insured? Are there shipping charges? What about tax? Are there any other charges? Are authorized dealers or repair services nearby? Are references available? Good vendors have them. Are satisfied customers in your area, real live human beings, a local call away? How long has the vendor been in business? With the rapid changes in technology of late, it may be to your detriment not to go with newer vendors because they may have the latest and greatest technology. The following checklist offers questions I use when making an important purchase:

❑ Any quantity discounts?

❑ Off-peak discounts, odd lot discounts?

❑ Money back guarantee, or other guarantee?

❑ Guaranteed shipping date?

❑ Toll free customer service line?

❑ Free delivery and installation?

❑ Are authorized dealer/repair services in my area?

❑ How long for delivery?

❑ Does the product come with a warranty?

Often, you can choose a service provider without going through elaborate procedures and still turn out OK. When you're dealing with a potential vendor, and you can talk to other satisfied customers in your local area, things will probably turn out fine.

Decisions with Less Work

I saw a study where two groups of executives were surveyed. Both groups were comprised of individuals facing a purchasing decision. The first group of executives made its decision based on articles, collected information, spec sheets, and other data. The second group made its decision based on instinct—gut feeling—with a dearth of data.

After three weeks, when each group had time to see the ramifications of their decision, everyone was polled again to determine how happy they were with the decision. As it turns out, the second group—those who chose based on instinct and intuition—were happier with their decision. How could this be? I initially had trouble with this. They were happier because they weren't deluged with data, but more important, because they weren't making a decision out of the blue.

What a Concept!

Instinctive decisions aren't made out of the blue, but are based on a complex set of decision-making guidelines that you have developed all your life. More data before choosing is not always desirable.

General Colin Powell said that one of the reasons he was able to make effective decisions in his military career was that he would wait until he had about 60 percent of the data and then make his choice, rather than wait for all the information.

Enough data exists to lead to multiple answers, which clearly gets in the way of choosing. Many people seek out information that confirms or reinforces what they already believe. By collecting more data are you defending against a worst-case scenario? Or are you supporting your initial position? What you're collecting could lack balance, which could lead to a poor choice.

Other Shortcuts Abound

Getting an answer with less effort is possible! You are three or four phone calls away from any expert on any issue. Suppose that you're making a big purchasing decision, deciding whether to relocate your plant, or contemplating terminating half your staff—any big decision.

Can you find an industry expert or someone who maintains a database or has similar case studies you could review? Perhaps you could call a librarian, look on the Internet, or contact someone in your organization. By the third or fourth phone call, you can reach a party who has some gems for you. *Perhaps you can find a trailblazer, someone who's gone through exactly what you're up against.*

It's also useful to become a consultant to yourself. President Richard Nixon did this often, referring to himself in the third person. He would ask himself, "Now, what should Nixon do next?" This gave him a measure of objectivity that he wouldn't otherwise have, much like the key questions you could pose to yourself as discussed in Chapter 18. Nixon often came up with different answers than he would have if he'd asked, "What should *I* do next?"

Pros and Cons

Benjamin Franklin used the "pros and cons" technique. He listed everything favorable and unfavorable about a choice. If the pros outweighed the cons, or vice versa, the decision was clear. Nowadays, with software, you can weigh pros and cons and perhaps assign them specific values or probabilities of occurring to make your decision making more objective.

The simple process of writing down what you're up against helps you in your choice process.

Choosing with Others

Many choices you face lend themselves to consensus or majority-rules decisions. Can you employ brainstorming, with the right group and the right facilitator? It can lead to a faster decision.

President Jimmy Carter was an analytical thinker who often devised seemingly practical solutions to tough problems, but had difficulty selling them to the American public. He often failed to see that in addition to logic and analysis, people like to be emotionally swayed to a decision.

Warning
If you've applied all the analytical processes but still have trouble persuading others you may not be selling them on the emotional appeal of a decision.

The Stress of Too Few or Too Many Choices

I visited Krakow, Poland, in 1985 when it was still under Communist rule. There, I was hailed by a small man in his 60s at the train station. His major revenue activity was going down to the train station and finding Western tourists who needed a good, clean, inexpensive room and didn't know a word of Polish. I balked at first, but it turned out he and his wife had a nice room indeed—the spare room in their two-room apartment.

During my stay at his apartment, I learned that he experienced the stress of too *few* choices in life. He couldn't leave the country. He couldn't travel without presenting a series of papers. There were many restrictions he faced regarding his residence.

Everybody has their stressors. When you have too much competing for your time and attention, you may long for a simpler life in a simpler era. When you meet people who, due to social, economic, or political conditions, don't have many choices, you find that they experience equal stress and anxiety about their confinement and about the freedoms they know they're missing.

Welcome to Your World

The reality of your life and the working world you inhabit is that you're going to face more decisions as life goes on—more than your counterparts in any other generation. You can flourish despite this if you stay focused each day on the few decisions that are vital.

You've made many decisions in your life, and many more face you. You've gotten this far, and you've done pretty well. And you can do as well in the future.

The Least You Need to Know

➤ Most of the decisions you make, in retrospect, don't have any significant impact on your life.

➤ You're only a few telephone calls away from an expert.

➤ Look for the trailblazer, the person who's already faced the decision confronting you.

➤ Can you arrive at an answer by consensus-building or majority rule?

➤ Make fewer decisions each day, but make them the ones that count.

NO, I'M SORRY. I DON'T HAVE THE TIME.

Choosing to Have Less Stress

In This Chapter

➤ New choices for a new way of living

➤ Choosing to embrace technology

➤ Choosing to handle change

➤ Choices about your career and success

➤ Choices about quality of life

What if you could *choose* to reduce stress, be more balanced, and live life with greater grace and ease? Guess what: you can! If you feel flustered, you can choose to embody grace and ease. If you're swamped by information, you can choose to have clarity.

Making profound choices is a simple, but deceptively powerful way to keep stress in check while handling the challenges that life throws at you—whether it's learning new technology, surviving a merger, or being laid off.

Choosing is not a feel-good formula. Choosing is not synonymous with "positive thinking." You make choices independent of how you feel. You gain power by directly addressing what you want or how you want to feel. By constantly making positive choices, you broaden your horizons while keeping stress in check.

Recall the discussion in Chapter 17 regarding self-talk. Making choices is a highly effective way to give yourself positive, specific self-talk. That's why it works so well. Often, you'll notice a difference within 21 days. Let's look at situations where powerful "choice" statements can help. Thereafter, you can directly use the statements I provide, or adapt them to your needs.

Choosing to Enjoy the Present

Has it been awhile since you enjoyed yourself in the present? Do you find yourself constantly preoccupied? Here are some key statements to use in your self-talk that will help you get back in touch with your present and your potential:

Go!
Devise all your choices to indicate what you want to have, not what you want to avoid—you gain no advantage when choosing to avoid something.

➤ I choose to relish my days.

➤ I choose to relish this moment.

➤ I choose to be fully present to others.

➤ I choose to fully engage in the activity at hand.

➤ I choose to proceed at a measured, effective pace.

➤ I choose to acknowledge all I have.

➤ I choose to focus on where I am and what I'm doing.

➤ I choose to acknowledge that this is the only moment I can take action.

Choosing to Master Your Finances

Because personal finances is cited as the number one stressor, perhaps you would like to put some of these statements to work for you:

➤ I choose to easily live within my means (i.e., to generate a surplus!).

➤ I choose to budget my cash resources appropriately.

➤ I choose to undertake comprehensive cash flow planning.

Go!
Using key words, such as "easily" or "readily" helps to boost the power of the choices you make.

➤ I choose to save for the long term.

➤ I choose to get qualified, professional advice.

➤ I choose to put away 15 percent of my salary each payday.

➤ I choose to plan for my child's higher education.

➤ I choose to provide for my retirement.

➤ I choose to invest my money with a stable, secure savings institution.

Notice the first item contains the magic word *easily*. You can insert this word or other modifying words when you feel they'll give your choice even more power.

Go!
To reinforce the use of choice statements, tape them on cassette so you can play them back over and over. Or make a wallet card with key choices that you can review anytime—like when you're waiting in line!

About That Divorce

Suppose you're among the millions of people whose marriage did not work out. What positive choices could you employ to reduce stress, make the best of things, and perhaps move on in life?

➤ I choose to feel good about my decision.

➤ I choose to have cordial relations with my ex-spouse.

➤ I choose to be an effective co-parent with my spouse.

➤ I choose to maintain a healthy outlook about marriage and relationships.

➤ I choose to easily and equitably divide our assets.

➤ I choose to reflect on what I've learned.

➤ I choose to engage in rewarding relationships.

➤ I choose to successfully remarry.

Handling Routine Upsets

"You're traveling in another dimension, a dimension of sight and sound. That's the signpost up ahead!" You're in the Toleration Zone!

Sometimes, stuff happens. Often, the best you can do is attempt to anticipate problems to minimize their impact. I frequently experience travel delays, convention halls and meeting rooms that aren't set up, and an occasional meeting professional who is more of an obstacle than a help. I've learned not to be unduly upset: This is part of my profession and comes with the territory.

Are there ways to prepare for the unexpected? Yes! The more rested you are, the less upset you will be when something doesn't go as planned and the "wider" your toleration zone will be. It helps to be alert, in general.

If you can keep some slack in your schedule, all the better. When I am scheduled to speak to a group, if I arrive at the meeting room 45 minutes early as opposed to 20 minutes early, I have 25 more minutes to deal with any potential concerns.

Choosing to Be Prepared

Having spoken to many groups over the years, I now automatically undertake contingency planning: I choose to easily prepare for speaking engagements. For example, I bring a timer with a large face because I can't count on a clock being in the room and I don't want to make the amateurish move of looking at my watch while I'm speaking. I place the timer several feet in front of me, so that no one else sees it.

Sometimes, I bring masking tape. If I'm speaking in a large lecture hall that may not fill up, I seal off the last several rows so that attendees will sit closer to the front, which is always more desirable for the success of the meeting. I also bring extra workbooks or handouts, tissues, and a water bottle.

If you're faced with making a presentation, what choices are available for you to make?

> ➤ I choose to handle difficult circumstances graciously.

> ➤ I choose to easily rise to the occasion.

> ➤ I choose to maintain calm in the face of a challenge.

> ➤ I choose to easily draw upon my resources to resolve tough situations.

> ➤ I choose to exhibit clear thinking when under pressure.

> ➤ I choose to become adept at on-the-spot problem resolution.

> ➤ I choose to easily find the opportunities that come with adversity.

> ➤ I choose to master the challenges of my profession.

What a Concept!

In your industry or profession, what choices can you make so you'll be better able to handle situations when things don't go according to plan?

Choosing to Work Effectively with a Tough Boss

The tougher your boss, the more you need good choices. Good or bad, your boss has enormous impact on your day. You may need to adapt some or all of these, but please use them:

> ➤ I choose to respect my boss.

> ➤ I choose to acknowledge that my boss is fallible.

➤ I choose to support my boss in ways that he/she hasn't even articulated.

➤ I choose to give my boss space.

➤ I choose to allow my boss the right to occasionally be upset.

➤ I choose to speak well of my boss to others.

➤ I choose to stand up for myself when necessary.

➤ I choose to learn from my boss.

➤ I choose to have my boss learn from me.

➤ I choose to form a powerful, effective, professional relationship with my boss.

And, if you really need it:

➤ I choose to remember that all boss-staff relationships are transitory.

Choosing to Master a Tough Profession

Suppose you're in a highly stressful position—the head of customer service for an auto-parts department. People call all day with questions, complaints, and off-the-wall requests. Every time you catch your breath, there is another fire to put out.

A fundamental choice to make is:

"I choose to easily learn from highly effective people in my profession."

From this choice, insights begin to open up. What behaviors, for example, can you adopt that have helped others handle this position even more effectively?

Suppose a new procedure is introduced within your department, and you have to learn it in short order. You feel scared, burdened, and fatigued. You also feel somewhat challenged and curious.

Instead of resisting the change, experiencing more stress, and not wanting to go to work in the mornings, what choices can you make to yield new approaches to this change?

➤ I choose to feel equal to the task.

➤ I choose to be rested and alert.

➤ I choose to easily absorb the new instructions.

➤ I choose to feel empowered.

Choosing to Overcome Technology Anxiety

Is the onslaught of new technology taking its toll on you? Does it seem like every time you turn around there's something else to learn? For many people, the main function of their computer has switched from word processing and data crunching to communications and presentations. If you're among this group, undoubtedly you'll feel a surge of anxiety in your attempt to learn new programs, new features, and new ways of proceeding.

The leap doesn't need to be painful, however. You can make choices that will help you become more technologically adept, without giving up your identity or your life in the process:

➤ I choose to readily take action on new ways of doing things.

➤ I choose to easily identify and resolve resistance to appropriate change.

➤ I choose to easily discover the opportunities of being on-line.

➤ I choose to be open to new ways of accomplishing my tasks.

➤ I choose to feel comfortable with new technology.

➤ I choose to easily identify technical mentors.

➤ I choose to fully embrace the new changes.

➤ I choose to have fun with the new ways of doing things.

What a Concept!

After the choices sink in, you find yourself almost automatically engaging in behavior that supports your choices.

What behaviors might kick in as your choices about handling new technology become internalized? Put your dream hat on and let's go for a ride:

➤ Each week you learn one new presentation or communications tool, particularly those that are already part of existing software packages that you use.

➤ You read at least one article a week related to communications or presentation ʰlogy. Perhaps the article is in a PC magazine, business journal, or your local

ʸou read a book related to technology, but you go easy on yourself. ˉariety of books that can help put technology in perspective for ˡ˰. friendly way.

➤ You choose one book on using software to navigate the Internet and using a modem.

➤ You explore more intently what your clients and customers are doing with technology.

➤ You focus on what others in your industry, particularly close competitors, are using. You even ask people how they accomplish certain tasks and what works particularly well.

➤ Amazingly, you join a technology group in your area. The business or calendar page of your local newspaper usually lists who's meeting, when, and where. You find PC and Mac user clubs, bulletin boards, support groups, and the like.

Go!
The Alpha and Que divisions of Macmillan Publishing, among other publishers, provide a complete line of books covering such topics as the Internet, DOS, Windows, CompuServe, America OnLine, and PCs in general, among many other topics.

One or more of the preceding items occurs because you are making choices about technology. You realize, perhaps, that others who once felt even *less* comfortable than you were able to embrace new technologies so that it became rewarding for them.

Flourishing in the Face of Constant Change

In the next several years, change is bound to accelerate, despite the feeling of many people that things are changing too fast right now. Below, I've sketched out some innovative approaches for handling change followed by supporting choices.

Jump starting   Initiating a small part of a project or activity in advance (getting a sneak preview) so as to gain familiarity for when the project or activity actually begins.

➤ I choose to readily initiate this project.

➤ I choose to readily take action on new ideas.

Total immersion   Surrounding yourself with *everything* you need to fully engage in the change process. This may involve assembling resources, people, and space, as well as ensuring that you have a quiet, secure environment, free of distractions.

➤ I choose to be a master of the new technology in my profession or industry.

➤ I choose to smoothly build change into my long-term plans.

Managing the beforehand   Living with the knowledge that change is continually forthcoming and preparing for activities or events in advance of the need to. This is enhanced by constantly establishing relationships with resourceful people who can help.

➤ I choose to recognize that change is an ongoing process.

➤ I choose to be open to new points of view.

Leap-frogging   Recognizing that although you can't keep up with all the changes in your industry and environment, you can periodically leap-frog over the developments of the last several months and "catch up" in a way. Combine other strategies above, such as jump-starting or total isolation, to give yourself the hours, or days, you need to read, study, and absorb what's occurring and to make decisions about how you'll apply new ways of doing things and new technology to your career, business, or organization.

➤ I choose to maintain clarity in the face of change.

➤ I choose to easily pinpoint new opportunities in the face of rapid change.

Picking your spots   Related to leap-frogging, pick your spots in the future, say six months, when you want a new product or service introduced, have some new technology fully integrated into your operations, and so forth. You can't ingest every development in your industry or profession.

➤ I choose to easily discover the opportunities in my industry.

➤ I choose to thrive on constantly changing market situations.

Go cold turkey   Not recommended unless you're hearty! Beyond total immersion, simply suspend operations and engage in whatever it takes to incorporate a new way of doing things. This is enhanced by ensuring that you'll have no disturbances, by bringing in outside experts, and assembling any other resources you need to succeed.

➤ I choose to be completely open to and readily accept major change.

➤ I choose to easily overcome resistance to change.

Go!
At the end of the grace period, be it a week or month, you'll be more than prepared to achieve a high level of productivity each day.

Days of grace   After deciding to implement major change, build in "days of grace" to allow yourself to proceed at half to three-quarters speed. Acknowledge that assimilating the new changes will take time and involve some disruption—and do not expect to achieve your normal productivity for now. Be gentle with yourself and recognize that you're doing your best.

With the changes you're implementing, you begin operating at a new level. Days of grace taper off as new, unfamiliar tasks become routine for you.

➤ I choose to seamlessly implement major change.

➤ I choose to embrace change with grace and ease.

Upping Personal Energy

The most appropriate choices for you, based on circumstances, may focus on having more personal energy. Here are some choices to help you draw energy from a variety of sources:

➤ I choose to be energized from my work.

➤ I choose to be easily energized by the ideas of others.

➤ I choose to be energized by my family.

➤ I choose to be energized by speaking to others.

➤ I choose to easily attract high-energy people into my life.

➤ I choose to be energized from life.

➤ I choose to expend my energy freely.

➤ I choose to easily replenish my energy.

Creative Choices to Recurring Stressors

Here are more choices for you, which focus on helping you tackle problems that otherwise seem insurmountable:

I choose to get started quickly. Sometimes, the easiest way to break through a logjam is to get started on something else. Or, to tackle what you have been putting off for so long that it has become a two-headed monster.

I choose to be more carefree. If you're always ready to go and your spouse routinely seems late, what if you did the opposite? What if you stop bugging your spouse and do something else while you wait? Perhaps you could have a magazine by the door, or a crossword puzzle, or simply a note pad.

What a Concept!

Rather than be stressed out over somebody delaying you, by not being concerned at all you might be pleasantly surprised. In the vacuum you leave, your partner may become more insistent about getting out the door on time.

I choose to easily share leadership. Do you have to lead all the time? Similarly, who says that you always have to be the one with the bright idea, or decide where the group needs to turn next?

I choose to be lighthearted. If you approach what you do as a sort of game, it can make things easier and less stressful. Without getting into Philosophy 101, some people approach their entire lives as if it's a game. They are not whimsical or frivolous; they understand that in the ebb and flow of life (over the span of 70 or 80 years), few things transpire that merit depleting one's health or well being.

I used to fret when I had an unproductive appointment that chewed up half a day and offered little return. Now, I realize that out of 240 working days a year, even if 24, a full 10 percent, turn out to be total busts, it has little long-term impact. I'm so productive on the other 216 days, I compensate for any down time. I'll bet it's the same with you, at least most of the time.

I choose to proceed with originality. If you're facing the same old same old, it's easy to fall into a pattern of routine responses. Dr. Roger von Oeck advises approaching challenges with off-the-wall creativity.

Go! Although controlling your personal environment is certainly important, on specific projects or instances, it's not always necessary or desirable.

It was 5:10 p.m. and the Suffolk County, New York, courthouse was closed. An attorney had missed the deadline for filing suit against a party who caused her client a substantial loss. A partner asked her, "Where would you like to be?" She replied, "San Francisco." Bingo! She made several calls to the San Francisco Bay area and found an attorney who, with 2 hours and 30 minutes before 5:00 p.m. Pacific Coast time, could easily prepare and file the papers.

Success in General

After all is said and done, more is said than done. But seriously, what if your quest is to simply be more of a success, personally and professionally? Here's a chapter-closing superlist!

➤ I choose to feel good about my success.

➤ I choose to easily capitalize on my success.

➤ I choose to easily maintain perspective on my success.

➤ I choose to acknowledge that career success is different from personal happiness.

➤ I choose to maintain humility.

➤ I choose to include others in my success.

➤ I choose to acknowledge those who have made a difference in my life.

➤ I choose to share the secrets of my success with others.

➤ I choose to be open to new opportunities for success.

➤ I choose to acknowledge the accomplishments of others.

➤ I choose to experience unlimited happiness.

➤ I choose to fully capitalize on my talents and skills.

➤ I choose to achieve the utmost in professional excellence.

➤ I choose to operate with the highest ethical standards.

➤ I choose to maintain clarity in my work and in my life.

➤ I choose to be a dynamic person.

➤ I choose to be widely acknowledged.

Name the challenge you face or quest for which you strive, and I guarantee that there is a choice you can make that will change the way you feel and hasten your progress.

The Least You Need to Know

➤ You can choose to reduce stress, have more balance, and live life with greater grace and ease.

➤ As choices sink in, you naturally engage in behavior that supports your choices.

➤ Using key words, such as "easily," helps to boost the power of the choices you make.

➤ Controlling your personal environment is important, but it's not always necessary.

➤ For every stressor, every challenge you face, there is a choice that you can make to reclaim the driver's seat.

Chapter 21

Stressed or Not, You're Probably Going to Live a Long Time

In This Chapter

➤ Guess what? You'll be here for a long time.

➤ Staying alert so change is less disruptive

➤ Approach your next 40 years

➤ Eternal truths

➤ The hard and fast rules

A couple who have been married for more than 70 years go to visit a divorce lawyer. The lawyer asks them why, after all these years, they want to get a divorce. The couple look at each other sheepishly and then say, "We were waiting for the children to die." I first heard this story told by Dr. Ken Dychewald, and it underscores the major theme in his book, *Age Wave*: You are going to live much longer than you think you will. Perhaps you'll reach 100, perhaps 120.

Surprise, You're In It for the Long Haul

New developments in science and technology all but guarantee that, barring some unforeseen catastrophe, you're going to live many, many more decades. Medical breakthroughs already in the pipeline, seemingly more akin to *Star Trek* than planet Earth, promise a new age to astound even the "New Agers".

You might see these breakthroughs in 10 years:

➤ The effects of aging reversed by growth hormones genetically constructed in laboratories

➤ New non-operative ways to treat prostate cancer that work without side effects and are as effective as surgery

➤ Organ transplants perfected by using immune therapies prior to surgery, without the need of antirejection drugs

And these in 20 years:

➤ Major victories in the onslaught of AIDS, including genetic therapies that offer a high cure rate

➤ Full recovery from spinal cord injuries via the development of artificial nerves

➤ The development of artificial body parts that function as well as or better than the original organs and are visibly undetectable

If you're here in 40 years:

➤ Replacement of body parts through cloning, which allows perfect genetic substitution *of one's own regenerated organs*

➤ The eradication of cancer and heart disease

➤ Human life spans averaging 100 years or more

In such an era, it's likely that you may stop and start work several times, go back to school, perhaps get a Ph.D., start a second or even a third family, and start your own business. Even if you can't see it now, you may find yourself taking time off to travel the world. You may retire and then come out of retirement several times.

What a Concept!

At 85 or 90, you may decide to run for political office. After all, there will be a large constituency of your contemporaries who will have no problem voting for a fellow octogenarian.

Although stress can certainly shorten a life span, most people still realize something close to their estimated life span. What counts is the *quality* of your life on the way there. Suppose I told you that you would live to be 115, but with the same amount of stress you experience currently. Would you do it? Would you want to? The quest of any rational person, I think, is to live a long, happy, healthy life, with relative grace and ease.

Substance Abuse Can't Be an Answer

There used to be a commercial on television that stated life got tougher, so the sponsor made its over-the-counter drug stronger. I cringed when I heard this commercial because it essentially said that the only way to face the work-a-day world was to medicate yourself at increasingly higher doses.

I wish it weren't true, but the rate at which people turn to "medication" as some type of temporary (or long term!) antidote for the stresses of working in contemporary society is alarming. In a given year, some five *billion* doses of tranquilizers are prescribed in the U.S. Suppose 150 million adults in the U.S. were to receive such prescriptions; that works out to at least 25 doses annually.

Warning
Given that you probably have decades to live, being chemically dependent simply can't be a solution for handling stress.

Without getting into the vile, vial details, all evidence indicates that the level of dosage and frequency of prescriptions is increasing. This is nothing short of appalling. People seem to have progressed from aspirin to Valium to Prozac to who knows what's next.

What a Concept!
Popping pills belies the majesty of your human potential. Your body is a wondrous mechanism, and it gives you the clues you need to stay healthy.

Your miraculous body lets you know what it needs. If you're "stressed to the max," if you have pounding headaches by the end of the workday, that's a definite sign. Popping a pill may bring predictable, temporary relief, but that strategy for getting through the day can't compete with the simple, tried-and-true measures discussed throughout this book, that will address the cause of stress, not just ease a symptom.

The scariest thing about chemical dependency as a vehicle for handling stress is that sooner or later, you'll be left with nothing. What if maximum doses of the pills or drugs are no longer enough? What will it be like if you simply cannot pause and reflect on your own?

The Last "Will" and Testament

I found the words of Dr. William R. Maples, Ph.D., in describing suicide victims to be most poignant. Maples is a forensic researcher; he diagnoses how and when people died. In *Dead Men Do Tell Tales*, he observes, "Many of the skeletons that come into my laboratory belong to suicide victims who behaved like shy hermits in their final hours.

Usually they are found in remote out-of-the-way places. People often go to some hidden place to kill themselves, whether from a desire to act alone and unhindered, or because they wish simply to disappear in solitude, spending their last moments in reflective silence."

Would these people have killed themselves if they could have attained reflective silence throughout their days? Was their quest to die alone simply an ill-advised solution to the stresses they faced?

> ### What a Concept!
>
> How would a suicide victim's life have been if he or she knew appropriate, reliable ways to find solace in the here and now, at home, at work, and everywhere in between?

To Thine Own Self Be True

Much of what I recommend in this book involves *not* following the crowd. The masses race though their days. The masses gobble down fast food. The masses take pills by the boatload. The masses, by and large, live lives of tension and turmoil. Stress has become the malady of the generation.

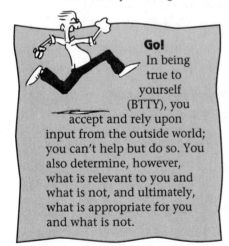

Go!
In being true to yourself (BTTY), you accept and rely upon input from the outside world; you can't help but do so. You also determine, however, what is relevant to you and what is not, and ultimately, what is appropriate for you and what is not.

Being true to yourself (BTTY) means doing what you need to do to stay healthy, balanced, and relaxed. BTTY means having inner directedness; the ability to call upon your knowledge, experience, and instinct to carve your own path; and less stress because you are less swayed by popular or prevailing norms. It is thinking and acting based on an ever-developing internal guidance system. It is learning what doesn't work and not repeating it, while learning what does work and making that work even better.

BTTY occurs when you fully acknowledge the circumstances and events as your life unfolds, and when you fully acknowledge your ability to make choices before, during, or after such events occur.

Out of the Mouths of the Rich and Balanced

I've talked to people who are highly respected in their fields, people who you can see have long been true to themselves. All are still working, including two of them who are in their seventies, although they don't have to—they all are financially secure many times over.

I asked them how the typical working man and woman could become a high achiever while keeping stress in check. To a person, they agreed about not going along with the crowd, particularly when the crowd is taking a seemingly easier road that results in unacceptable outcomes. Sometimes, suboptimizing ends up creating more problems than it solves, and a lot more stress.

Here's what else they said:

➤ Pace yourself. Especially if you've got big goals.

➤ Don't be afraid to aim high, but at the same time, make sure that you approach tasks with a realistic notion of what it will take to be successful.

➤ Take frequent breaks, however short in duration.

➤ Anticipate setbacks. Nearly everyone faces a long and winding road, on occasion, on the way to real breakthroughs. Everyone is subject to mistakes. Those who recover quickly are the ones who achieve success.

➤ Follow up. When it looks as if you're near the goal line, don't make the mistake that so many people do and coast in the rest of the way. Put in a little more time and effort to make sure that your quest will pay off.

Next, for your enlightenment, and funny bone, I've listed some of my own "Eternal Truths" in regards to handling stress. How many of these can you relate to?

➤ The hardest step is simply doing something differently from the way you have always done it.

➤ You don't know how a stress-reduction technique will work for you until you commit to putting it into practice.

➤ The best results start to come a day or two after you thought they would.

➤ You never quite get all the time you want to engage in a technique.

➤ Although you would like to try yoga or T'ai Chi, you're too embarrassed to be seen practicing them.

➤ It's hard to feel stressed when you're looking good.

➤ The quiet space that you have found will soon be found by others. So, find several.

➤ A break feels best when you need it the most.

➤ Working with stress, day after day, is an unnatural act, but it doesn't stop you from doing it.

➤ The less that you enjoy doing something, the more potentially stressful it can be.

➤ No one really wants to hear about your stress, unless you pay them to do so.

➤ No matter what techniques you discover, someone will always know a better way.

➤ It's almost impossible to be the most stressed person in your organization.

➤ A stressful day seems the worst in the middle, when it feels like it's never going to end.

➤ When your mother says you look tired, it really means that you're highly stressed.

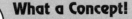

What a Concept!

Reducing stress is a stage that you pass through on the way to becoming a balanced person.

You don't necessarily get better at handling stress with age; it all depends on what you learn and put into practice.

Remaining Alert

The sage wisdom you develop for yourself and what you learn about handling stress in general, are bolstered by your understanding of changes occurring in society.

Go! Start a file of intriguing trend articles as you encounter them, so that you have a better understanding of what's brewing in society and to become a better forecaster for personal ends.

Understanding the changes in society, especially those forthcoming, can help you to better prepare for them, and hence, reduce some of the stress related to rapid change.

Since the start of the 1990s, I've been regularly adding to a roster of emerging trends as I see them, or become aware of them, to diminish being caught off guard should they occur. I call them *soft forecasts*—phenomena not based on known technological developments, such as the medical breakthroughs cited earlier in this chapter.

For the foreseeable future, here's the Jeff Davidson lineup of soft forecasts arranged by subject area.

My forecasts for relationships:

➤ There will be more single adults as a percentage of our population. More people will "marry" their work and mistakenly accept the idea that there isn't enough time for a spouse, friends, or a social life. Choosing to avoid intimacy is, in part, a reaction to feeling overwhelmed.

➤ The divorce rate stays high. It takes significant time and energy to develop and grow an intimate relationship.

➤ The notion of limited term marriage will be introduced for periods of 5, 10, or 15 years. The fundamental issue surrounding term marriages will be whether the couple intends to have children.

Social forecasts:

➤ The gulf between the information "haves" and "have nots" will get wider and wider, until technology enables all individuals to access a computer simply by speaking English.

➤ There will be a return to standards socially, educationally, and politically. People won't condone disruptive behavior, illiteracy and innumeracy, or fabrication of the truth to reach public office.

➤ Welfare as we know it will end. Time limits per recipient will go into effect.

Economic things to look for:

➤ Those who received high school diplomas but lack basic skills, will prompt corporations to undertake mass remedial education efforts.

➤ There will be an increase in the servant class—the fast food worker in the $5 to $8 per hour category. Many of these people will be forced to take on two jobs; many will never become part of the economic mainstream.

➤ The entrepreneurial economy comes into full bloom. Starting one's own business is a logical, creative response to the confining straightjacket of the 9 to 5 world.

➤ The work at home movement accelerates.

➤ The typical American household will own its own fax, and in most cases, faxes or fax/modems will be part of most standard telephone equipment. More consumer orders will be placed by fax, and more companies will offer 800 fax numbers.

➤ The proliferation of orders by fax and secure e-mail will prompt a dramatic increase in overnight and second-day delivery of goods.

➤ There will be a proliferation of 800 numbers; it will be commonplace to call any business toll free, especially as competition to serve specific targets multiplies.

➤ Many long-standing associations will fall by the wayside as members opt to join smaller, more temporary groups that meet specific needs. Major, long-standing associations will serve more as umbrella organizations for a variety of subgroups.

➤ More edge cities will develop around major metro areas; not because anybody wants them, but because the virtual community is replacing real communities. The long-term planning and care in developing mixed-use land in suburbs will diminish.

➤ Inflation will return in the U.S., prompting people to begin hoarding goods and precipitating a boom in real estate buying and selling.

Information/communications items to come:

➤ Books will be regarded as commodities, packaged with software, videos, or other media. It will become common to call authors who serve as direct long-distance coaches, via 900 numbers.

➤ CD-ROMs, videos, CDs, and other entertainment vehicles will all come with rating labels.

➤ The emergence of the flat-screen TV will enable people to hang them on walls. Thereafter, "smart homes" will be built in greater numbers. Such homes will have computers built into the walls that respond to English language requests, freeing people from handling keys and TV remote controls.

➤ Ultra-friendly software will proliferate, marking the end of instruction manuals.

➤ The information superhighway will initially lead to several years of information overload, as people learn to sort out what they need and when. The Internet eventually will become the preferred and dominant entertainment, information, and communication vehicle.

➤ Concurrently, we'll need new types of software and filters to protect us from the explosion of on-line messages and communications competing for our attention.

➤ Due to its extensive grip on the global entertainment industry, every country will have American English as its second language.

➤ As more vendors recognize the power of reaching customers online, snail mail will decline. This will be good news for our environment.

➤ Conspicuous recycling becomes commonplace. Regions, states, communities, and individuals will seek to outdo each other, seeing that everything that can be recycled is recycled.

Political stuff:

➤ Ecology becomes the single biggest issue, while the green entrepreneur, conspicuous recycling, and a Green political party all flourish. People's deep instinct for self-preservation will finally allow them to see the necessity of biodiversity.

➤ Provinces, states, and sections of nations will seek to secede from their nations of origin. This will be true even in the United States.

➤ The states will continue to grow in power and in autonomy, with the federal government handling more administrative tasks while making fewer policy decisions.

➤ A black or Hispanic male will be elected U.S. President sometime before 2016.

➤ Islam will become more influential in the West.

➤ The breakdown of national borders continues. Yuppie U.S. expatriates try Canada, Iceland, Ireland, Switzerland, Germany, and Italy among others in their search for countries where they think the pace will be more conducive to living a sane, comfortable life.

➤ The notion of bilingual education falls out of favor everywhere as English predominates.

The View From Here

You don't build a secure house in the middle of quicksand, you need a solid base on which to build. The same holds for managing stress. The more solid the base on which you build, the more readily you position yourself to maintain control.

Here I am at what could be my midpoint in life. Here is the view from here; a base, a set of observations, in the following list, about life in general, upon which you can build. May these aid you in your journey. May you have less stress and a better, long life.

1. You are born and you receive a physical shell—your body. It may be strong or weak. It may support you or cause unending problems. Still, it's what you have to work with.

2. Someone will raise you, well or poorly, whether it's your parents or surrogate parents. Yet, you got to where you are today.

3. You will have many experiences in life, some joyful, some frightening, some profound, most forgettable. Many will come from trial and error. Lessons will derive from teachers, mentors, and peers. All experiences and lessons, even the bad ones, have some value.

4. The brains and skills you were given at birth, plus what you've added to your repertoire, are sufficient to see you through to the end of your days, if you put them to use.

5. Youth passes quickly. So does young adulthood. It happens to everyone. No regrets if you've squandered some of your youth. You have a long time to go. Make the best of it.

6. Growth is part of the human experience. Early in life, you grow taller. Later, you try not to grow wider. Everyone needs to grow—emotionally, mentally, socially, and spiritually. In general, stagnation is your only problem.

7. Your productive work life is finite. Change is guaranteed. Staying productive in the face of ever-increasing change becomes a major challenge. Don't worry; everybody is facing the same thing.

8. While you're still breathing, there is more to learn, more experiences to process, more lessons to complete. You never do get to graduate; you never actually arrive. You simply get to a resting place for a little while, and then move on. Be especially careful whenever you think you've arrived. Instead, enjoy the process.

9. Life is finite, so you can only choose a handful of life priorities. If you have a couple dozen priorities, paradoxically, they can't all be priorities. For some, choosing priorities is easy. For others, it takes courage and discipline. Either way, you can only have a few priorities.

10. As you thinketh, so shall the world be. If you regard the world as a beautiful place, it will show up as beautiful. If you think society is going to hell in a hand basket, then hand baskets postmarked for hell will appear.

11. The little voice—the one you keep ignoring—has some great ideas. Don't be afraid of instinct or intuition. You have most of the answers you need right inside of you.

12. Over the course of your 20,000 to 28,000 days, most of what transpires in your life is the result of choices you make. Yes, occasionally stuff happens from out of left field. Mostly, you make the choices that impact your life.

The Least You Need to Know

➤ The final wish of many suicide victims is to spend their last moments in reflective silence, experiencing what they did not give themselves in life.

➤ Being true to yourself means having inner directedness, carving your own path.

➤ Understanding social changes helps you prepare for them, and reduce some of the stress related to rapid change.

➤ Pace yourself. Especially if you have big goals.

➤ Being true to yourself will help keep stress in control.

➤ Reducing stress is a stage that you pass through on the way to becoming a balanced person.

Word Power Glossary

anticipatory stress Worry or concern with endless stressful possibilities.

bad stress Known as *distress*; a response to some type of pressure, which can be both external and self-imposed, that prompts psychological and real physiological changes within you of an undesirable nature. It results in your being anxious or irritable, can dampen your spirits, and possibly shorten you life.

burnout An umbrella term used to describe a particular type of stress manifested by diminished personal accomplishment, emotional exhaustion, and depersonalization.

chronic stress Stress that builds over time, possibly stemming from a tough experience over which you have no control except to endure or accept, such as the loss of a loved one, an illness, accident, or other trauma.

etymology Charting the origin of something.

good stress Also known as *eustress*; stress that provides stimulation and challenges; is essential to development, growth, and change; and helps to make your life enjoyable, even interesting.

insomnia Sleeplessness.

Luddites People who look upon the intrusion of technology in everyday life with disdain. Those who would prefer to have society return to an era in which technology was not so intrusive.

megalomania The unrealistic desire to be in control and on top of everything within your grasp.

micro-sleep A five- to ten-second episode where your brain is effectively asleep while you are otherwise up and about.

mismanaged stress   Non-adaptive ways of coping with stress, such as relying on drugs or alcohol.

modus operandi   A Latin term still in use today, which translates to the standard way of doing things.

narcolepsy   A malfunction of the central nervous system that results in daytime sleepiness including sudden, temporary losses of muscle control and brief paralysis when falling asleep or waking. Sleep attacks may occur while driving, operating dangerous equipment, or simply in midsentence.

neo-Luddite   Those who believe that the best chance of social survival is via the abandonment of modern technology and a return to a more harmonious relationship with nature. Neo-Luddites loathe television.

oxymoron   An unlikely pairing of two words or concepts, such as "government efficiency."

presenteeism   Being at work, appearing to be productive, but in reality, being too tired or too unfocused to be effective.

rapid eye movements (REMs)   A crucial part of your overall sleep cycle. If your REM pattern is disrupted, even eight hours of sleep may not yield the benefits you need to be effective.

recomplicating   Making something more complicated than it was originally. For example, technology was developed that would enhance the process of making, say, fare changes and new reservations in the airline industry; instead, the process has become more confusing and more involved.

reframe   Looking at a situation from another perspective.

residual stress   Stress of the past representing an inability or unwillingness to let go of old hurts or bad memories.

situational stress   An immediate threat, challenge, or agitation; something that demands attention now.

sleep apnea   The cessation of breathing during sleep, usually due to obstruction. Usually, the sufferer is aroused from sleep by an automatic breathing reflex. Thus, he may end up getting little sleep at all.

stress   A by-product of pressures (real or perceived), changes, demands, and challenges that one faces.

stress response   When you experience the consequences of exposure to stress such that you suffer some adverse effect.

Sources

Blankenhorn, David, *Fatherless America* (Basic Books, 1995).

Bridges, William, *Job Shift* (Addison-Wesley, 1995).

Davidson, Jeff, *Blow Your Own Horn* (Berkley, 1991).

Davidson, Jeff, *Breathing Space: Living & Working at a Comfortable Pace in a Sped-Up Society* (MasterMedia, 1991).

Davidson, Jeff, *The Complete Idiot's Guide to Managing Your Time* (Macmillan, 1996).

Donald, David H., *Lincoln* (Simon & Schuster, 1995).

Drucker, Dr. Peter, *The Effective Executive* (Harper & Row, 1967).

Dychewald, Dr. Ken, *Age Wave* (Tarcher, 1989).

Dyer, Dr. Wayne, *Your Erroneous Zones* (Harper, 1993).

Dyer, Dr. Wayne, *Pulling Your Own Strings* (Harper Collins, 1991).

Fanning, Robbie, *How to Get it All Done and Still be Human* (Chilton, 1979).

Frankl, Dr. Victor, *Man's Search for Meaning* (Beacon Press, 1963).

Fritz, Robert, *The Path of Least Resistance* (Fawcett Columbine, 1989).

Gallagher, Winifred, *The Power of Place* (Poseidon Press, 1993).

Gross, Martin L., *The Psychological Society* (Random House, 1978).

Hardison, O.B., *Disappearing Through the Skylight* (Viking, 1992).

Hardy, Dr. Charles, *The Age of Paradox* (Harvard Business School Press, 1994).

Jackson, Phil, *Sacred Hoops: Spiritual Lessons of a Hardwood Warrior* (Hyperion, 1995).

Lively, Lynn, *Managing Information Overload* (AMACOM, 1996).

Mantell, Michael, *Ticking Bombs: Defusing Violence in the Workplace* (BusinessOne-Irwin, 1994).

Maples, Dr. William R., *Dead Men Do Tell Tales* (Doubleday, 1994).

Moore, James F., *The Death of Competition* (HarperBusiness, 1996).

Morris, Desmond, *The Human Animal* (Crown Publ., 1995).

Posner, Gerald, *Case Closed* (Random House, 1993).

Roszak, Dr. Theodore, *The Cult of Information* (University of California, 1994).

Schor, Dr. Juliet, *The Overworked American* (Basic Books, 1991).

Sisken, Bernard, *What Are the Chances?* (Crown Markers, 1989).

Index

A

abusive supervisors, 108-109
accepting responsibility for
  situations, 210-211
acknowledging feelings, 217
addresses
  The Direct Marketing
    Association, 164
  DMA Mail Preference
    Service, 165
  family services organiza-
    tions, 36
  Federal Trade
    Commission, 164
  Mail Order Action Line, 165
  television networks, 141-142
adequate sleep, signs of, 157
advertisements, as stressors,
  143-144
affirmations (stress
  reduction), 101
The Age of Paradox, 10
anger
  alternatives to, 22
  responses to, 189-190
anticipatory stress, 18
  defined, 251
aroma therapy (stress reduction), 199
articles commissioned by
  public relations firms,
  142-143
average work week, determining overwork hours, 59-61

B

bad stress
  compared to good stress, 17
  defined, 251
balance in news reporting, 141
balancing work/non-work
  activities (stress reduction), 59
beepers, 87-88
best companies to work for,
  79-80
biofeedback cards, 194
bosses
  abusive, 108-109
  accentuating positive
    aspects, 78
  dealing with, 232-233
  diplomatic skills, honing, 79
  empathizing with, 78
  responses to about high
    expectations, 74-75
  revenge against, 79
  as stressors, 5
breathing (stress reduction), 188
  deep, 201-202
  fresh air, 201
BTTY (being true to
  yourself), 244
burnout, 72-74
  defined, 251

C

call forwarding, 87
call waiting, 87
calling office during vacations,
  215-216
calm people, reactions to stress,
  211-212
car phones, 88
carefree (stress reduction), 237
Case Closed (JFK conspiracy
  theory), 137
casual days (stress
  reduction), 62
catalogs, shopping by, 121
cell phones, 88
centering (stress
  reduction), 205
certified massage therapists
  (CMTs), stress reduction,
  199-200
change of routine (stress
  reduction), 26-27, 100
chaos, completions during,
  175-176
checklist for purchase
  decisions, 225
chemical dependency
  reactions to stress, 243
  as stressor, 7
Chicken Soup for the Soul, 197
children, as stressors, 34
children's sporting events, 215

chlorophyll (stress reduction), 199
choosing to reduce stress, 229-230, 237-239
  bosses, handling, 232-233
  divorce, handling, 231
  energy, increasing, 237
  enjoying the present, 230
  finances, mastering, 230-231
  preparing for unexpected, 231-232
  rapid change, handling, 235-237
  technology anxiety, overcoming, 234-235
  work-related stress, mastering, 233
  see also decision-making
chronic stress, 18
  defined, 251
closure, *see* completions
clutter, as stressor, 166-167
CMTs (certified massage therapists), stress reduction, 199-200
co-workers, as stressors, 5
cold turkey, handling change, 236
communications
  development of high-stress society, 9
  forecasts for, 248
commuting
  stress reduction strategies, 39, 121
  as stressor, 8
companies
  best to work for, 79-80
  objectives, distinguishing yourself at work, 50
  responses to violence in workplace, 104-105
competition
  eliminating at work, 46
  with yourself, 44-45
completions, 172-173
  during chaos, 175-176
  compared to perfection, 179-180

concentrating on single projects, 179
courtesy for others, 177-178
  with loved ones, 173-174
  organizing information, 176-177
consensus decisions, 227
contract employees, 51
contrarians, defined, 121
control, need for (stress reduction), 25
controlling stress, 25-26
coping with rejection, 23
costs, federal government information overload, 127
creative sanctuaries (stress reduction), 90-92
creativity (stress reduction), 238
crediting group efforts, distinguishing yourself at work, 49
cycles of productivity, 75-77

D

de-personalization (burnout), 73
decision-making, 219-220
  in business, 223
  deciding by not deciding, 221-222
  identifying importance of decisions, 222-223
  instinctive decisions, 226
  narrowing priorities, 223-224
  purchase decisions, 224
    checklist, 225
  shortcuts, 226-227
  as stressor, 220
  too many versus too few choices, 220-221, 227-228
deep breathing (stress reduction), 201-202
difficult bosses, coping with, 77-79
diminished personal accomplishment (burnout), 73

diplomatic skills, honing, 79
The Direct Marketing Association, address for, 164
disruptions, 95-97
  dealing with, 94-96
  mental reduction techniques, 100-102
distinguishing yourself at work
  crediting group efforts, 49
  doing unwanted tasks, 47-48
  know job description/ company objectives, 50
  make supervisor look good, 49
  mentoring others, 49
  praising supervisors, 49
  productivity when supervisor is away, 48
  volunteer to help others, 48
distress (bad stress), 17
  defined, 251
divorce, stress reduction techniques, 231
DMA Mail Preference Service, address for, 165
downloaded information, organizing, 176-177
dress-down days (stress reduction), 62
drinking water (stress reduction), 13, 52
driving, dangers of sleep deprivation, 151-152
drugs/medication
  reactions to stress, 243
  stress reduction, 193-194

E

e-mail, 89
economy
  ages, 124-126
  forecasts for, 247-248
The Effective Executive, 212
eliminating competition at work, 46
emotional exhaustion (burnout), 73

empathizing with bosses (stress reduction), 78
employees
    stress of moving on spouses, 186-187
    termination, reducing violence in workplace, 106-108
energy, increasing, 237
enjoying the present (stress reduction), 230
entertainment, as stressor, 138-139
environment
    mastering, 190-192
    as stressor, 7
etymology, defined, 210, 251
eustress (good stress), 17
    defined, 251
exercise
    meditation during, 203
    stress reduction, 13, 61-62
exhaustion
    dangers of driving, 151-152
    men, effect on, 153-154
    napping, effect on, 156-157
    personal sleep needs, 150-151
    physical impact of, 149
    reducing, 154-157
    signs of, 149-150
    while traveling, 156
    trends in, 148
    women, effect on, 152-153
    work-related problems, 148-149
expectations at work, 67-68
    burnout, 72-74
    reasons for increasing, 68-71
    responses to supervisors, 74-75
    stress reduction techniques, 71-72
experiences, learning from, 213-214

F

family concerns, as stressors, 34, 36
family services organizations, addresses for, 36
fatigue
    dangers of driving, 151-152
    men, effect on, 153-154
    napping, effect on, 156-157
    personal sleep needs, 150-151
    physical impact of, 149
    reducing, 154-157
    signs of, 149-150
    while traveling, 156
    trends in, 148
    women, effect on, 152-153
    work-related problems, 148-149
fax machines, 89-90
fax-on-demand, 90
Federal Express, relationship to increasing expectations, 68
federal government, information overload, 126-127
Federal Trade Commission, address for, 164
feelings, acknowledging, 217
fertility rates, effect of over-population, 119
fight or flight, 4
finances
    mastering, 14, 230-231
    as stressor, 7, 31-32
forecasts
    communications, 248
    economy, 247-248
    politics, 248-249
    relationships, 246-247
    societal problems, 247
Frankl, Dr. Victor (violence in workplace), 109
fresh air (stress reduction), 201
future
    forecasts for
        communications, 248
        economy, 247-248

        politics, 248-249
        relationships, 246-247
        societal problems, 247
    visualizing, 196-197

G

good stress
    compared to bad stress, 17
    defined, 251
grace periods, handling change, 236
group efforts, crediting (distinguishing yourself at work), 49
guided imagery (stress reduction), 197-198

H

hand grippers (stress reduction), 13, 52
health-related concerns, as stressors, 33, 35
helping others
    distinguishing yourself at work, 48
    stress reduction, 216-217
high expectations at work, 67-68
    burnout, 72-74
    reasons for increasing, 68-71
    responses to supervisors, 74-75
    stress reduction techniques, 71-72
high-stress society, development of, 8-10
hiring out household chores (stress reduction), 37-39
home
    clutter, 166-167
    privacy, 159-161
        junk mail, 164-165
        phone solicitations, 163-164
        solicitors, 161
        uninvited guests, 161-163

hot tubs (stress reduction), 194
hours in work week, determining, 59-61
household chores (stress reduction), 37-39
humor (stress reduction), 14, 52, 195-196

I

identical twins, research on, 12
imaging (stress reduction), 196-197
importance of decisions, identifying, 222-223
inability to choose, too few versus too many choices, 220-221
incompletions, 171-172
    concentrating on single projects, 179
    information overload, organization techniques, 176-177
    with loved ones, 173-174
    perfection, compared to completion, 179-180
    preventing for others, 177-178
    procrastination, 178
    turning into completions, 172-173
        during chaos, 175-176
    worrying about, 169-171
increasing
    energy, 237
    life spans, 241-242
incremental progress on projects (stress reduction), 53-54
Information Age, 124-126
information overload, 123-133
    advertisements as stressors, 143-144
    economic ages, 124-126
    eliminating waste, 132
    federal government, 126-127

forecasts for, 248
    handling, 132-133
    Library of Congress holdings, 127-128
    Living on the Margin, 10
    organizing information, 131, 176-177
    publishing industry, 126-128
    reducing, 121, 130
    selectivity of information intake, 128-130
    technology as stressor, 84-85
    tickler files, 131-132
insomnia, 148
    defined, 251
instinctive decisions, 226
interruptions, 95-97
    dealing with, 94-96
    mental reduction techniques, 100-102

J

JFK conspiracy theory, 137
job burnout, 72-74
job description, distinguishing yourself at work, 50
job market, effect of overpopulation on, 119
job security
    distinguishing yourself
    at work
        crediting group efforts, 49
        doing unwanted tasks, 47-48
        know job description/ company objectives, 50
        make supervisor look good, 49
        mentoring others, 49
        praising supervisors, 49
        productivity when supervisor is away, 48
        volunteer to help others, 48

self-employment, 50-51
Job Shift (future of self-employment), 50
jump starting, handling change, 235
junk mail, 164-165

K-L

Kettering, Thomas (finding solutions within problems), 218
leadership sharing (stress reduction), 238
leap-frogging, handling change, 236
learning
    from mistakes, 213-214
    from stress, 216
Library of Congress holdings, information overload, 127-128
life observations, 249-250
life spans, increasing, 241-242
lighthearted (stress reduction), 238
limiting television/newspapers (stress reduction), 144
Living on the Margin, 10
loneliness, as stressor, 7, 34-35
loved ones, completions with, 173-174
Luddites, defined, 84, 251

M

Mail Order Action Line, address for, 165
Managing Information Overload, 129
manifestations of stress, 20-22
marriage, as stressor, 33
massage (stress reduction), 199-200

mastering
  finances (stress reduction), 230-231
  your environment, 190-192
medication/drugs
  reactions to stress, 243
  stress reduction, 193-194
meditation (stress reduction), 202-204
megalomania, defined, 251
men, effect of sleep deprivation on, 153-154
mental interruption-reduction techniques, 100-102
mentoring others, distinguishing yourself at work, 49
micro-sleep, 151
  defined, 251
misinformation, perpetuated by television, 137
mismanaged stress, defined, 252
mistakes, learning from, 213-214
mobile phones, 88
modus operandi, defined, 58, 252
monetary pressures, as stressors, 7
moving, as stressor, 186-187
multitasking, 96-97, 97
Murrow, Edward R. (balance in news reporting speech), 141

N

napping, effect on sleep deprivation on, 156-157
narcolepsy, 148
  defined, 252
narrowing priorities (stress reduction), 223-224
natural resources, scarcity of, 117-118
negativity of news, effect on society, 140
neighbors, as stressors, 36-37

neo-Luddites, defined, 84, 252
news, as stressor, 139-141
newspapers
  articles commissioned by public relations firms, 142-143
  limiting for stress reduction, 144
  tabloids, 142-143
nutrition, as stressor, 6

O

observations on life, 249-250
occupational stress, 5-6, 43-44, 55
  average work week, determining overwork hours, 59-61
  beepers, 87-88
  best companies to work for, 79-80
  burnout, 72-74
  call forwarding, 87
  call waiting, 87
  calling in during vacations, 215-216
  car/cell phones, 88
  commuting, stress reduction tips, 39
  competing with yourself, 44-45
  decision-making during change, 223
  difficult bosses, 77-79
  distinguishing yourself
    crediting group efforts, 49
    doing unwanted tasks, 47-48
    know job description/ company objectives, 50
    make supervisor look good, 49
    mentoring others, 49
    praising supervisors, 49

productivity when supervisor is away, 48
  volunteer to help others, 48
e-mail, 89
eliminating competition, 46
factors for, 19-20
fax machines, 89-90
high expectations, 67-68
  reasons for increasing, 68-71
  responses to supervisors, 74-75
  stress reduction techniques, 71-72
indications of overwork, 56-58
interruptions, mental reduction techniques, 100-102
overworked, 55-56
pacing yourself, 63-64
physical symptoms, reducing, 64-65
presenteeism, 21
reducing, 51-53, 99-100
  balancing activities, 59
  through choice, 233
  dress-down days, 62
  exercise, 61-62
  incremental progress on projects, 53-54
  via productivity cycles, 75-77
  via respectful interactions with others, 109-110
self-employment options, 50-51
sleep deprivation, 148-149
sped-up sense of time, 62-63
telephone interruptions, 85-86
timing of shift, 99
unnecessary work, evaluating, 212-213
vacation time, lack of, 56
Office of Thrift Supervision, information overload, 127

organizing information, 131, 176-177
originality (stress reduction), 238
Overachievers Anonymous, 211
overcrowding (population density), 115-117
  fertility rates, 119
  scarcity of resources, 117-118
  stress reduction strategies, 120-122
  traffic problems, 119-120
  unemployment, 119
  in United States, 120
overload, information, 123-133
  advertisements as stressors, 143-144
  economic ages, 124-126
  eliminating waste, 132
  federal government, 126-127
  forecasts for, 248
  handling, 132-133
  Library of Congress holdings, 127-128
  Living on the Margin, 10
  organizing information, 131, 176-177
  publishing industry, 126-128
  reducing, 121, 130
  selectivity of information intake, 128-130
  technology as stressor, 84-85
  tickler files, 131-132
overworked, 55-56
  average work week, determining hours, 59-61
  balancing activities to reduce stress, 59
  dress-down days to reduce stress, 62
  exercise to reduce stress, 61-62
  indications of, 56-58
  pacing yourself, 63-64
  physical symptoms, reducing, 64-65

  sped-up sense of time, 62-63
  vacation time, lack of, 56
The Overworked Americans, 55
oxymoron, defined, 95, 252

P

pacing yourself (stress reduction), 63-64, 71
paperwork
  federal government information overload, 126-127
  reducing amount, 98
pausing (stress reduction), 184-185
  consequences of neglecting, 186
  places to practice, 188-190
  suggestions for, 187-188
perception of self, as stressor, 7
perfection, compared to completion, 179-180
personal finances
  mastering, 14, 230-231
  as stressor, 7, 31-32
personal sleep needs, 150-151
phone solicitations, 163-164
physical environment, as stressor, 7
physical impact of sleep deprivation, 149
physical reactions to stress, 4-5, 12, 16-17
  reducing work-related, 64-65
politics, forecasts for, 248-249
poor nutrition, as stressor, 6
population density, 115-117
  fertility rates, 119
  scarcity of resources, 117-118
  stress reduction strategies, 120-122
  traffic problems, 119-120
  unemployment, 119
  in United States, 120
positive actions, turning stressors into, 24-25
Postal Service, violence in workplace statistics, 105

posture (stress reduction), 13, 52
praising supervisors, distinguishing yourself at work, 49
prayer (stress reduction), 195
preparing for unexpected (stress reduction), 231-232
presenteeism, 21
  defined, 252
priorities, narrowing (stress reduction), 223-224
privacy, 159-161
  junk mail, 164-165
  phone solicitations, 163-164
  solicitors, 161
  uninvited guests, 161-163
problems, finding solutions within, 218
procrastination, 178
productivity cycles, 75-77
productivity when supervisor is away, distinguishing yourself at work, 48
pros and cons technique (decision-making), 227
public relations firms, commissioning newspaper articles, 142-143
publishing industry, information overload, 126-128
purchase decisions, reducing stress of, 224-225

Q-R

quiet settings (stress reduction), 90-92

rapid change
  decision-making during, 223
  stress reduction techniques, 235-237
rapid eye movement (REM) sleep, 154-155
  defined, 252
rate of change, 10-12
Rather, Dan (balance in news reporting speech), 141

reactions to stress
  calm people's reactions, 211-212
  fight or flight, 4
  physical, 4-5, 12, 16-17
    reducing at work, 64-65
  signs of, 20-22
  sleep deprivation, 148
    dangers of driving, 151-152
    men, effect on, 153-154
    napping, effect on, 156-157
    personal sleep needs, 150-151
    physical impact of, 149
    reducing, 154-157
    signs of, 149-150
    while traveling, 156
    women, effect on, 152-153
    work-related problems, 148-149
  substance abuse, 243
  suicide, 243-244
  violence in workplace, 103-104
    abusive supervisors, 108-109
    company responses, 104-105
    subversion, 106
    terminating employees, 106-108
    U.S. Postal Service, 105
recomplication, defined, 84, 252
reducing stress, 12-14
  acknowledging feelings, 217
  anger, responses to, 189-190
  aroma therapy, 199
  balancing work/non-work activities, 59
  beepers, 87-88
  breathing techniques, 188
  BTTY (being true to yourself), 244
  calm people's reactions to stress, 211-212

car/cell phones, 88
centering, 205
changes of routine, 26-27
children's sporting events, 215
through choosing, 229-230, 237-239
  bosses, handling, 232-233
  divorce, handling, 231
  energy, increasing, 237
  enjoying the present, 230
  finances, mastering, 230-231
  preparing for unexpected, 231-232
  rapid change, handling, 235-237
  technology anxiety, overcoming, 234-235
  work-related stress, mastering, 233
clutter, eliminating at home, 166-167
commuting, 39
completions, 172-173
  during chaos, 175-176
  with loved ones, 173-174
  organizing information, 176-177
creative sanctuaries, 90-92
deep breathing, 201-202
difficult bosses, working with, 77-79
dress-down days at work, 62
drink water, 13
e-mail, 89
exercise, 13, 61-62
family services organizations, 36
fax machines, 89-90
financial management, 14, 31-32
finding solutions within problems, 218
focus on one task, 96-97
fresh air, 201
guided imagery, 197-198
hand grippers, 13
helping others, 216-217

high work expectations, coping with, 71-72
  responses to supervisors, 74-75
hiring out household chores, 37-39
humor, 14, 195-196
incompletions
  concentrating on single projects, 179
  eliminating excessive worry, 170
  perfection, compared to completion, 179-180
  preventing for others, 177-178
ineffective measures, 193-194
information intake, 130
  eliminating waste, 132
  organizing information, 131
  tickler files, 131-132
instinctive decisions, 226
interruptions, 95-97
  dealing with, 94-96
  mental reduction techniques, 100-102
junk mail reduction strategies, 164-165
learning from experiences, 213-214
limiting television and newspapers, 144
massage, 199-200
mastering your environment, 190-192
meditation, 202-204
moving, 187
narrowing priorities, 223-224
need for control, 25
overcrowding reduction strategies, 120-122
pacing yourself, 63-64
paper, reducing amount of, 98
phone solicitations, 163-164
physical symptoms at work, reducing, 64-65

posture, 13
prayer, 195
procrastination, strategies to
reduce, 178
purchase decisions, 224
checklist, 225
reframing situations, 214
respectful interactions with
coworkers, 109-110
self-talk, 198-199
shortcuts to decision-
making, 226-227
sit still, 13
sleep, 154-157
strategic pauses, 184-185
consequences of neglect-
ing, 186
places to practices,
188-190
suggestions for imple-
menting, 187-188
stress inventory, 204
T'ai Chi Ch'aun, 206-207
talking to someone, 195
telephone interruptions,
dealing with, 85-86
television viewing, 138
timing of work shift, 99
tips from successful people,
244-246
uninvited guests/solicitors,
161-163
visualization, 13, 196-197
vitamins, 200
volunteering, 14
work-related, 51-53, 99-100
incremental progress on
projects, 53-54
productivity cycles, 75-77
yoga, 205-206
reflecting (stress reduction),
184-185
consequences of
neglecting, 186
places to practice, 188-190
suggestions for, 187-188
reframing situations, 214
defined, 252
rejection, coping with, 23

relationships
forecasts for, 246-247
as stressors, 6, 33
relatives
completions with, 173-174
as stressors, 36
relaxation tapes (stress reduction), 53
REM (rapid eye movement)
sleep, 154-155
defined, 252
residual stress, 19
defined, 252
resources, scarcity of, 117-118
respectful interactions with
coworkers (stress reduction),
109-110
responses to supervisors about
high expectations, 74-75
responsibility for situations,
accepting, 210-211
retaining versus tossing clutter,
166-167
revenge, 79
routine changes (stress reduction), 100
rule violations, telemarketers,
164

S

Sacred Hoops (reducing interruptions), 101-102
sanctuaries (stress reduction),
90-92
scarcity of natural resources,
effect of overpopulation,
117-118
selecting, *see* decision-making
selectivity of information
intake, 128-130
self-employment, 50-51
self-image, as stressor, 135-136
self-induced stress, 5, 16
sleep deprivation, 148
dangers of driving,
151-152
men, effect on, 153-154

napping, effect on,
156-157
personal sleep needs,
150-151
physical impact of, 149
reducing, 154-157
signs of, 149-150
while traveling, 156
women, effect on,
152-153
work-related problems,
148-149
self-talk (stress reduction),
198-199, 229-230, 237-239
bosses, handling, 232-233
divorce, handling, 231
energy, increasing, 237
enjoying the present, 230
finances, mastering, 230-231
preparing for unexpected,
231-232
rapid change, handling,
235-237
technology anxiety, over-
coming, 234-235
work-related stress, mastering, 233
sense of humor (stress reduction), 52, 195-196
sense of time, work-related
stress, 62-63
sex, as stressor, 35
sharing leadership (stress
reduction), 238
shopping (stress reduction), 121
shortcuts to decision-making,
226-227
showers (stress reduction), 53
signs
of adequate sleep, 157
of sleep deprivation,
149-150
of stress, 20-22
single projects, concentrating
on for completion, 179
sitting still (stress
reduction), 13
situational stress, 18
defined, 252

sleep, signs of adequate, 157
sleep apnea, 148
    defined, 252
sleep deprivation
    dangers of driving, 151-152
    men, effect on, 153-154
    napping, effect on, 156-157
    personal sleep needs,
        150-151
    physical impact of, 149
    reducing, 154-157
    signs of, 149-150
    as stressor, 6-7
    while traveling, 156
    trends in, 148
    women, effect on, 152-153
    work-related problems,
        148-149
Smithsonian Institution,
    information overload, 128
society
    forecasts for, 247
    television's effect on,
        136-138
    violence in, 103-104
soft forecasts
    communications, 248
    economy, 247-248
    politics, 248-249
    relationships, 246-247
    societal problems, 247
solicitors, 161
solutions within problems, 218
spamming (e-mail), 89
sped-up sense of time, work-
    related stress, 62-63
sports, children's sporting
    events, 215
spouses, stress of moving on,
    186-187
statistics, violence in work-
    place, 105
strategic pauses, 184-185
    consequences of
        neglecting, 186
    defined, 184
    places to practice, 188-190
    suggestions for implement-
        ing, 187-188

stress
    defined, 15-17, 252
    responses, defined, 252
    signs of, 20-22
stress control cards, 194
stress inventory for stress
    reduction, 204
stressors, 5-8, 30-37
    advertisements, 143-144
    anticipatory, 18
    beepers, 87-88
    bosses, 5
    call forwarding, 87
    call waiting, 87
    car/cell phones, 88
    chemical substances, 7
    children, 34
    chronic, 18
    clutter, 166-167
    co-workers, 5
    commuting, 8
    controlling, 25-26
    decision-making, 219-220
        in business, 223
        deciding by not deciding,
            221-222
        identifying importance of
            decisions, 222-223
        instinctive decisions, 226
        narrowing priorities,
            223-224
        purchase decisions,
            224-225
        shortcuts, 226-227
        too many versus too
            few choices, 220-221,
            227-228
    e-mail, 89
    entertainment, 138-139
    fax machines, 89-90
    financial, 7
    health-related concerns, 33
    incompletions, 171-172
        during chaos, 175-176
        concentrating on single
            projects, 179
        with loved ones, 173-174
        organizing information,
            176-177

        perfection, compared to
            completion, 179-180
        preventing for others,
            177-178
        procrastination, 178
        turning into completions,
            172-173
        worrying about, 169-171
    information overload,
        123-133
        economic ages, 124-126
        eliminating waste, 132
        federal government,
            126-127
        handling, 132-133
        Library of Congress
            holdings, 127-128
        organizing
            information, 131
        publishing industry,
            126-128
        reducing information
            intake, 130
        selectivity of information
            intake, 128-130
        tickler files, 131-132
    interruptions, 95-97
        dealing with, 94-96
        mental reduction tech-
            niques, 100-102
    junk mail, 164-165
    learning from, 216
    loneliness, 7, 34-35
    moving as, 186-187
    multitasking, 96-97
    neighbors, 36-37
    news, 139-141
    occupational, 6
    paper, reducing amount, 98
    personal finances, 31-32
    phone solicitations, 163-164
    physical environment, 7
    poor nutrition, 6
    rate of change, 10-12
    rejection, coping with, 23
    relationships, 6, 33
    relatives, 36
    residual, 19

self-image, 7, 135-136
sex, 35
situational, 18
sleep deprivation, 6-7
    dangers of driving,
        151-152
    men, effect on, 153-154
    napping, effect on,
        156-157
    personal sleep needs,
        150-151
    physical impact of, 149
    reducing, 154-157
    signs of, 149-150
    as stressor, 6-7
    while traveling, 156
    trends in, 148
    women, effect on,
        152-153
    work-related problems,
        148-149
solicitors, 161
subordinates, 5
tabloid newspapers, 142-143
technology, 84-85
telephone interruptions,
    dealing with, 85-86
television, 136
    addresses for networks,
        141-142
    misinformation perpetu-
        ated by, 137
    violence in, 137-138
time pressures, 8
turning into positive
    actions, 24-25
uninvited guests, 161-163
uniqueness to you, 22-24
violence in workplace,
    103-104
    abusive supervisors,
        108-109
    company responses,
        104-105
    subversion, 106
    terminating employees,
        106-108
    U.S. Postal Service, 105
waiting in line, 8

work-related, 5-6, 43-44, 55
    average work week,
        determining overwork
        hours, 59-61
    balancing activities to
        reduce stress, 59
    best companies to work
        for, 79-80
    burnout, 72-74
    calling in during vaca-
        tions, 215-216
    competing with yourself,
        44-45
    difficult bosses, 77-79
    distinguishing yourself,
        47-50
    dress-down days to
        reduce stress, 62
    eliminating
        competition, 46
    exercise to reduce stress,
        61-62
    factors for, 19-20
    high expectations, 67-68,
        71-72
    indications of overwork,
        56-58
    make incremental
        progress on projects,
        53-54
    overworked, 55-56
    pacing yourself, 63-64
    physical symptoms,
        reducing, 64-65
    presenteeism, 21
    productivity cycles,
        reducing via, 75-77
    reasons for increasingly
        high expectations,
        68-71
    reducing, 51-53, 99-100
    respectful interactions
        with others to reduce
        stress, 109-110
    responses to supervisors,
        74-75
    self-employment options,
        50-51
    sped -up sense of time,
        62-63

    timing of shift, 99
    unnecessary work,
        evaluating, 212-213
    vacation time, lack of, 56
stretching (stress reduction), 52
subordinates, as stressors, 5
substance abuse, reactions to
    stress, 243
subversion, workplace vio-
    lence, 106
successes, choosing to reduce
    stress, 238-239
successful people, tips for
    reducing stress, 244-246
suicide (reactions to stress),
    243-244
supervisors
    abusive, 108-109
    accentuating positive
        aspects, 78
    dealing with, 232-233
    diplomatic skills, honing, 79
    empathizing with, 78
    responses to about high
        expectations, 74-75
    revenge against, 79
    as stressors, 5
surroundings, mastering,
    190-192

T

tabloid newspapers, 142-143
T'ai Chi Ch'aun (stress reduc-
    tion), 206-207
talking (stress reduction)
    to someone, 195
    to yourself, 198-199
technology
    anxiety, overcoming,
        234-235
    development of high-stress
        society, 9
    as stressor, 84-85
telecommuting (stress reduc-
    tion), 121
telemarketing, as stressor,
    163-164

Telemarketing and Consumer Fraud and Abuse Prevention Act, 163
telephones
call forwarding, 87
call waiting, 87
car/cell phones, 88
interruptions, dealing with, 85-86
television
addresses for networks, 141-142
effect on society, 136
misinformation perpetuated by, 137
violence, 137-138
limiting for stress reduction, 144
news, as stressor, 139-141
stress reduction, 138
terminating employees, reducing violence in workplace, 106-108
tickler files (reducing information overload), 131-132
time pressures, as stressors, 8, 62-63
timing of work shift (stress reduction), 99
tossing versus retaining clutter, 166-167
total immersion, handling change, 235
traffic problems
effect of overpopulation, 119-120
stress reduction strategies, 121
Transcendental Meditation, 202
transportation advancements, development of high-stress society, 9
traveling, sleep enhancements, 156
twins, research on, 12
Type A personalities, 26

U

U.S. Department of Justice, information overload, 127
U.S. Postal Service, violence in workplace statistics, 105
unemployment, effect of overpopulation, 119
uninvited guests, 161-163
uniqueness of your stress, 22-24
United States, population density, 120
universality of stress, 10-12
unnecessary work, evaluating, 212-213
unwanted tasks, doing to distinguish yourself, 47-48

V

vacation deficit disorder, defined, 56
vacations
calling office during, 215-216
lack of, 56
violence
in society, 103-104
on television, effect on society, 137-138
in workplace, 103-104
abusive supervisors, 108-109
company responses, 104-105
subversion, 106
terminating employees, 106-108
U.S. Postal Service, 105
visualization (stress reduction), 13, 196-197
vitamins (stress reduction), 200
volunteering to help others
distinguishing yourself at work, 48
stress reduction, 14

W-Z

waiting in line, as stressor, 8
walking (stress reduction), 52
Washington National Record Center, information overload, 126
water, drinking (stress reduction), 13, 52
women, effect of sleep deprivation on, 152-153
work-life programs, 80
work-related stress, 5-6, 43-44, 55
average work week, determining overwork hours, 59-61
beepers, 87-88
best companies to work for, 79-80
burnout, 72-74
call forwarding, 87
call waiting, 87
calling in during vacations, 215-216
car/cell phones, 88
commuting, stress reduction tips, 39
competing with yourself, 44-45
decision-making during change, 223
difficult bosses, 77-79
distinguishing yourself
crediting group efforts, 49
doing unwanted tasks, 47-48
know job description/ company objectives, 50
make supervisor look good, 49
mentoring others, 49
praising supervisors, 49
productivity when supervisor is away, 48
volunteer to help others, 48
e-mail, 89

eliminating competition, 46
factors for, 19-20
fax machines, 89-90
high expectations, 67-68
  reasons for increasing, 68-71
  responses to supervisors, 74-75
  stress reduction techniques, 71-72
indications of overwork, 56-58
interruptions, mental reduction techniques, 100-102
overworked, 55-56
pacing yourself, 63-64

physical symptoms, reducing, 64-65
presenteeism, 21
reducing, 51-53, 99-100
  balancing activities, 59
  through choice, 233
  dress-down days, 62
  exercise, 61-62
  incremental progress on projects, 53-54
  via productivity cycles, 75-77
  via respectful interactions with others, 109-110
self-employment options, 50-51
sleep deprivation, 148-149

sped-up sense of time, 62-63
telephone interruptions, 85-86
timing of shift, 99
unnecessary work, evaluating, 212-213
vacation time, lack of, 56
workplace violence, 103-104
  abusive supervisors, 108-109
  company responses, 104-105
  subversion, 106
  terminating employees, 106-108
  U.S. Postal Service, 105
worrying, 169-171

yoga (stress reduction), 205-206